Autobiography,
Sermons, Addresses, and Essays
of Bishop L. H. Holsey, D. D.

LARGE PRINT EDITION

PREPARED FOR PUBLICATION BY HISTORIC PUBLISHING

All Rights Reserved
San Antonio, Texas
©2017

Slavery Books & African American History Resources
https://slaverybooks.blogspot.com

BISHOP L. H. HOLSEY, D.D.

Autobiography, Sermons, Addresses, and Essays of Bishop L. H. Holsey, D. D.

By
Bishop L. H. Holsey,
[1842-1920]

Autobiography, Sermons, Addresses, and Essays

AUTOBIOGRAPHY, SERMONS, ADDRESSES, AND ESSAYS OF BISHOP L. H. HOLSEY, D D.

By

Bishop L. H. Holsey

LARGE PRINT EDITION

ATLANTA, GEORGIA:
THE FRANKLIN PRINTING AND PUBLISHING CO.
(Geo. W. Harrison, State Printer, Manager.)
1898.

CONTENTS.

- PREFACE
- INTRODUCTION
- AUTOBIOGRAPHY
- SERMONS

SERMONS.

SERMON I.
MAN AN IDEAL EMPIRE IN MINIATURE.
Psalms 8:4.--"What is man, that thou art mindful of him? and the son of man, that thou visitest him?"

SERMON II.
THE IRREPRESSIBLE CONFLICT.
I. John 3:8.--"For this purpose the Son of God was manifested: that he might destroy the works of the devil."

SERMON III.
THE FATHERHOOD OF GOD AND THE BROTHERHOOD OF MAN.
Romans 1:14--"I am debtor both to the Greeks, and to the barbarians; both to the wise, and to the unwise."

SERMON IV.
CHRISTIANITY SHILOH'S EMPIRE.
Genesis 49:10.--The sceptre shall not depart from Judah, nor a lawgiver from between his feet, until Shiloh come;

unto him shall the gathering of the people be."

SERMON V.
THE SONG OF BELIEVERS.
Psalms 101:1.--"I will sing of mercy and judgment: unto thee, O Lord, will I sing."

SERMON VI.
THE RICH AND THE POOR.
Proverbs 22:2.--"The rich and the poor meet together: the Lord is the maker of them all."

SERMON VII.
THE PERPETUITY OF THE NAME OF CHRIST.
Psalms 45:17.--"I will make thy name to be remembered in all generations: therefore shall the people praise thee forever and ever."

SERMON VIII.
FROM REPENTANCE TO FINAL RESTITUTION.
Acts 3:19-21.--"Repent ye therefore, and be ye converted, that your sins may be blotted out when the times of refreshing shall come from the presence of the Lord; and he shall send Jesus Christ, which before was

preached unto you: whom the heaven must receive until the times of restitution of all things."

SERMON IX.
DEEP CONCERN FOR THE WELFARE OF ZION.
Isaiah 62:1.--"For Zion's sake will I not hold my peace, and for Jerusalem's sake I will not rest, until the righteousness thereof go forth as brightness, and the salvation thereof as a lamp that burneth."

SERMON X.
LIFE AND DEATH.
II. Timothy 1:10.--"Who hath abolished death, and hath brought life and immortality to light through the gospel"

SERMON XI.
THE INSUFFICIENCY OF THE WISDOM OF MAN.
I. Cor. 2:5.--"That your faith should not stand in the wisdom of men, but in the power of God."

SERMON XII.
WHY WE SHOULD LOVE GOD.
Matt. 22:40.--On these two commandments hang all the

law and the prophets."

SERMON XIII.
THE WORK OF AN ENEMY.
Matt. 13:28.--"And he said unto them, an enemy hath done this."

SERMON XIV.
HOLINESS AND PEACE.
Hebrews 12:14.--"Follow peace with all men, and holiness, without which no man shall see the Lord."

SERMON XV.
THE UNITY OF CHRISTIANITY.
I. Cor. 3:21.--Therefore let no man glory in men; for all things are yours."

ESSAYS; ADDRESSES, ETC.

The Christmas

The Unity of Force

The Colored Methodist Episcopal Church

The Origin and Place of Religion in Civilization

Amalgamation or Miscegenation

Speech Delivered before Several Conferences of the M. E. Church, South

Religion

Southern Methodism and the Slaves

The Papacy

The Image of God in Man

The Trend of Civilization

The Great Presence

The Connection of the Spirit and Body

Autobiography, Sermons, Addresses, and Essays

PREFACE.

This book is published with the hope of doing good in more ways than will be expedient to state at this time. It is intended not only to disseminate the truths and glory of the gospel system, but also, as far as possible, to inspire the Negro to think, and to encourage investigation, literary advancement and authorship by men of my race.

The sermons, essays, etc., are selected from what I have been preaching and writing for the last decade. Originally, the sermons were not designed for publication, but for private use. The lectures and essays, with few exceptions, were designed for the public, and most of them have appeared in the public prints. I have written as I have thought, always following what seemed to be the truth, the conclusions of others, save the inspired Word, to the contrary notwithstanding.

Rev. Prof. John W Gilbert; A.B., A.M., of The Paine Institute, is the immediate cause of the appearance of the book upon the arena of thought and action. Often he has urged me to publish a book of sermons for the sake of helping the church and race of which I am a representative. He has gone so far as to become sponsor for its publication. Also, he has, in collaboration with Rev. Geo. Williams Walker, D.D., President of The Paine Institute, read the manuscript and corrected the proof. Gladly do I take this opportunity of thanking these two distinguished scholars for the labor which they have so patiently and willingly bestowed upon these pages. I am incapable of expressing the high appreciation and esteem which their labor upon this book begets.

Their labor, of course, was confined to the mechanical make-up of the book. For its doctrines and sentiments I am solely and independently responsible.

Twenty per cent. of the net proceeds of the sale of this volume I shall give to The Paine Institute.

If by this book the kingdom of Christ and the uplift of mankind are promoted even in the slightest degree, my prayers will have been abundantly answered.

THE AUTHOR.

Atlanta, Ga., March 31, 1898.

INTRODUCTION.

I take real pleasure in introducing this volume of sermons to the public. Not that a volume of sermons is a rarity, but the present one occupies in several respects a unique position, in that it represents the production of an ex-slave, who without the aid of school, and, despite untoward circumstances, exemplifies what aspirations the missionaries to the slave awakened and that civil law could not put down. This pleasure is enhanced by an acquaintance with its author for fourteen years that has endeared him to my heart as an honored friend.

Bishop Lucius H. Holsey was a member of the Methodist Episcopal Church, South. He represents a faithful product of the missionary zeal of this church that was awakened by Bishop Capers in founding the missions to the slaves. His fidelity to trust and zeal for the salvation of souls caused him to be appointed a local preacher before emancipation. So that when the changed conditions that followed in the wake of the civil war came upon the church he was an active exponent of that conservative force that resulted in the organization of the Colored Methodist Episcopal Church in America. Not only is the Bishop one of the organizers of his church, but he has ever been promotive of its highest and best interests, and the source by far of its public documents. He has supervised the editorial work of all his church's literature, compiling its hymn book, discipline, manual of the discipline, etc. He discerns in slavery a providential blessing to both white and black--a harsh measure to bring the ignorant Negro in contact with the educated Caucassian. He as firmly regards emancipation as the very best measure for the development of the highest interest alike for the white man and the black. His views are to be seen in his autobiography and in his recent address delivered before many of our annual conferences.

Deprived of the advantages of the school room, he has been a close student of men and nature. He gives us a partial insight to the manful effort he put forth to educate himself as best he could. We see in his autobiography what books he read. What influence these books had upon him is seen in many of his sermons. He was in a situation to appreciate the great need of school training. He has for years represented the foremost demands and zeal of educational endeavor in the interest of his own church. He presented the first plans for a school for the youth of his church which developed into The Paine Institute. He was the first colored man to give money to the erection of such a school. While Rev. W. C. Dunlap, of the Methodist Episcopal Church, South, was Commissioner of

Education, just before Rev. W. M. Hayes, of the same church became commissioner, Bishop Holsey, by advice of Bishop E. R. Hendrix, of the Methodist Episcopal Church, South, went before the Missouri Conference of the same church, and presenting the claims of The Paine Institute, collected between three and four hundred dollars for a much needed building. Thus providentially thrust out he kept on before the conferences of this church until he had collected about $3,000 from only a few of the conferences. As it was largely through his influence that the Methodist Episcopal Church, South, was aroused to the demand of the Colored Methodist Episcopal Church for Christian education of her children, so it was eminently fit for the burden of awakening a deeper enthusiasm in the educational work to devolve upon him.

Therefore, at the urgent solicitation of the Board of Education of the Methodist Episcopal Church, South, backed by appointment and request of the Board of Trustees

of The Paine Institute, the Bishop went before this church with an appeal for $25,000 to erect a building at this school to be known as the Haygood Memorial Hall. He is not in any wise a commissioner of education, but at the urgent solicitation of his brethren is actively asking money for the erection of this hall. As if this were not enough he contributes a handsome per cent. of the sale of this volume to the erection of the Haygood Memorial Hall.

Bishop Holsey is the best known Bishop of the Colored Methodist Episcopal Church. He has represented his church on several occasions, both by pen and person. In the New York Independent his church has been presented to the public by articles from his pen. At the Ecumenical Conference in London, he represented his church as her chosen delegate. His appeal to the General Conference of the Methodist Episcopal Church, South, in behalf of a school for the youth of his church resulted in the establishment and maintenance of The Paine Institute, at Augusta, Georgia.

Bishop Holsey is an eloquent preacher whose mind has a decidedly philosophical trend. He has appeared before many large gatherings of the people, sometimes made up wholly of white persons, as preacher, lecturer, orator. In each sphere he has acquitted himself well and brought about most beneficial results. He is the Munsey of the Colored Methodist Episcopal Church.

Without further delay I present this book to the public. Whatever is found in it that is helpful and praiseworthy attribute to the heart and mind of its author; whatever of shortcoming or imperfection, attribute to the lack of education, training and culturing development.

GEORGE WILLIAMS WALKER.

AUTOBIOGRAPHY OF BISHOP L. H. HOLSEY.

I was born in Georgia, near Columbus, in 1842, and at that time was the slave of James Holsey, who was also my father. He was a gentleman of classical education, dignified in appearance and manner of life, and represented that old antebellum class of Southern aristocracy who did not know enough of manual labor to black their own shoes or saddle their own horse. Like many others of his day and time he never married, but mingled, to some extent, with those females of the African race that were his slaves--his personal property. My mother was named Louisa, and was of pure African descent. She was of fascinating appearance and comely parts. Her father was named "Alex," and was an African of the Africans. He was short, thickset, and of a stubborn and massive build. He lived to be nearly a hundred years of age. So far as I know, all his children were daughters, of whom my mother was the youngest. She was an intensely religious woman, a most exemplary Christian, and belonged to the M. E. Church, South. She had fourteen children, myself being the oldest. I lived with her until about six years of age, when my father died, and I became the property of Mr. T. L. Wynn, who lived in Sparta, Ga. Mr. Wynn was my second owner. I served him as body servant until 1857, when he died. A few days before his death he called me to his bed and told me that, he was going to die, and wanted me to choose one of two of his intimate friends as my master. He named the two friends and I chose Col. R. M. Johnston, with whom I lived until the emancipation of the slaves. As he was a very kind man to his slaves, I remained on the plantation with him one year after the emancipation. From the fall of 1857 until the emancipation, I was his house servant, and looked after his domestic interests in general. He had great confidence in me and trusted me with money and other valuables. In all things, I was honest and true to him and his interests. Though young, I felt as much interest in his well-being as I have felt since in my own. I made it a special point never to lie to him or deceive him in any way. I felt that I could not afford to be false even to those who appeared to be my enslavers and oppressors, and I have never regretted this course in after years. The training that I received in the narrow house of slavery has been a minister of correction and mercy to me in all these years of struggle, trial, labor, and anxiety. I have no complaint against American slavery. It was a blessing in disguise to me and to many. It has made the Negro race what it could not have been in its native land. Slavery was but a circumstance or a link in the transitions of humanity, and must have its greatest bearing upon the future.

Col. Johnston, my last owner, had an interesting family of seven brilliant children and a brilliant wife. For them I have the best wishes and the highest esteem.

In 1867-68, I cultivated a cotton farm in Hancock County, Ga., on rented land. My wife and I labored to make an honest living. Assisted by two young men whom I hired, I made a competent living. My house was built of skinned pine poles and contained two large rooms and a hall. It was so constructed that every part of the spacious building had windows, so that I was out of doors while I was in doors. In my humble palace on a hill in the woods beneath the shade of towering pines and sturdy oaks, I felt as a king whose supreme commands were "law and gospel" to my subjects. Here I dwelt for two years cultivating the cotton farm and preaching at the same time. This was in the years of 1868-'69. Prior to this in 1866, I farmed on the old plantation of Col. Johnston. My wife then "took in washing" and I ran "a one-horse farm." Col. Johnston, the owner of the place, conducted a large boarding school, and my wife was laundress for the students. By this combination of interests, we made a "handsome living," and all was well.

From my youth I felt a call to preach the gospel, although I saw no opening for such a thing in the days of slavery; but still there was a hope and a lingering anticipation that somehow, in the divine arrangements, I would ultimately have an opportunity to proclaim God's truth. In the little church that stands beneath the oaks and cedars, in the village of Sparta, Ga., I was licensed to preach. It was in February, 1868, under the pastorate of Rev. A. J. Garrell, that I appeared before the Quarterly Conference. Rev. W. H. Potter, D.D., was the Presiding Elder. Bishop George F. Pierce being present, I had to be examined by him. He was a wonderful preacher, with wide influence, and august presence. Everybody loved, respected, and some almost adored him. Coming before such a high personage, I was scared out of my wits, and all that I had previously known seemed to have taken the wings of the winds and fled away. But I was examined pretty closely, especially on the doctrines of the church, and the Bible, yet, somehow, I came out all right. In 1862, I was married to Miss Harriett A. Turner, a girl then fifteen years of age, who had been reared by Bishop Pierce, and given by him to his son-in-law, Mr. Turner, as a maid for his wife. We were married in the spacious hall of the Bishop's residence by him on the 8th day of November, 1862. The Bishop's wife and daughters had provided for the occasion a splendid repast of good things to eat. The table, richly spread, with turkey, ham, cake, and many other things, extended nearly the whole length of the spacious dining hall. "The house girls" and "the house boys" and the most prominent persons of color were invited to the wedding of the colored "swells." The ladies composing the Bishop's family, dressed my bride in the gayest and most artistic style, with red flowers and scarlet sashes predominating in the brilliant trail. As the gorgeous flashes of waving scarlet and white softly moved across the spacious hall and stood in the glare of the light, I thought I saw in my Harriett an angel in the dwarfed splendors of heaven as if ornamented with gems set upon a background of gold. In the vision of life that then threw its brightness upon me, I saw nothing but the roseate splendors of its triumphs and its glory. But since then I have seen something of its opposite phases, and know much of its trials, reverses and disappointments. From the union thus formed fourteen children were born, but only nine of them lived. One of them, the first child, a daughter, died in her seventeenth year. The others died at birth. I have at present, eight living children, four of whom are boys.

    After I was licensed to preach in 1868, I belonged to the M. E. Church, South, as all colored people did who were Methodists in the slave States. In 1868 and 1869, I was on the Hancock circuit, which covered the entire county. Rev. E. B. Oliver and myself were the pastors. I was senior and he junior. There were seven churches on the circuit, and we followed each other in rotation. Brother Oliver was a great preacher, also great in prayer and song. He was the popular man among the people and their ideal man and pastor. He had a clear, loud, high, ringing voice, with a rare depth of pathos and sweetness. He could make his voice thunder, thud, or scream, as the occasion required, and a few blasts, as it were, of his silver clarion, in that "age of stone" was considered a wonderful sermon. One of the most difficult things with which I had to contend, was to get from under the withering blight of his trumpet voice. The man that had the loudest voice and the most dramatic emotions in pulpit or on platform, was necessarily, irrevocably, infallibly, and eternally in the estimation of the people, the great preacher, the flying angel of the everlasting gospel. But as I was farming, and not depending on the people for a living, I continued common sense preaching, which was considered by the undiscerning multitudes as very dry. My hearers would often take a nap while I was trying to do my little talking. My voice was very poor, weak, and defective, which greatly militated against me as a preacher. As a preacher's ability, in those days, was measured by his voice, a poor fellow like I was in a bad fix. It was noise that moved the multitudes, held the public ear, and like magic, swayed the public heart. For a long time I did not know where the trouble lay. I could not move the multitudes to tears like the junior preacher, although it was understood by the people that I was "the deeper reasoner," as they used to say, but was "no preacher." However, I never was discouraged by the adverse verdict of the people, because I had higher aims, ambition, and an unflagging industry, which never faltered, but pressed every moment and opportunity into service that could be spared from the farm and circuit work. But it was voice that I needed more than learning or gospel. What shall I do to make it thunder, scream, screech, howl, or roar as did the junior preacher. I had heard of a great Grecian orator, who, to improve his voice, put pebbles of stone in his mouth, and spoke against the loud roar of waves on the seashore. As I lived in the hill country away from the great waters and as "there was no more sea" for me, I often spent an hour in the woods, and from a pine stump, serving as a temporary pulpit, I would take the text to be used on the next Sabbath, and from it preach in a loud voice. I went through with all the gestures and attitudes with some respect for silent nature as was to be given to the listening congregation. A stump was my pulpit, the trees, grapevines, and the smaller daughters of the woods were my congregation, and the open heavens were the high dome under which I proclaimed the truth as best I could to a silent and emotionless multitude. This practice helped me wonderfully, and soon I began to thunder and rattle like the other big preachers.

    No salary was fixed for the circuit preachers. Each man made his living in the sweat of his face, and preached on Sunday as best he could. But at the end of the second year, it was proposed by some of the members of one of the churches to give the preachers a collection, and they willingly and generously gave us both the magnanimous sum of four dollars for the two years' services. We both were present, and a wide-awake and generous brother paid us the money, and with a triumphant air on his beaming countenance, said to us, in the tone of self-congratulation, "We are glad you don't preach for money, but for souls." Thus ended my first two years as circuit preacher. The memory of those two years is still fresh and green with its romance and "spiritual revelries." The following year (January 4th, 1869) Bishop Pierce called all the preachers of color, belonging to the M. E. Church, South, in the State of Georgia to meet in Trinity church at Augusta. On the day appointed, about sixty of the preachers assembled in Conference, and here, under the presidency of Bishop Geo. F. Pierce, the first Annual Conference was organized. Up to this time, all the colored preachers were merely local, and but few had received ordination. The material was very raw and untrained, and the men presented that uncouth appearance that belonged to the earlier days of freedom. A few had on long coats, and "plug" or "stove-pipe" hats, and all who could, wore long hair so as to look venerable, which was thought to be very becoming to ministerial dignity. To be in style and maintain the exalted dignity of the venerable parsons, I was adorned with a bushy head of red hair, parted in the middle, and covered by a "stove-pipe hat" of indefinite length. Like many other young circuit riders, fresh from the "bushes," I began to suspect that I was a very wonderful personality, based especially upon the length of my hat, and the enormous amount of "the insufferable wool" upon which it was pillared. I made the same mistakes that I have often observed in young preachers in later years. I was too big a fool to know that I was a fool. But the wear and tear of years will correct such errors, and force our erratic manhood into line. Of this conference of "raw recruits", I became a member. As there had to be a starting point, all the preachers who attended became at once full members of the Conference, and deacon's orders were given to most of them. At this Conference, I was ordained a deacon by Bishop Pierce and sent to Savannah, Ga. After I had received the appointment I returned home, sold out my farming interests, abandoned the plow, gathered my family, and went to Savannah to take charge of the colored church known as "Andrew Chapel." But this church was seized upon by the A. M. E. Connection, and was then in litigation. As there was no way for me to get or use the church, the white people of Trinity church in Savannah gave me their library to preach in, which was located upstairs in the rear of the church. Lest we should come in conflict with the white congregation because of our noise, we held our meetings only in the afternoons on the Sabbath. Here I preached and labored as pastor with a membership of about fifteen for six months. As the church was in litigation and could not be obtained until the decision of the court, I returned to my home near Sparta, Ga. Up to this time I was very deficient in that training that was almost absolutely essential for successful work in the ministry. I had a wife and three children to care for, and a very little of this world's goods. It is true, it required but little for their support, but then that little was essential. Happily for us, we lived two miles in the country from the town, where we had no rent to pay, no wood to buy, and were surrounded by plenty of vegetables and fruits. My wife milked a cow that was given to us by the owner of the place. We had chickens and eggs besides. I had learned to read to some extent in the days of slavery, and I thought that I knew it all, but going to Savannah was an "eye-opener," and I now had begun to see myself in the true light. Savannah was too big for me, and I was too little for Savannah. I learned by the dint of adverse conditions that the world had more in it than I had hitherto calculated.

As stated before, in 1857, when my second owner, Mr. T. L. Wynn, died, I became the property of Col. R. M. Johnston. In the early winter of that year, he went to Athens, Ga., and became a professor in the State College. As an important part of his effects, I was carried along with him and his family as carriage driver, house servant, and gardener. I was then fifteen years of age. As soon as I arrived in Athens, I felt an insatiable craving for some knowledge of books, and especially I was anxious to learn to read the Bible. What must I do? I was a slave and could not attend school, and it was considered unwise, if not dangerous for slaves to read and write. But my owners, although strict, were very kind, especially my master. So I determined to learn to read at all hazards, and take whatever risks there might be connected with it. There was a junk house in the city where rags were sold. I gathered and saved all the rags that I could, and sold them that I might get some money with which to buy books. After weeks of toil and intense vigilance in gathering and watching for rags that belonged to the first man that laid hands upon them, I had accumulated about thirty pounds. These I stuffed into the legs and seat of a pair of old white pantaloons, the cast-off garment of a large and long-legged man. At nights after tea, I was allowed to "go down town" for recreation. I hired a boy to help me carry the rags to sell them to the rag merchant. The boy put one leg of the pants on one shoulder, and the other leg on the other, and we both marched to town with bright dreams of wealth. Reaching the store, I lingered in the darkness in front of the door, and when the boy walked in with something that had the appearance of a fat man on his shoulders, the man said in a loud voice as if astonished at the strange sight, "What in the h-- is that you have on your back?" "Some rags," replied the boy. "Well, lay them on the scales," said the merchant. So we did, the rags were sold and the money was mine. With this money, I bought books. I purchased at one time, two "Webster blue back spellers," a common school dictionary, Milton's "Paradise Lost," and a Bible. These then constituted my full stock of literary possessions, a library more precious than gold to me. There were several colored people in town that could "spell to baker," in the old speller, while others could go to "the a, b, ab's" or to "the b, a, ba's." The white children and an old colored man taught me the alphabet, after which I fought my way unaided through the depths of my ponderous library. Day by day I took a leaf from one of the spelling books, and so folded it that one or two of the lessons were on the outside as if printed on a card. This I put in the pocket of my vest or coat, and when I was sitting on the carriage, walking the yard or streets, or using hoe or spade, or in the dining room, I would take out my spelling leaf, catch a word and commit it to memory. When one side of the spelling leaf was finished by this process, I would refold it again with a new lesson on the outside. When night came, I went to my little room, and with chips of fat pine, and pine roots that were grubbed up from the woods nearby, I would kindle a little blaze in the fireplace and turn my head toward it while lying flat on my back so as to get the most of the light on the leaves of the book. Thus lying on the floor with pine knots at hand and my blankets around me, I reviewed the lessons of the day from the unmaimed book. By these means I learned to read and write a little in six months Besides, I would catch words from the white people and retain them in memory until I could get to my dictionary. Then I would spell and define the words, until they became perfectly impressed upon my memory.

In 1858, in Athens, Ga., I was converted, and became a member of the Methodist church. At that time, Rev. W. A. Parks was sent as pastor to the colored church, while his uncle, Rev. H. H. Parks, was pastor of the white people's church. During April and May of this year, Rev. H. M. Turner, (now Bishop) came to Athens and preached every night to appreciative congregations, and under his powerful sermons, I experienced a change of heart, and became a zealous member of the church. I was taken into the church by Rev. Mr. Parks, and baptized and fellowshipped by his uncle, the Rev. H. H. Parks.

In 1861 when the war began, my owners moved back to Hancock County where I remained until freedom came to the slaves. After returning from Savannah in 1869, I began afresh my studies. That I might be retired and placed in the best condition to prosecute my studies, I purchased a number of schoolbooks and theological works, and sought a convenient place in the woods nearby where I was then living. Every day when the weather would permit I resorted to this place for study, contemplation, and prayer. By the bank of a little rippling brook that came murmuring down the rocky hillsides, I found an over-hanging boulder that ran up perpendicularly, mildly facing the east. A cluster of maple trees, interspersed with sweet gum, that constantly dropped their fragrance along the brook beneath, I selected as a silent boudoir. Wild grapevines interlaced with yellow jessamines, wrapped around the slim trunks of the towering wood, and threw a crown of green and tangled meshes of vines and flowers on the waving limbs above. The murmuring brook that rolled below whispered to me the presence of God, the wonders of his providence, and the marvels of his hand. Here, in the deep solitudes of silent nature, retired and alone, I spent the greater part of two years. Here I studied reading, writing, geography, grammar, arithmetic, astronomy, history, and theology. I read Milton, Dick's Works, Watson, Wesley, Stevens' History of Methodism, and a number of other books. Among them were "Barnes' Notes," and "Newton on the Prophecies." I gave close attention to the English language, as I would need that more than anything else. When I came to a word that I did not understand I would turn to the dictionary, spell it and define it, and with a cedar pencil I would write down every word thus acquired. On the next day, I first had a thorough review of all the words and all that I had read and studied the day before. I cared nothing for gold and silver, nor the presence and company of mankind, nor anything that would divert the mind from its deep thoughts of God or intense application. At the end of about twenty months, I was lost and bewildered in the deep things of God. However, I rose from my hermit home with spiritual powers and convictions that have been a wonderful help to me through all these years of struggle and toil. I became so intensely interested and profoundly engaged that sometimes I seemed to have been out of the body and in another sphere where God and angels stood nearer to men. There are no months and days in my life more precious to me than those days of mental struggle and silent contemplation. Then it was that my intellect was broadened and deepened, my religious proclivities intensified, and my character fixed.

In the fall of 1869, the colored conference of Georgia met in Macon, having Bishop Pierce for its President. Here I was ordained Elder and elected delegate to the organizing General Conference, which met in Jackson, Tenn., the 15th day of December, when the Colored Methodist Episcopal Church in America became a separate organization. I was present as a delegate during the session of the conference and voted upon all the measures that were put forth for the organization of the C. M. E. Church into a separate body. I was also the strongest advocate for the election of W. H. Miles, of Kentucky, to the bishopric. I first entered his name as a suitable person for the bishopric, and on the first ballot, he was triumphantly elected.

In January, 1871, the Conference convened in Augusta, Ga. Three Bishops were present, Miles, Vanderhost and Pierce. Bishops Miles and Vanderhost were the presidents, and presided on alternate days. Bishop Pierce was the distinguished and honored guest. When the appointments were read out, I was appointed to Trinity church, then the leading church in the conference, and perhaps in the connection. Here I was pastor two years and four months. In the fall of 1872, the conference was held in Columbus, Ga. Bishop Miles presided, and I was elected delegate to the called session of the General Conference, which met in Augusta, Ga., in March, 1873. I received every vote in the Annual Conference cast for delegates to the called session of the General Conference. When the General Conference assembled in extraordinary session in Augusta, in 1873, I was then pastor of Trinity church in which the conference was held. The business for which the General Conference was convoked in extraordinary session, was the election and consecration of three Bishops. Bishop Vanderhost was dead, and the whole presiding fell upon Bishop Miles. Bishop Pierce was present by special invitation.

Three men were elected Bishops, namely: J. A. Beebe, L. H. Holsey, and Isaac Lane. I was elected on the first ballot with Bishop Beebe, and I think I received every vote cast but two. I assisted Bishop Miles in preparing the Bishop's message for the conference, and took a leading part in all its work. Bishop Pierce preached the ordination sermon on the Sabbath, and at that time, I was ordained Bishop by Bishop Miles, assisted by Bishop Pierce. Here also, Bishops Beebe and Lane were ordained. The respective fields of labor for the new Bishops were laid off, and I was sent to Texas, Arkansas, Alabama, and Tennessee. The Bishop's salary was fixed at eight hundred dollars, his traveling expenses to be paid by the work he served. The work was poorly organized, and, indeed, was scarcely organized at all. I had with myself, seven in family. It was hard to get bread to live on and pay traveling expenses. My wife and children lived mainly on peas, bacon, and corn bread, having biscuits for Sunday morning breakfast. None of them had any shoes but went barefooted, and nearly naked, and lived in only a two-room house in Augusta. The first ten years was a struggle, a terrible struggle to keep our heads above the wave.

I have been so pushed for fuel on a cold night that I would take the coal ashes and wash them in water and drain out the burnt bits of coal in order to make a fire. In these years of suffering and almost starvation, my vegetable garden was the main and real dependence for a living. My good wife being strong and muscular stood by our garden, and often at night when the moon was shining, she and I would put the little ones to bed, and work until twelve o'clock. She would often cut short the rations for the family that I might have money to reach the appointments and build up the connection. No one knows the anxiety, the sorrow, and the depth of suffering through which I have had to pass for the church of my choice. The annals of God alone can tell. I cannot. But on I went, struggling up the hill of difficulty, often staggering and trembling beneath the heavy load. At an earlier period of my history (1869-70), my small amount of money once gave out and I taught a little school that kept the wolf of hunger from the door. This process of training to which I subjected myself, in its results, is, of course, infinitely better than ignorance; but it is far inferior to a regular course in the schools. I have found that it is patchwork, a kind of crazy quilt education; and yet this form of training has its blessings and advantages. It teaches a man to rely upon his own efforts, and by experience, he is convinced that nothing is impossible for him to accomplish by industry and faithful application. Since I have been a Bishop, I have been in the regular work. I have tried to do the work assigned to my hands with an eye single to the glory of God, the good of the race, and the salvation of men. I have traveled and preached all over the Southern States many times, and have been intensely interested in the establishment of the Colored Methodist Episcopal Church in America. Not because I thought it to be the best church in itself, not because I thought it purer and better than other such organizations, but because I thought it to be the most fitted religious power to meet the peculiar conditions that exist in the Southern States. Harmony between the two races is what is needed.

There can be no great progress in the betterment of the people of color without peace and harmony. The pulpit has much to do with human sentiment, and consequently with the actions of men. A semi-civilized people are necessarily greatly controlled by their religious feelings and sentiments. Often they are very religious, and at the same time very slow to comprehend their true status and the best modes of procedure in the chief things that make for their peace and prosperity. Many conditions and facts come in to make the Negro race unique in this country. The diversity of manhood brought about by the diversity of character presents to the calm judgment of the philanthropist intricate questions that involve the life and safety of the race. Moral purity and Christian excellence being equal, the best church for them is that religious organization that can, without compromising its great fundamental principles, adapt itself to present conditions. From the time of the emancipation of the slaves by the fortunes of war, I have not seen any reason why the Southern people should not be the real and true friends of the Negro race. The very religion that they taught, and practiced, and preached to the Negroes, directed them to be the friends of the ex-slaves. Consequently, I can see no reasons why they should not teach Negroes in the schoolroom. I saw from the first no reasons for any feelings of hate and revenge, either on them part of the one or the other. Accordingly, at the Conference held in Macon in 1869, I wrote and offered a paper on Education, in which I advocated the establishment of a church school by the M. E. Church, South, for the training of Negro preachers, said school to be taught by some of the good white people of that church. I knew that colored ministers of the gospel were far behind in those accomplishments that best fitted them for that important work, and that up to that date there had been but few opportunities presented to them for improvement. It was also clear to my mind that the white ministry was the only standard of excellence by which the colored ministers could be inspired to reach a higher plane of fitness. True, the Bible lay open before them, but in the conduct of the white ministers, the teachings of the Bible were displayed in visible, tangible form, and in its best practical phases. I thought then, and still think, the nearer the colored and white preachers are to each other in the work of the ministry, the better it would be for us all. This view of things caused me to be a perpetual and persistent advocate of the establishment of a school for the training of our preachers under the care and complete control of the M. E. Church, South, with teachers from the same source. "The Paine Institute" is the outcome of this sentiment. To enforce this idea I wrote a series of letters upon the subject in 1870 just prior to the organization of the Colored M. E. Church in America. The letters were published in the Christian Index while Dr. Watson was editing and publishing that paper for the colored people. At that time, and for some years after, many people, white and colored, thought that I was a "crank," and that it was the one thing impractical if not impossible.

In 1882, I was sent as Fraternal Messenger to the General Conference of the M. E. Church, South, which assembled in

Nashville, Tenn. I was especially instructed, first, to bear to them the friendly greetings of the colored church, and then to ask them to establish a school for us wherein our ministry might be properly trained and fitted for evangelistic work among their own people. When the General Conference of that church was held in Atlanta four years before, I addressed a rather lengthy communication to them upon the same subject. Some things I then said were thought to be a little reproachful, or reflective on them.

Their noble endeavors to preach the gospel in heathen countries, while they neglected the heathen at home, appeared to me to be inconsistent with the teachings of Christ and the Apostles. I meant not that the evangelical work in foreign countries should be neglected, or left to perish, but that the needy people at home should have some attention given to them as was done in the days of slavery. It was true, there were many barriers in the way, but no more in this country than in foreign lands. It ought to be said, however, that after emancipation the Negroes held themselves aloof from the Southern people to such extent that no proposition made by the latter could reach the former. Consequently, the margin for evangelistic labors among Negroes by Southern white people was narrow. When The Paine Institute became a reality, but few of the colored people approved of it, and the men of my own "faith and order" were more against it than those on the outside. My own preachers fought it bitterly as an untimely and unwise measure. They fought it because they thought that other Negro organizations would reproach us for being under the Southern sentiment and bowing to the verdict of pure prejudice upon the race question. Already all the colored churches had branded us as "Democrats," "bootlicks," and "white folks' niggers," whose only aim was ultimately to remand the freedmen back to abject bondage. This was, as subsequent events have proven, a distorted view of a great movement. But prior to the organization of the school in 1883, I traveled over the States, agitated the question, and spoke in its behalf in public and private. In the early fall of 1882 I held the Virginia Conference in Front Royal, and there I made a speech on the question, and laid the first dollar on the table that was ever given to it. Rev. W. T. Thomas followed with a like amount.

When I made my speech before the General Conference of the M. E. Church, South, in Nashville, in 1882, in behalf of the school, it was well taken and highly appreciated by the large and intelligent audience. The venerable John B. McFerrin put his arms around my shoulders and congratulated me for its timeliness. So did a large number of others. While I knew that all was agreeable and pleasant, yet I had a sense of fear and a thrill of doubt, lest I should make a failure, and the chief end for which I came should be defeated, and the whole project lost. But the golden eagle of success perched upon my staff, and I felt as a plumed knight beneath its wings. I had but one object in view and that was to help my fellowman. As this General Conference authorized the establishment of the school, and appointed a committee to put the thing in motion, Bishop Pierce being the chairman, called that committee to meet in Atlanta. In the summer of 1882, it convened in the First Church. Bishop Pierce and Dr. Haygood, and all the Bishops of the colored church were present. I wrote to our Bishops and urged them to be present, and all agreed to come but Bishop Miles. But I wrote him again to be present, lest he should hinder the initiatory of a great work, and to my surprise, he came. The whole matter was discussed pro and con. It was agreed to locate the school at Augusta, Ga., and ask the church for two hundred thousand dollars for facilities and endowment. Early in January, 1883, Rev. Morgan Calloway, D.D., then the vice-president of Emory College, and Rev. Geo. W. Walker, of the South Carolina Conference of the M. E. Church, South, came to Augusta and organized the school. For this purpose, rooms were rented in the heart of the city, and I gathered up the students by personal solicitation and public appeals until the number reached about thirty. Still it was a dark day for the school. Popular sentiment, among white and black, was widespread and bitter against it. But my friends were numerous, and Dr. Calloway used to say that I had more friends than any man he ever saw. I paid the first hundred dollars that were ever given for that purpose, a few days before the organization of the school, and since that time I have given myself, and collected from others almost continuously whatever I could for it.

In 1886, at the request of Rev. W. C. Dunlap, who was then its commissioner, I wrote a strong paper upon The Paine Institute, and sent it to him, and he sent it to the Nashville "Christian Advocate" to be published. But as it was so long before it appeared in the "Advocate," I concluded that it had found its way to the wastebasket. Finally, it appeared and I afterward learned from Mr. Dunlap the reason for this delay. He told me that the editor hesitated in publishing it because he believed it to be somebody else's production, and, consequently, "bogus." It was thought that the paper was an abler one than I could produce. It was published on the first page of the great church paper, a place where only the best documents appear.

In 1890, I was impressed that enlarged facilities were almost essential to the successful work of the school, and I started out of my own accord, with almost infinite misgivings, to make speeches before as many Conferences of the M. E. Church, South, as I might be permitted to reach. This I did with good results, as to the aid given the school. Although I was self-appointed, these conferences gave me the warmest reception and responded librally to the cause. This conference year (1897-'98), I am out on the same work. The trustees of the school and the Bishops of the Colored Church, and others, thought it wise, and so steadily urged me to take the field again in behalf of the school. This I have done, and have spoken before fourteen of the Conferences. In 1886 the General Conference of the Colored Methodist Episcopal Church in America, met in Augusta, Ga., and at that session, I wrote our "Financial Plan" by which Paine Institute and the other schools have received a considerable amount of money for their running expenses. I wrote this financial plan with special reference to the support of the schools of the church, which at that time were only two--"The Paine" and "The Lane." Perhaps there is no single act of legislation connected with the history of the church so significant and far-reaching in its effects as our "Financial Plan." Prior to its adoption in 1886 there was no way of a practical nature for the collection and disbursement of the general funds or general revenue of the church; but since the "Financial Plan" has been operated, the whole connection and the schools have felt the advantages, and owe their life, in a large measure, to its operation.

    For twenty years, I was the Secretary of the College of Bishops, and kept the minutes of our meetings from year to year at my own expense. Also, for the same length of time, I was the statistician and corresponding secretary of the connection, and replied to all communications of a public nature. I have written every Message for the Bishops except the one written by Bishop

Miles, in 1873, and I assisted him in that one. Only two of these Messages have ever been changed in a single word or sentence by the Bishops after I had written them, and consequently nearly all of the acts and legislation of our general conferences have been governed by them. I have read and passed upon every book in manuscript that has been published in our church from its organization until the present time, and have written their introductions. By authority of the General Conference, I have written and compiled the only hymnbook and the only Manual of Discipline that we have ever had, without any aid from the church whatever.

In 1881, four delegates were selected by the Bishops to represent the church in the Ecumenical Conference that was held in London, England, and no one went but myself. As yet, I am the only C. M. E. representative that has ever gone to a foreign port on an official errand. I read a paper before that splendid and august body according to the program. While in London, I preached in City Road Chapel, the distinguished mother of Methodism, from the same little box pulpit from which John Wesley preached the gospel of free grace. I did what I could upon the same great subject. During my stay in this the largest city of the world, I preached many times, perhaps with more force than I have before or since. On this trip to the first Ecumenical Conference of Methodism, I visited Paris and spent a week in "sight-seeing," weighing and measuring the world's greatest civilization, which no man can know until he comes in contact with it. I was delegate to the Centennial Conference of American Methodism that was held in Baltimore in 1884, and wrote a paper that was read in that conference. I was not present on account of ill health, but the paper was read by Rev. F. M. Hamilton, M. D. I was also a member of the last Ecumenical Conference that was held in Washington, D. C.

From 1870 until the present time (1898), I have written a great many papers and public communications on the history and polity of the church, a large number of which have been published in the Christian Index, the official organ of the church. I have given the reading public the greatest part of what permanent literature the church, up to the present time, has been able to produce. A great deal of what I have written in the last twenty-eight years never has been and never will be published. Much of it has already been suppressed, the other in all probability will be. I have often written sermons and afterwards destroyed them. This I have regretted, but they are gone beyond recalling.

As orator or writer, philosopher or preacher, I leave the estimate of myself to the candid judgment of those who have known me. As a citizen, I have tried to do the right, no matter how far I have come short of it.

My history is the history of the church of which I am a member. Its history cannot be written, nor its records compiled without me as one of the chief actors in its drama, and one who has deeply impressed himself upon its character and productions.

At present, I am the editor-in-chief of "The Gospel Trumpet," associated with the Rev. R. A. Carter A.M., who is the managing editor. I was elected to the office of Bishop when I was in my thirtieth year of age, and have held the position for twenty-five years. When I was elected it was said by some prominent man that I was the youngest man ever elected Bishop in any age or church.

I have not sought to get rich, nor make money, and have in no way made my office, position, nor the church an instrument of power or worldly gain. All that I have received above a bare living, I have made it a habit to return to the church, and to help on to a better state suffering humanity. At this time I have no "cottage in the wilderness" that I can call my home, and I have been in debt ever since I have been a Bishop. From youth to the present, life has been an unremitting struggle and a perpetual series of trials and conflicts. I have helped every man, woman and child that I could, and have tried to bear the burdens of others as the Scriptures direct.

L. H. HOLSEY.

Atlanta, Ga., February 23, 1898.

SERMONS.

SERMON I.

Man an Ideal Empire in Miniature.

"What is man, that thou art mindful of him? and the son of man, that thou visitest him?"--Ps. 8:4.

However small and insignificant man may appear to be in physical parts and bodily proportions amid the marvelous wonders of creation, and however insignificant in weight, height, and girth, when compared with the cloud-kissed hills or the towering mountains of eternal snows that lift their cones to the cloudless zones, and however light and ponderable he may be, compared to the infinite masses of tangible materialities that compose the universe in which he lives and moves, and of which he is a part, yet he is an ideal and realistic empire within himself. He has not only a realistic and enduring self, but he within himself is a real and ideal empire composed of all those powers and elements and inherent qualities that seem needful to complete the same. As a great steam engine may be built in miniature with its wheels, cogs, pulleys, cylinders, boiler, steam chests, piston rods, and gear, and as such a miniature engine may be as real and as perfect as a great engine which it may represent, so man is as perfect an empire as the little or model engine is an engine. As extension of parts and immensity of materiality have nothing to do with perfection of quality and character, so there need be no real difference in the two engines except in degrees. Indeed, man is a perfect creation in the fundamental facts and constituent elements of his being; and in these respects, he is an emanation of the Divine.

Humanity is divine, not in its moral purity and perfection, but in its mental capacity and corporal delineations. In everything but moral standing, the mental humanity is made in the image of its Creator. Man's mental humanity is the most real and the most conspicuous, indeed the only real enduring and essential attribute of his being. This mental individuality is in the image of God, the Supreme Mentality, that universal spirituality whose exterior building is the universe. This universe is the temple of God--the empire of the Supreme Mentality. Somewhere in this temple or empire, is the seat of universal government, authority, and power, the central location of one almighty thrilling force that acts upon and centralizes all the forces, energies and activities of all the universe. Gravitation, so called, can be nothing less than the operation of universal mentality in perpetual activity, by whose coercive energy the mindless elements and their infinitely various combinations sustain their harmonious interrelations. Thus, God is the life and soul of the universe in the same sense that man's soul is the life and light of his body. In this high metaphysical sense God is the life of the universe, the life of all the worlds, and the light of men. Evidently, man is the little God, the microcosm, an image of the macrocosm, which is God's larger universe. I need not dwell upon the indestructibility of human nature. It is as enduring as the ages. The tardy steps of centuries and cycles, the abrasions and indentures of all eternity, will leave the divinely imaged mental humanity fresh and green, forever blooming from its own deathless inherent vitality, because it is the image of God. Man's body is the temple of his soul. It is the splendid super-cosmopolite from the cosmopolitan center, tenting and dwelling for a season on this sub-lunar sphere. Its style and outlines and delineations are from heaven. It is the human form divine from the skies. The body is materialistic, because there is nothing in the universe other than matter of which it may be composed, and, therefore, desolation and decay shall overtake it. Its pillars and columns and towering arches shall fall down, and its stately roof and star-crowned turrets shall be broken and buried, but the image of God--the heavenly Visitant--that dwells within, in all its divine completeness and ethereal brightness, shall remain intact and untarnished amid the wonders of the cycles and the evolutions and transitions of the endless future. Truly, man shall live forever. Death is simply a removal from one sphere of being to another, a shuffling off a coarser and earthly coil, and a flight from a lower to a higher, purer and sublimer altitude in another sphere. It is the heavenly mentality abdicating an earthly throne, and reascending to its high place to be in perfect unison with kindred spirits, and vie in the splendors of the ethereal.

I. What is man in his physical constitution?

The psalmist says, "I am fearfully and wonderfully made." None but God can make man. No angelic fingers nor seraphic handicraft, nor wonderful mechanism, though contrived and manipulated by the skillful touch of angelic operators, can spin into threads and weave in golden looms the warp and woof, and manufacture into grace and beauty the delicate fabric of which man is made. None but God could throw the silver shuttle and bring from the evolving intricate mechanism of nature a mighty product like man. What a wonderful organism is this man empire! In this man empire, there are two hundred and sixty-three bones, five hundred muscles, and three hundred millions of brain cells, about three thousand of which are destroyed every minute. Therefore, every man has a new brain every sixty days. Every man that has lived to be seventy years of age has had, therefore, four hundred and twenty-nine sets of brains. Allowing that the average brain weighs sixty ounces, the man of seventy years would have had two thousand five hundred pounds of the precious thing.

Every day there are in each head more than four millions of the brain cells destroyed and replaced by new ones. The alimentary canal is thirty-two feet long. Man has a heart six inches in length and four in diameter, beating seventy times per minute, four thousand two hundred times every hour, one hundred thousand eight hundred times a day, and two billion six hundred millions in three score years and ten. At each beat, two and a half ounces of blood are thrown out of it at the rate of one hundred and seventy-five ounces per minute, six hundred and fifty-six pounds per hour, seven and a half tons a day, lifting it two thousand one hundred and twenty-two feet in the same length of time. We breathe twelve hundred times an hour, using twenty-four gallons of air a day. The breathing surface of the lungs is twenty thousand square inches, equal to the floor space of a room twelve feet square.

There are ten millions of silken cables or nerve cords that permeate and ramify the man empire, and center in the brain or the seat of government, making the greatest army of bodyguards that ever defended a kingdom or assembled upon the field of battle. The atmospheric pressure upon each square inch of the human body is fourteen pounds, making the weight upon a single human body of medium size forty thousand pounds. There are three thousand five hundred perspiratory pores, one-fourth of an inch long, making a little drainage canal forty miles long. Beyond and beneath all of these there is the great ganglia system of nerve tissues, so fine and minute that the point of a sewing-needle covers a whole system, in which there are thousands of little elastic threads, too fine to be seen except by glasses of the highest magnifying power known to man. Indeed, there are thousands of wonders and marvels in the physical constitution and operations of the human organism that are beyond the power of the mind to comprehend and explain. As God, the Supreme Mentality, presides over the universe, governing all its forces under the reign of law, so man is presided over by the mind, which is the supreme king of the man empire, governing all its parts and forces under the reign of law.

As God's mind is everywhere in the universe as an all-powerful and infinite activity, so the mind of man is everywhere the infinite activity in the man empire, filling all its parts and ramifications with its own ineffable light and glorious power. The God empire and the man empire are images the one of the other. The first is absolute and infinite in fact and abstract; the second is only absolute and infinite within its prescribed bounds. Both are the same in kind, but different in degrees. Therefore, the mind of man is the reigning king, the monarch and master of the man empire. Hence, man is an empire in miniature, with all the elements and inherent capacities of a kingdom, with its presiding monarch highly exalted upon the throne of the brain. Here lives and rules the mind king from whose dictatorial throne edicts are issued and commands sent forth into all the realms, provinces and the ramifications of the universal dominions. Indeed, man is an empire, having all the realms, provinces and the ramifications of the universal dominions. Indeed, man is an empire, having all the elements, forces and powers of nature in co-operative harmony, with its solids and liquids, and with its flora and fauna. It has lands, skies, seas, brooks, rivers and sparkling rills, that convey life and light and vitality to every part; from its fertile plains and golden fields, the metropolis and seat of empire draws tribute and support. The brain is the throne and seat of government and the mind is monarch. At his command ministers fly, cables hiss, sinews quiver, fluids dash, bones quake and sensations play like electric volts on the strings of the nerves. The mind king has eyes, ears, hands, feet, lips and tongue. He is the real and divine personality, the mind monarch whom God "from old times" has crowned, sceptered and clothed with the royal robe and insignia of state. He has judgment, discretion, tastes, will, choice and sensibility. Around him are his courtiers, diplomats and flaming ministers, hung on threads of gold and cables of silver, ever ready in reverential attitudes to execute his high behests. By these, space is blotted out and time annihilated. They fly on wings of thought and dance as it were on the lightning's flame, unifying and binding the states of empire with his arm of glorious power.

God's power is absolute, and his government executive, ministerial and dictatorial. "He maketh his angels spirits, and his ministers a flame of fire." As the empire of God moves about his throne as the center of attraction, so the man empire moves about the brain as the center of will force, rule and authority. This man empire has reservoirs of blood, lakes of water, rills of oil, and repositories of fluids that make up its gulfs, seas, inlets and bays. It has cables of elastic steel that thread and permeate all its parts, wrapped in silken integuments, and of the finest mould. Over these elastic threads and living cables, fiery dictates and high behests from the throne of the mind king dance and play and preach his will and proclaim his laws upon every hill, through every plain and valley, till every leaflet, rock, and tree, and all the deep gorges and mountain passes are resonant with his voice and filled with his commands. Deep in its seas there are flowing currents and boiling springs, from whose agitated waters come pearls of thought, folios of science, books of wisdom, bringing up from their hidden archives curriculums of study, deeper, vaster, broader and higher than ancient sages, approximating the ken of angels and the wisdom of seraphs.

There are mountains of bone, hills of cartilage, ledges of gristle, and ropes of sinew, to give form and beauty, and hold intact the rolling, jostling empire, with its leaping rills, restless seas, agitated gulfs and quaking land. It has a fertile soil of flesh and blood where roses blush and lilies bloom, through which a thousand streamlets flow to perpetuate its virgin days of youth, and crown its high meridian with the flora of light, wisdom, and strength, and its hoary years with a diadem of silvery harvest. This man empire has its winds, storms, cyclones, hurricanes, typhoons and trade winds, that roar among its caverns, whistle along its dales, hum among its rocks, play on its seas, shout over its hills, and strew its valleys with awful wreckage and direful ruins of uprooted forests. This man empire has its sun, the central luminary, meting its days and years, shining over its hemispheres, continents, seas and islands, giving light and life to its flora and fauna, producing towering trees of knowledge on its mountains of wisdom, from whose sunny peaks the mind king makes the sunbeams his horses and the ethereal currents his chariot wheels. Or through the lofty constellations of judgment, discovery, and golden thought he flies toward God until his wings of flame sets aglow all the widespread areas of air, sea, and land, until the lakes and rivers and island homes are filled with the life of God, the anthem of the ages and the symphonies of the skies, until every granite bone, elastic cord, and nerve cable is filled with heaven, and suffused with songs of seraphs and the melodies of the spheres. In orbital grandeur, around the miniature empire's sun shine the satellites of truth, virtue, will, purpose and the designs of life, while each planetoid of disease--the fragment of broken worlds--"walketh in darkness" through its cities, states and provinces, corrupting its fountains, contaminating its seas, and planting the baleful seeds of death and dissolution along its flowing currents and prolific soils. By flying fragments of broken worlds, many upheavals occur. Rivers overflow their banks, seas forsake their ancient beds, volcanoes explode, islands are submerged, mountains quiver on their rocky foundations, isthmuses sink, the land quivers while all its elements groan at the approach of the great catastrophe--death. Yea, by these fragments of broken worlds (diseases) many a joint is dislocated, cables of elastic steel are broken, and silken links of ligaments, sinews of brass, and bones of granite yield amid the general "wreck of matter and the crush of worlds." But the text says, "When I consider thy heavens, the work of thy fingers, the moon and the stars which thou hast ordained; What is man, that thou art mindful of him? And the son of man, that thou visitest him."

II. What is man in his spiritual or mental nature?

Whence came he? It is said there is nothing great in the world but man, and there is nothing great in man but mind. Indeed mind is the man--the true hidden man that thinks, conceives, judges and forms mental images; measures time and space, calculates in numbers, weighs even the imponderable masses of materialities, comprehends the sublime majesties of the universe, and has the power of will, choice, taste and thought, and indefinite continuity of individual consciousness. Deeply pervading all the attributes of his nature, the faculty of imagination like an angel of flame in splendid trim, with his golden sandals buckled on his feet, is ever ready to sweep the azure floors of the skies, or pierce the illimitable bounds beyond, where planets, stars and suns revolve on their rounds. By this faculty, space is blotted out and time annihilated. It is swifter than lightning, faster than electricity and outflies its volts that dance, as it were, on ethereal vibrations. In a moment, in the twinkling of an eye this cherub of the airy deep leaps heavenward or hellward, rejoicing in the happiness of the saved, or revolting at the horrors of the lost millions. It sweeps the tracks of lesser stars, pierces the orbits of planets, the belted splendors of Jupiter, the golden rings of Saturn, and visits "Arcturus, Orion, and Pleiades, and the chambers of the South," and wraps itself in the fiery sheets of the sun. It delights to flee through "The Milky Way" and the gem studded and constellated highways of God. Above stars, planets, suns, in the zoneless seas and unhorizoned spheres where the wings of seraphs battle for decades with the tides, the imagination lingers not, but lifting its fiery eye as system after system recede and sink in the shaded distances of eternal space he seems to cry to all the children of eternity, "On to Alcyon, on to Alcyon," the greatest system known to man, and which once seemed to be the center of universal power, and the place of the throne of the Most High. Here alone, at the throne of God, this wonderful faculty is foiled and baffled, but still radiant in its glory; and virgin strength. The wings of this mighty visitant can carry thought no farther. Here all ends meet and all explorations end. And here she cries--

>Eternal Power, whose high abode
>Becomes the grandeur of a God:
>Infinite lengths beyond the bounds
>Where stars revolve their little rounds.

>The lowest step beneath thy feet
>Rises too high for Gabriel's seat;
>In vain the tall Archangel tries
>To reach the height with wondering eyes.

In the transitions of eternal wonders, or those spiritual metamorphoses and evolutions that await us in the future, this faculty will dwell with us as the great photographer that never sleeps, but ever pictures upon the expanding canvas of the memory all the images with their exact forms that have ever been presented to the mental man.

III. But what is man in his moral constitution?

Man is a sinner, for the "Scriptures of Truth" declare that "All men have sinned and come short of the glory of God." Again, "Sin is the transgression of the law." Not a visionary or arbitrary command, but it is the violation of the law, the high, holy, and eternal law that governs the mental and moral universe. The law here spoken of is the embodiment of those underlying principles by which the universe is governed, and by which it maintains its successive and harmonious relations. By this law all of its elements, physical, and mental, act in concord. Whoever violates this law, or, if you will, these laws, is a sinner, a sinner against God and against all those spiritual beings, or mental individualities that have kept the laws of God, and thereby maintained their perfect estate. But this man empire, like others in which there is sin, is in perpetual throes, discord, and agitation, through all the years of its sublunar existence. Its restless inhabitants, with its rebellious states and provinces, constantly threaten the dissolution and subversion of its earthly domains. They threaten to transplant their interests and move the seat of empire to sublimer realms in those sunny plains of eternal day, where they may vie in the altitudes and majesties that live in their bright abodes. On earth storms arise upon the empire's seas, cyclones move and twist its mountains upon their rocky bases, shake its hills, sweep down its forests, filling its plains and valleys with howling destruction and the broken ruins of his kingdom. This is dying, so-called. As the mind king doffs his crown, lays aside his royal insignia of state, drops the sceptre and abdicates the throne, the silken cables and elastic cords break, the chambers of the king's palace are closed. All his courtiers, diplomats and flaming ministers cease to do his biddings and sink in eternal muteness. The nerve centers with their ten millions of body-guards in decadence die. On come the whirlwinds of death, over the coagulated seas of blood, up the streamlets of oil and channels of fluids. It climbs the vertebrated stairs of the spiral mountain of sinews and the hills of cartilages, crushing the granite of bones and scattering the parts of the magnificent pile. Its sun ceases to shine, its moon is turned to blood and all the stars of his lofty firmament are covered with the thick blackness of the night. The kingdom is demolished and the strength of the empire broken; but "the soul of man, Jehovah's breath," like an eagle from its cage, soars away on its wings of flame to dwell with God, to live and reign with Jesus, the Christ, "and through eternal ages will shout beyond the skies."

SERMON II.

The Irrepressible Conflict.

"For this purpose the Son of God was manifested, that he might destroy the works of the devil." 1 John III:8.

The text brings before us the two most conspicuous and renowned characters that have ever appeared in the world, acted upon the theatre of life or written their deeds upon the scroll of the ages. The annals of the ancients and the records of the nation's cannot produce their equals in the least degree whatever. Indeed, they stand out in bold relief of character and incomparable individuality. In their respective relations and natures, they are without a compeer. If all the greatness of mankind that has been displayed in the wisdom of the sages, the sagacity of statesmen, the valor and prowess of heroes, the sweetness of poets, the melodies of bards, were compressed into one great personality, he could not be so great, so wonderful, so matchless in consummate skill, profound wisdom, and exhaustless resources of those principles and things that make up the sum of greatness, as to rival the great characters mentioned in the text. Add to the control of such a personality, the rubies of kings, the diamonds of queens, the scepters of emperors, the gems and gold of princes, the sacerdotal scarlet of popes, the royal splendors of imperial courts, and the wealth of the ages and nations, yet such a character could not be compared to either of the distinguished individuals mentioned in the text. Then give such an individual a thousand years to display all this mighty wealth and dazzling splendor, yet in celebrity and influence, he could not approximate the ideal representatives of the irrepressible conflict--the Son of God and the devil. They both occupy the most exalted, lofty and most conspicuous position in the world, and in their work, influence and relations, they affect every nation, people, tongue and age. Their influence runs parallel with all times, epochs, and dispensations, ramifying all human governments, institutions, orders, fraternities and administrations. They affect the administration of all civil laws and the adjudication of every lawsuit. The one or the other has paved the pathway of every war, feud, conflict and revolution that has swept the zones of human civilizations, and fixed the destiny of men and nations. They affect all events in the world's written and unwritten history; from its incipient civilization and birthday, until in the sable drapery of its solemn requiem, the world shall cease to be aglow with the burning cinders that fly from the two great swords of Beelzebub and the conquering Messiah. Their influence stops not in time, but crosses the dark and trackless sea of death, and, rekindling on the shores of the spiritual world, will continue through all the great millenniums of eternal duration. Heaven and hell, with their crowded intelligences, will feel their potent and lavish influence by which their unnumbered billions of indestructible individualities will be forever swayed. Their imprint of character, for good or for evil, for hell or for heaven, for life or for death, will be made and deeply engraved upon the life and spiritual nature of every man, woman and child that has ever lived, or ever will live. They are not private but public individuals--federal heads--and representatives and embodiments of the two great diversities of the moral universe--good and evil. They are the representatives and heroes of the two great spiritual empires of the world, representing the two great moral ideas of the universe, which are founded upon the immortal principles of right and wrong, and of truth and falsehood, and of life and death. There is an infinite distinctiveness --constitutional, innate and irrevocable-- between these two individuals, in their nature, work and the great outcome of their career. This difference is essential, absolute and necessary. Therefore, it is as much impossible to operate them together in harmony upon the same plane so as to produce the same results, as it is to bring the north and south poles together. They are not only antagonistic, but antipodal. Two distinct principles inspire the work of the one, and the efforts of the other. The one is the principle of good and heaven, and the other is the principle of evil and hell, each in battle array, and perpetual conflict. The one is from heaven and the other from hell; one is life, and the other death; one is eternal happiness, the other eternal misery; one is of God and godly, the other is of the devil and devilish; one seeks the good of all, and one the death of all; one dignifies and deifies human nature, the other strips man of his glory, and leaves his prostrate form on the ground--"a splendid palace in ruin." Ever since sin hath entered into the world, and death by sin, these two great leaders and powers have exhibited themselves in the children of men in all the departments and diversified features of human society. In the courts of kings, in the palace garden, in the halls of justice, on the rostrum, in the realms of legislation, in commerce, field, and store, their prowess is seen. On the battlefield, in prisons and camps of horrid war, in the diplomatic circles, and stealthily along the quiet veins and avenues of thought and learning, all along, and everywhere, these two great majestic powers and principles confront each other and beset humanity round about. Hence, they have made the children of men good or bad, right or wrong, lifting them to heaven, or casting them down to hell. Therefore, whatsoever exists in the moral world, exists under the generic terms of good and of evil. Whatever is good is not evil, and whatever is evil is not good. Good cannot produce evil and evil cannot produce good. Life cannot produce death and death cannot produce life. Out of the depths of falsehood and darkness arise no truth and light, and out of the depths of truth and light come no darkness and no untruth. Darkness flees before approaching light, and falsehood loses hold when truth enters. Both cannot fill the same moral space at the same time, because they are moral spheres, filling the utmost limits of the mighty circles of the moral universe.

But to our conception, good and evil are best known by their effects upon those who follow the one, and pursue the other. If certain actions of moral creatures-- whether they be men or angels--render them happy or miserable, we know that those actions are good or evil, and spring from the good or the evil one. The practice of the two principles, in their respective relations and tendencies, always and forever produces and reproduces the same results in every case. They are eternal evolutions, but their evolutions never evolve out of themselves so as to produce something different from themselves. They produce their own likeness and superscription. Heaven is heaven, and hell is hell, a thousand times so in all their intrinsic natures throughout eternal duration. Good redeems her children, washes them clean and white in the blood of the Lamb, and sends them up the shining way to God and gives them the endless felicity of heaven. But evil, hideous, dark, and treacherous, sends her multitudinous squadrons to hell, giving them the misery that hath no end. Every word and work of men and angels, is, therefore, significant. There is a meaning, deep, profound, and far-reaching in every word, thought, and deed that enters the broad realm of being. Our thoughts chisel their forms upon the disc of the soul. Our words are written upon the folds of the heart, and our actions are the pent-up fires that leap out, leaving the dead volcanic cinders within. Like causes produce like effects, and like effects are produced by like causes. For every effect, there must be a cause, and the cause is best understood by the results. In the moral world, this is a truism. Now, every moral action that takes place among intelligent beings, is actuated by, and receives its momentum from the will and volition. The will is the motive power--the sheet anchor of the soul--that moves and stimulates the actions. Therefore, every moral action must have the consent of the will, otherwise they cannot be moral actions for which men and angels are responsible. All actions, therefore, are good or evil, and must be classified as such. The former lead to heaven, the latter lead to hell. At the end of every man's road stands life or death, hell or heaven, which is the inevitable and final destiny of all the living. When the sundering blade of death shall cut the vital threads of life, the soul--the heaving spirit--emancipated from its house of clay, shall then be transported away and up to God, or away and down to hell, and the day of preparation shall then be closed, when the inexorable fiat of Almighty God shall forever seal the irrevocable life of the one, and the changeless damnation of the other. No man can tell where hell is, but it is, it does exist, and whatever it is, and wherever it is, is a matter of small moment. But we are certain of two things: (1) It is a state and place of punishment. (2) That punishment is eternal in its duration. This arises out of the nature of the case, and the nature of God's government. When the sinner lands in hell, he will then be nearer to God, heaven, and life, than he will ever be again in all the cycles and evolving millenniums of eternity. Every surging wave and fleeing current of rolling years, will thrust him farther and farther out into the mid-ocean of hell's seething and boiling billows. Every turn of the wheel of the centuries will but augment his sins, and enlarge his capacity for transgression and sink him lower and lower.

Man is a progressive being. Progression--eternal progression--characterizes his innate constituency whether in the human body or out of it; whether in a state of bliss or state of misery; whether in earth, heaven or hell, or whether as applied to the three realities of his nature--physical, moral and mental. Change of place or condition cannot change his nature and indestructible selfhood or spiritual identity. Man is man in all the relations and conditions in which he may be placed. The immortal mind, the conscious self, with all the moral sensibilities, are incapable of decay, and therefore, of necessity, he is eternal in conscious duration. It seems, also, a truism, that the functions of the moral and mental man are never in a state of perfect quietism. There is a perpetual unrest, or rather, there is rest only in motion, progression, and development. Absolute quietism is incompatible with life, and there can be no such thing as vital energies in absolute quietude. Activity, in a greater or less degree, is the law of all living and is operative in all intelligent beings, whether in a state of bliss or state of woe. The saved will continue in obedience, the lost will continue in sin, since mere punishment has no redeeming qualities, and since obedience has no element of misery. As one wave of the sea produces another, and these produce others indefinitely, so one act of sin produces others through the eternal rounds of the dreadful series of transgressions. One hell will rise above and crowd the burning crest of another, each more dreadful and pressing harder upon the heels of the other, adding force and fury to the mighty avalanche of the fiery flood.

This text, like others, gives us the key to the origin of evil in the world, a question long debated by "the wise and prudent," and philosophic schools of the ancients. "The devil sinneth from the beginning," "for in the day that thou eatest thereof, thou shalt surely die," is the plain declaration of holy writ. Long was the world in darkness on this subject, and many were the vain and absurd theories entertained by the wisest of human kind. They were greatly troubled, puzzled, and bewildered to account for the advent and work of evil in the world. The fertile imagination of the ancient thinker set about to invent theories and invest probabilities with the habiliments of truth, hoping thereby to explain the mystery. Hence, then ecessitarians tell us that evil arises out of the nature and constitution of things; and that the Creator himself could not hinder its manifestation in the world. The Manichean theory is that there are two deities, the one good and the other evil; one the author of the body and the other the author of the soul; and that, therefore, the body is evil because it comes from the evil deity, and that the soul is good because it comes from the good deity. How absurd! But this is the result of human wisdom, when it sets at naught the word of God. "In the day that thou eatest thereof, thou shalt surely die." This positive command, given to Adam by the Creator, placed him, as a free moral agent in a state of probation and trial, clothing him with power to stand, yet liable to fall, because he could not be free as an agent unless it was in his choice to obey or disobey. But he fell. He "kept not" his first estate. By the influence of the devil, he became a sinner, "and brought death into the world and all our woes," because:

> "She plucked, she ate,
> Earth felt the wound,
> And nature from her seat,
> Gave signs of woe,
> That all was lost,"

Thus, sin entered into the world, and death by sin. Death, with all his howling furies came in pompous state, drawing the dreadful phalanxes of hell at his chariot wheels. Here then is that long and dreadful reign of the king of hell, called in Genesis, "The seed of the serpent." The declarations of the Scriptures, his natural character, and his real work in the world, prove that he is a real being, possessing individuality, and identity of personality. He is endowed with all the properties and characteristics that constitute an intelligent being. He is not the principle of evil personified, as some would have it to be, by assigning to it all the qualities and actions of an individual. He is not a mere myth, a fable or fabulous being--the outgrowth of man's fear, or product of human imagination. He is not an allegorical being without body or parts, but he is a great and astute being, mighty in power, skilled in wisdom, profound in knowledge and is thoroughly acquainted with the history of the world and the acts of the nations. In Genesis (3:15) he is the seed of "the serpent," and the singular personal pronoun is used to describe his personality and unity of being. In Job, he is called "Satan," the adversary, the great enemy of God. He is called "the prince of this world" (John 10:31), "The prince of the power of the air" (Eph. 2:2). He is "a roaring lion seeking whom he may devour." He is called "the God of this world" (2 Cor. 4:4). He is said to be a "murderer from the beginning, and abode not in the truth, because there is no truth in him. When he speaketh a lie he speaketh of that which is his own: for he is a liar and the father of it" (John 8:44). In Revelation he is the king of hell, for says the Apostle, "And they had a king over them, which is the angel of the bottomless pit, whose name in the Hebrew tongue is Abaddon, but in the Greek tongue hath his name Apollyon" (Rev. 9:1.1). Moses, the venerable lawgiver of Israel was well known by the Devil. He knew also his relation to God and to Israel, and that Israel venerated him above all men living or dead. But Moses died, and was buried in the land of Moab, in a valley over against Beth-peor. Satan knowing that Moses was dead went in search of his body, that if possible, he might devise some plan by which the body might be given to the children of Israel, that they might fall down and worship the lifeless corpse of a great man, as was the custom in Egypt, and thus bring down the wrath of God upon Israel, and nip the plan of salvation in the bud. But God in his goodness, foreseeing what would follow, placed an archangel there to watch over the body, and defend it against the violence and intrigue of hell's greatest legate. This is the work of a character, and the diplomacy of hell.

St. Peter declares that "God spared not the angels that sinned, but cast them down to hell, and delivered them into chains of darkness, to be reserved unto judgment" (2 Peter 2:4). Jude substantially declares the same thing, using almost the same words. From these, and similar passages of Scripture, we learn:

1. That the Devil is not a principle personified, but that he is a real substantial and individual character.

2. That he was in a state of happiness and probation --under positive law, well understood by him, and his fellows, or "the angels that sinned" and "kept not their first estate."

3. That he rebelled, or "sinned" against the laws of God and the government of heaven, and thereby lost his first estate and was cast "down to hell and delivered into chains of darkness," awaiting the just vengeance of the judgment day of Almighty God.

4. That he is a powerful prince, a mighty king and a great captain with an empire of spiritual darkness of immense proportions, and that he stirs the hearts and minds, and works through and in the children of disobedience.

Let us study his nature, work, and history, its it is written in the history of the world. He is wise, astute, stalwart. Standing up like a spiritual giant of massive proportions, and roaring like a lion when he thirsts for blood, he sounds his clarion voice, which, like an electric shock, flashes along all the zones and parallels of the habitable earth, convulsing the nations, and spreading far an intensive discord through all the tribes of men. His footprint and handiwork is seen and felt in every land, state, and age--wherever men live and die. The operations of his hand are simply marvelous--dark deep, intricate, and profound. His devices are multiplex and serpentine. His aim is one. He lives through the ages with illustrious strength and indomitable will that forever spring with elastic and virgin strength, which nerves his spirit and inspires his obdurate soul with a fiery zeal that "no languor knows." Changes in the world of man make no changes with him. Yoking the whirlwinds to his rolling car, he traverses the misty deep, plods and plows the surging seas, and as a bold corsair in quest of treasures new and old, he seeks the heathen in his jungle heath island home to pour hell and denser darkness upon his moral and mental day. He throws the somber pall of sin and death high upon the disc of his shield, while his black pinions shade and darken the path and contract the highway of the world's civilizations. As a warrior, he stands at the head and is the dictator of a multitudinous, powerful, and well-organized

army, equipped and skilled in all the military tactics of diabolical and spiritual warfare. His soldiers are the bold spirits, the thunder-driven and hell-bred legions from the infernal cave of the damned that kept not their first estate; being goaded on by the hell in their conscience, they are ever ready for the scenes of war and carnage. The weapons of their warfare are mighty, formidable and tried upon the spiritual battlefields of the nations and ages. Each soldier-devil is armed with barbed spears and swords of adamantine steel whose dreadful play in the air shows that they are in the hands of spirits bold and spirits daring. Their quivers are filled with winged arrows, polished and tempered, and tipped with poison of asps and venom of serpents. Precision and dexterity characterize the engagements of these diabolical archers and sharpshooters of hell. But open war is resorted to only when cunning and intrigue fail. The devil is great in cunning

and stratagem. Hence, the Apostle tells us that "we are not ignorant of his devices." He stirs the passions, lust and pride, and the baser nature of kings, princes, rulers and potentates, and perpetually foments civil and national strife among the nations of the earth, causing the plowshare of destruction to glide through the flourishing fields of human society, uprooting the temples, of civilizations and flooding their open halls with human gore, and piling high around their fluted columns the broken bones and bleeding bodies of the dead and dying, causing the widow to weep and the orphan to sigh and clamor for bread. Often he seeks his seat in the church of God, throwing discord and confusion among the saints of the Most High. He is not omnipotent, nor omnipresent, but mighty, and is the antipodal force and antagonistic power against Christ, God and humanity. Messiah on the one side and the devil on the other are great leaders and captains. The battle began in the Garden of Eden six thousand years ago. Both have had varying success and defeats upon the arena of the nation and rostrum of the ages. Still the battle rages. Neither has entirely defeated the other, but onward and fiercely rolls the battle cry. But hush! hush!! I hear the silver notes of the golden clarion of Messiah coming with martial tread and haughty tramp. He is "clothed in a vesture dipped in blood." He rides upon the great white horse of truth and on his head are "many crowns." By his side hangs a potent double-edged blade of "heavenly temper keen" that never turns back from the blood of the slain. His armies are upon white horses robed in the bright and shilling habiliments of divine purity. Their swords are forged upon the anvil of God in "the house of David," and made of the best old Jerusalem steel dug out of the mountains of God. Other blades may break or shatter, but these never. Dreadful are the incisions they make in the rank and file of the enemy. "How shall one chase a thousand and two put ten thousand to flight?" "For the weapons of their warfare are not carnal, but mighty through God to the pulling down of the stronghold of the devil." Christ cannot fail. Hell is great, but heaven is greater. Christ is rich in all the fathomless depths and endless heights of eternal power. He is more than a match for the Devil. "He is the same to-day and yesterday and forever," and on through the eternal series of great and glorious achievements he repeats his mighty deeds and stupendous acquisitions in the redemption scheme. While this and more is true, yet dark and dreadful were the closing scenes of the world's greatest drama, for it is said in Genesis by the mouth of God, "Thou shalt bruise his heel." The "Thou" here spoken of is the Devil himself, and the expression comes from the custom of pursuing an enemy so closely that the heels of the fleeing are trod upon by the front part of the foot of the pursuer. This implies that the contest was to be close, fearful and irrepressible, and that Satan would pursue the Son of God even to the gates of death. This is also the turning point in the great and long struggle for the mastery, and the ascending of the one over the other. Here the Son of God must conquer or be conquered. Here he must rise victorious over the power of darkness, or he must fall under shame and defeat. Christ says, "The prince of this world cometh, and hath nothing in me." He felt the dreadful tread of Satan crowding upon "his heels," while his steps in the Garden of Gethsemane were marked with his own blood, sweat, and tears. He felt the powers of hell surrounding him on every side and hedging in the pathway of the Son of God. Four thousand years of conflict had passed, but now the culminating hour is reached at last. Now is the dreadful hour when his strength and power are tried and hope flickers in the golden sockets of life. Now the Redeemer of the world was to stand off no longer, and from the red mouth of heaven's artillery rain hail and burning thunderbolts upon the hideous head of the demon; but he must meet him face-to-face, and arm-to-arm, and measure swords and spears. Ten thousand devils peep up from the bottomless pit and hiss and howl and clamor for the blood of the Son of God. Swift winged messengers pass in rapid transition from earth to hell, and also from earth to heaven, bearing dispatches and news of the dreadful hour and of the culminating scenes of the great and irrepressible conflict. O, dreadful hour, fraught with life or death for the millions of the sin enslaved of Adam's race! The Son of God now falls upon his knees upon the cold ground, while his humanity passes through the fearful ordeal and crucial test and the augmented sorrows of the ages, but amid anguish, pains, sorrows and temptations, he says, "My soul is exceeding sorrowful even unto death." The sins of the world were upon him, and for that reason he must be fearfully chastised by the hand of his Father. But he went a little farther, and fell on his face and prayed, saying, "O, my Father, if it be possible, let this cup pass from me! nevertheless, not as I will, but as thou wilt." This prayer he prayed three times. He begins to sweat blood and bleed at every pore, and his tears thrown up from the depths of an aching heart fell in Gethsemane's Garden. Not only his body, but his soul, the intelligent, the sensitive inner man, was "exceedingly sorrowful even unto death." How deep was that sorrow, and how painful the situation! He looked up, and behold, Judas with his band of ruffians came with swords and staves, and the Son of man is betrayed into the hand of sinners and taken to the judgment seat of the wicked. "Surely he hath borne our grief's and carried our sorrows; yet we did esteem him stricken, smitten of God and afflicted." Having ascended the hill of sacrificial death, he is nailed to the cross. The rough iron spikes pierce his feet and hands, and he is cruelly transfixed to the rugged wood. Every sinew is stretched, every tendon distended, every joint dislocated, and every nerve cable thrills with pain. Here hangs in agony and blood the Prince of Peace, the incarnate Son of God, the Alpha and the Omega of all creation. But he dies! "It is finished." But the great tragedy is not yet ended. Another scene is yet to be acted In the world's greatest drama. Joseph of Arimathea deposits the dead body in his new tomb. The disciples scattered and all seemed lost. Nature by her internal throes "gave signs of woe." Hell laughs and shouts in triumph. Hope seemed fled away. upon the dying zephyrs of the last breath of the expiring Messiah. But on the third day, Messiah calls back and, resumes his ancient power. The bars, bolts, and rock-ribbed jaws of the grave began to swell and heave as if moved by the omnificent hand of God. Death and hell heard the rattling chariot wheels of the heavenly legates as they leaped from the heavenly gates and fled to the rescue of the sleeping Jesus. They pour the message of life from God into the dungeon of death, and the Son of God rises from the dead. Heaven laughs, hell is astonished, and, universal humanity is thrilled by the triumphal declaration: "I am he that liveth and was dead, and behold I am alive forever more, amen; and have the keys of hell and of death."

SERMON III.

The Fatherhood of God and the Brotherhood of Man.

"I am debtor both to the Greeks, and to the Barbarians; both to the wise and to the unwise."--Rom. 1:14.

From the language of the text, it is evident that the great Apostle to the Gentiles designed to represent or set forth the universal family of man as one whole and perfect race in so far as a common humanity goes. But when he comes to consider the civil, social and religious status of humanity, he divides mankind into two very distinct divisions, and grades the human race under the appellation of "the Greeks," and "the Barbarians." This view of the apostolic idea is emphasized and paraphrased by the words, "The wise and the unwise." Hence, the difference between "the Greeks" and "the Barbarians" is a state or condition, and not a fundamental. The difference between the two representative specimens of the human family here presented is not constitutional or inherent in the nature of man; but the evident or manifest superiority of the one over the other, grew out of those conditions, elements, and phases of civil and religious life that proceed upon natural law, and have always characterized, to a great or less extent, the race of mankind. Whatever aspect of human progress or retrogression has presented itself to the student of ethnical science and the philosophy of history, nothing founded on bottom facts warrants the conclusion that one man is, by nature and certainly not by grace, superior to the other. But there is a common humanity with a common interest, destiny and parentage that unify all the nations and peoples of the earth. Manners, habits, customs, the forms of governments and civil institutions change according to the tastes of men and the evolutions of human nature; but the innate manhood knows no change in that sense whereby one man or people is made inherently superior to the other. Human nature is found by experience as well as by history and philosophy to be the same in quality and essentials, in all ages, states and conditions. State or condition, whether national, racial, or personal, has nothing to do with those great immortal and high mental parts or constituencies that belong to the human individualism. All men are created with the same number of mental faculties, the same number of those attributes of mental and physical parts that have characterized all the individuals of the race from its inception in the Garden of Eden to the present day. Neither does time, in its steady and onward flow through the centuries, nor do those advancing and changing forms of government under which man has lived, have any tendency to change his innate nature in the slightest degree whatever. No improvement in civilized life, no matter how far and how high it may advance the human character in the scale of progress, can add to or take from man one single faculty of his nature. So far as the kind and number of the human faculties are concerned, they are complete. And it seems that his present number of faculties is sufficient to put him and keep him in touch with the spiritual, mental and physical universe by which he is surrounded, and of which he is a part, as well as a citizen. The capacity to do and to know and to comprehend the phenomena of mind and matter on this plane of life, or it may be even in the life to come, does not demand new faculties or other innate constituencies, but only the culture, the development and the indefinite expansion of those that now belong to him. At present, man seems to be in the morning twilight of his being. He is on the inclined plane from the days of his infancy, ascending those loftier graded altitudes of perfections of being and character that are demanded by the very nature of his existence. But so far as the real attributes of his nature are concerned in their deepest and broadest realisms, there will be no more change in him than there is between the man when he is an infant and the same man when he is grown to riper years. In the growth, training and culture of such an individual, great changes have taken place. His body has grown, enlarged and taken on its majesty, beauty and stateliness. His mind has been cultured and all the faculties have become active, keen and incisive, and with the fullness of a finished and rounded manhood, he is far different from what he was when lulled to sleep by the sweet, soft melody of a mother's song. But mark you, he is the same individual. There has been added no new nature, attribute or faculty, either in his physical or mental being, but he is the same character with the added expansions and developments of the human essentials. It denotes progress in the potentialities of the mental and immortal humanity that constitute the real man, whose continuity of consciousness is eternal. If these statements are not true, then man's identity is not possible, and his moral obligations with his moral nature are destroyed, and there can be no punishments or rewards. Indeed, man is man wherever found, with the same connections, relations and affinities of life and character. Every man is made by the same hand, according to the measure, mental contour and personal and original endowments. Neither can racial distinctions, color, climatic or geographical situation of birth and growth make any difference in the characteristics of his real manhood. This proves the unity of the race of man, the oneness of interest, origin and destiny. What, therefore, is possible for one man is possible for all men under the same conditions and circumstances. All are made in "the image of God," after the same pattern, in the sublime fundamentals of the original. Hence, the great Apostle says: "I am debtor both to the Greeks and to the Barbarians, both to the wise and to the unwise." In plain words, "I am in debt to all men, whether they be the polished, educated, and refined philosophic Greeks, or the crude, wild and untutored Barbarians." Again, there is but one religion for all men. There is one God and Savior--"Jesus Christ, the same yesterday and to-day and forever." God has presented to mankind but one living, active and forceful Christianity, which is adapted to, all states, ages, and conditions of universal intelligence. God has adapted its requirements, tenets, doctrines, practices and all its splendid elements and agencies to reach and save his intelligent offspring's in any and in all the possibilities of life and human probation.

I. What then is the greatest work to be done under heaven?

Answer: To save both the polished Greek and the ignorant Barbarian. Both have souls that must be redeemed or lost. This is a great work, the greatest that can be done by men or angels. For this, the great universal church of God was established in the earth. For this the great world of man has groaned, oppressed beneath the heavy and sable bands that beclouded as with a heavy-laden pall of death his social and civil horizon in the dreary and sluggish moving centuries of the past. But dead centuries cannot save, nor sleeping cycles atone for the sins and transgressions of men. Time can do nothing of itself without the superior power and agency of the Son of God. We are all debtors one to all the others, and all the others are indebted to that one. God demands of all men to do all that they can to save the race of man from sin. Our duty, in this respect, is never accomplished until we have done our best to reach the ends of the salvation of the one and universal humanity. All the great works, achievements, and wonderful discoveries of the centuries cannot be compared to the work of redemption. Man is lost. The vital threads and living strings that played in harmonious relation between heaven and earth, threading and thrilling the deep ethereal seas, were broken off by the cruel hand of sin. Somewhere in the great ocean between God and man, the ends of the broken cables lie buried in some vast depth, sleeping embedded amid the unfathomable mysteries in the wonders and plentitudes of those awful seas of pandemonic and howling space. Over these broad seas of unfathomable depths, tented Night threw her canopy of thick darkness, heavier than mountains of iron and stronger than hills of brass, over which the thunders of God and the winged lightnings of wrath played in gorgeous and awful splendors filling the space of empire between God and man with all the obstructive elements, agencies, and forces of sin and disobedience. No seraphs bold, nor angels daring, ever penetrated the darkened highways or flashed on flaming pinions over the howling seas, gyral cataracts and leaping billows of that wide and black waste that divided the empire of sin from the empire of life. Man is lost. The planet on which he lives has broken her moral relations with God, life and glory. The silver cables and steel chains whose adamantine links were older than the angels and stronger than the cycles and more wondrous than the centuries have been broken. The rebellious planet is lost somewhere in "the void immense," and rolling away far from God and peace she wheels her flight covered with the thick and unyielding nebulæ of sin. God strikes the keys of the diapason of being, and all the cords, pulleys, wheels and threads of the universal mechanism are still attuned but one. He strikes again all the keys, and pulls all the lines and threads of the infinite and universal mechanism and all respond to their God and their Maker but one. There is a harsh sound, a broken thread that causes a discordant note in the mechanism of the moral universe, breaking the melodies of the centuries, the harmonies of millenniums, and severing from the throne of God and the bosom of his love an alien planet. The cables break, heaven feels the tremor, and the rocking chimes of a lost empire of man and God come flashing on ethereal volts faster than ever lightning flashed. They danced into the outer space of "the lost Pleiades," when God thundered in the heavens and sent it in billions of flaming parts, broken shafts and splintered spars as flaming messengers to execute his high behests in the illimitable empire of space. He looked out on the extended seas of the ethereal deep, counted the stars, weighed their imponderable masses in scales and called them by name. Every sun is still shining, and every star in the vaulted chambers of creation is twinkling in its orbit and dancing and singing on its eternal lines, making schedule time. Hard by the throne of God a thousand millions of sparkling and singing worlds roll on in their awful majesty, and yet in meek submission to their awful King. On they fly, wrapping their belted splendors and burning webs of golden flame around the throne of the great "I Am"-- all but one, and that is the one called earth. "Oh, earth, earth, hear thou the word of the Lord." Who will go in search of the lost planet calledearth? unite the cables, tie their broken ends and severed cords and again hitch them to the throne of God? Who among the ancient sons of God and the tallest archangels of eternity hath the arm of power to sound the infinite mains, gather the cables with hand omnipotent, and relink their broken fibres? O, ye bright sons of heaven, ye morning stars that sang together when "all the sons of God shouted for joy," can you not go and do wonders and work the works of gods in the mighty deep? Heaven stood mute, seraphs dropped their crowns, victors cast their palms, choirs hushed their voices, the Te Deum of the cycles lost its melody, and unstrung harps their euphony. Millions of towering spirits, each wrapped in the splendors of a morning sun, with uplifted wings of sheeny brightness, with eyes of flame whose focal gleam swept the orbits of a thousand suns, measured the rims of moons and traced the track of comets, stood in listening attitude but dared not move. The temple of the tabernacle in heaven was opened and the house of the lords of creation ceased the eloquent and profound deliberations upon the things which "the angels desired to look into." Bulls and briefs, edicts and behests, and all the wide commands of the temple court that flamed on lip and tongue, and glowed in the hearts of the tall minds and intellectual majesties of the universal metropolitan center, felt the tremor and the moving forces of the approaching crisis. The crowned and mitered sentinels who stood on the jasper walls of heaven while cycles perished and millenniums died, left their golden towers, and like burning splinters of broken suns, sweeping from the azure peripheries to the diamond centers, they joined the heavenly perturbation and stood with bated breath and uncovered heads in the great congregation. Fiery squadrons on electric steeds whose thrilling circuits quiver with the living energy of heaven, faster than flashes of lightnings, thread and ramify the illimitable "fields of light," the kingdoms, thrones, dominons, principalities, powers, heights, depths, lengths and breadths, and all the multitudes that dwell in those eternal and extended areas under the gem-studded and the arch-flaming concavity of heaven's high ceiling are summoned to the tabernacle of the great congregation. It was "a great multitude which no man could number" of all the great personalities and eternal kings and princes and queens of the ages that swept along the streets of gold with sandals of rubies, crowns of diamonds and amaranthine robes of sunbeams, whose glorious forms and splendid trim glittered like pyramids of incandescent flame and glinted blushes of a sun sifting through the seven colors of the rainbow. Mighty legates and plenipotentiaries in their dazzling ermine and brilliant paraphernalia of state, with their broad phylacteries and embossed folios, containing the legal lore of the eternal annals, sat upon thrones of judgment. One hundred-forty and four-thousand legations, representatives of as many dominions, filled the diplomatic circles with their nodding plumes and royal credentials. Far out in the open sea towards heaven's impalpable periphery the loyal legions of the royal dominions stand with stately mien and awful muteness, while a thousand suns peep up from the horizon, uniting their blended splendors in graduating zones of light as if pinned together by the sheeny tails of comets and veiled with the radiance of the morning stars.

But "there was silence in heaven about the space of half an hour." It was a silence whose mighty influence was like the stillness that comes after the haughty steps and heavy tramp of cycles and centuries have crushed the nations, ground their temples to dust, broken the scepters of kings, calcinated cast-iron dynasties, corroded and gnawed asunder empires of brass and monarchies of steel. And still the world feels the iron heel of the ages. The despot's spear is not broken, he still maintains his throne, riding down the centuries, drinking the blood of the nations and wielding the scepter of universal dominion. So the profound silence and awful muteness was deep, distinct, decisive, and heaved the deep bosom of heaven as the ocean currents heave the mighty bosom of the deep. But a world is lost. A planet, like a ship on the high seas that has broken its cable, thunder-struck and storm-driven, is tossed upon the ocean of sin and the vasty deep of moral pollution. Who is able to recover it? Who is able, oh, who? John says, "And I saw a strong angel proclaiming with a loud voice, Who is worthy to open the book and loose the seals thereof? And no man in heaven nor in earth, neither under the earth, was able to open the book, neither to look thereon. And I wept much because no man was found worthy to open and to read the book; neither to look thereon. And one of the elders saith unto me, Weep not; behold the Lion of the Tribe of Judah, the root of David, hath prevailed to open the book and to loose the seven seals thereof." Again, "Then said I, lo, I come * * * to do thy will, O God." Again, "Here am I, send me." This is the voice of God the Son to God the Father, loud and strong, and ringing high above all the mighty powers, altitudes and massive conclaves and sublime actualities of the assembled dominions, states and kingdoms of the universe. Heaven was satisfied. God smiled, musicians leaped to their harps, seraphs flashed their wings, tuned their ivory lutes and grasped their golden cymbals and all the choirs and multitudinous hosts cast down their crowns, regathered the silver chords of the ancient anthems and the eternal melodies of the spheres, waving in sweet and dulcet octaves the mighty chorus, "Saying with a loud voice, blessing, and honor, and glory, and power be unto him that sitteth upon the throne, and unto the

Lamb for ever and ever." Yea, "for ever and ever," and the doxologies rolled and echoed, reverberating over "the sea of glass," resounding along "the river of life," until every hill and mountain, valley and plain, and all the wide arenas, highways and lofty courts of the skies were filled with the music of his name and resonant with the redemptive anthem. There is a chorus in that song for you and for me. A golden harp for every hand, and deep sweet melodies for every lip, tongue and heart, and a silver cord and ivory key for every finger. There is a palm for every victor and a crown for every conqueror. So he comes, and so he is here. Behold he standeth at the door, he is at our elbows, he is in this place.

Isaac Watts touches the central chord in the universal diapason when he sings:

> Plunged in a gulf of dark despair,
> We wretched sinners lay,
> Without one cheering beam of hope,
> Or spark of glimmering day.

> With pitying eyes the Prince of grace
> Beheld our helpless grief:
> He saw, and (O amazing love!)
> He ran to our relief.

> Down from the shining seats above,
> With joyful haste he fled,

Entered the grave in mortal flesh,
And dwelt among the dead.

O for this love, let rocks and hills
Their lasting silence break,
And all harmonious human tongues
The Saviour's praises speak.

Angels, assist our mighty joys,
Strike all your harps of gold;
But when you raise your highest notes,
His love can ne'er be told.

SERMON IV.

Christianity Shiloh's Empire.

"The sceptre shall not depart from Judah, nor a lawgiver from between his feet, until Shiloh come; and unto him shall the gathering of the people be."--Gen. 49:10.

The text is a prophecy uttered by the Patriarch Jacob upon his dying bed to his sons in the land of Egypt. Passing through the troubles of life, he came at last to his dying day. The words that he spoke were inspired predictions respecting the things that should befall the house of Israel in future generations. His prophetic vision being touched by the finger of God, and enlarged by his Spirit, he sang a song of triumph that he never sang before, and threw the verses of its enchanting melodies down through the illustrious line of great princes, priests, and kings, until the great Messiah became haloed and wrapped in the brilliant splendor of his expanding kingdom.

The Shiloh here spoken of is Jesus Christ, the Son of God, and the son of David. He was the son of David according to the flesh, and declared to be the Son of God with power. Jacob felt that power while the bright rays of its light flashed upon his soul and strewed his pathway to the grave with the leaves of the tree of life and the blushing petals of perennial flowers. Shiloh was his hope. He looked through the kingdom of Israel to the kingdom of Shiloh, that should come in the fullness of time, and by whose power the yoke of sin should be broken from the necks of the nations, and the mild sceptre of Shiloh should sway the life and hearts of men.

We need not produce any elaborate argument to prove that the term Shiloh refers to Christ. From the scope of the prophecy, the depth of its subject, and the nature of its prediction, especially in its application to a person, Shiloh can only refer to Christ, the Messiah of God. David and Solomon were great characters. They were men of God, and in their official capacity were symbols and metaphorical representatives of Christ. The kingdom over which they presided represented that which was to come. Hence it is said, "The Lord God shall give unto him the throne of his father David; and he shall reign over the house of Jacob forever; and of his kingdom there shall be no end." The Shiloh then here spoken of is the same as he who should "reign over the house of Jacob forever," to whose "kingdom there shall be no end, because unto him shall the gathering of the people be."

But the text says, "The sceptre shall not depart from Judah, nor a lawgiver from between his feet until Shiloh come." That is, the theocratic government of the Jews was to have its kings and rulers coming from the tribe of Judah until Christ should come and take the throne whose by right it was.

1. Let us consider the Christian system as a progressive force.

Christianity is a growth as well as a principle. While its fundamental doctrines are eternal and form the basis of eternal government, yet the application of its principles and practices is adapted to all conditions of humanity, whether collective or individual. It has the same power over a single person that it has over a nation of single individuals. Indeed, this is the first fruit of its operation. It takes hold upon personal life and personal character. It seeks the individual members of a nation and the distinct characteristics of a people. It often begins with the smallest number, and sends them as messengers and forerunners to open a highway in the wilderness and make a royal pathway for our God in the desert. Step after step, it adds one by one to its army of heroes and princely warriors. It appeals to each and every one as a distinct consciousness, and calls upon the perceptive faculties and reasoning powers to consider its claims upon the attention, presenting its attractiveness to the sons and daughters of men. It appeals to personal interest and human consciousness on the highest plane of the eternity of being, and proposes to solve the profound and intricate relations that exist between God and man. It reaches deep into the moral and spiritual entities that relate to the incomprehensible and the incomparable Deity. As a moving force, it threads our being, ramifies the conscious individuality, speaks in thunder tones to the sensibilities and all the properties and potentialities of intelligent creatures. It stimulates, stirs and lifts the legitimate aspirations of man to those sunny altitudes, where alone God and man walk in peace, and blend in the splendors of reconciliation and a glorified union. It moves and propels man upward to his designed dignity and the eternal harmonies of the universal spheres, where the stars of God "forever glow in the fervent warmth of His love." Religion is a secret power. It plies the currents beneath the waves of human nature. Men may see you, they may think of you, and speak of you, and weigh you in the scale of their judgment. They may reach a true or false conclusion respecting you as a man and a citizen; but there is a divinity that dwells within, whose shape or form they cannot see, whose stately steps and steady march through the deep chambers and hidden receptacles of the soul they cannot measure. It is a thing of personal possession and personal experience, deep and resonant with the music of heaven that fills the soul with the reigning Shiloh, the living Christ of God.

Again, Christianity suits every man, fits every age, and is adapted to every sphere of being in the universe. It is the need of every being, the joy of every soul. It crowns life with honor, embellishes its devotees, makes its followers conquerors and gives light in the darkest night and opens the royal highway to the throne of God. It softens the dying bed, bridges the river of death, and in chariots of fire takes God's Elijahs to the paradisaical city of the Great King

2. "The sceptre shall not depart from Judah till Shiloh come."

That is, Christ was to come and grasp "the sceptre" that Judah held. Judah was to hold it until Messiah should appear on the scene and take his rightful authority. Christ did come. He came at the predicted time, and "in the fullness" of the purposes of God. Here he must stay and "reign until he hath put all enemies under His feet." This is his earthly work, and his great mission in the world. It will not be completed until this is done. "The sceptre" here spoken of is the royal insignia of the Messiahship. It is the emblem, or symbol of His authority, and His right to reign over all the earth. Ancient kings and monarchs had their sceptres, which signified their complete and extended jurisdiction. Before them the millions prostrated the body. With trembling heart and hand they bowed to earthly masters. But their sceptres have departed, their authority has gone, their empires are broken, and their kingdoms calcinated by the hot tramp of the centuries and destroyed by the giant worm of time. Where are they proud kingdoms of old, that rose, towered, and glowed in their might and majesty? Where is the kingdom of David and Solomon, that stretched "from the river to the ends of the earth?" Where are the great kingdoms of the Babylonians, the Medo-Persians, the Macedonians, and the iron empire of Rome? Nay, my friends, they have passed away and sleep the eternal sleep of death. Their sceptres are broken, their crowns fallen, and all their greatness is gone; but the sceptre of the Shiloh of God still abides. Why does it abide? Because it "is a right sceptre," a true kingdom of righteousness, harmony and peace, and presents to the judgment and wisdom of men God's idea of government. It is stronger than Bessemer steel, harder than adamant, more incorroding than the gold of Ophir, and more enduring than the precious diamond. It is more enduring than the schools and systems of thought and philosophy; for while these perish amid the march of years and the death of centuries, and fall in the grave of time with their dead masters and hoary sages, Shiloh's empire still abides, and its magnetic embodiment in the person of the living Christ, marches on in stately tread, traversing the breadth of centuries, measuring the decades, and wrapping the string of days and the fibre of hours around his hand, and buckling the aged cycles and the countless trend of years to his belt. Columns, arches, mausoleums, pyramids and the immortal sarcophagi of famous heroes and dead philosophers quivered and shivered and tumbled upon their rocky foundations at the command of conquering time; but the sceptre of the "Shiloh" of God still sways in triumph above the din of war, the clash of elements, and the stroke of years. Seas shift their beds, rivers change their channels, continents grow old with the weight of years and hoary crowns bestud the islands, while ocean currents grind their rocky feet to dust and scatter their flinty ribs in the secret chambers of the deep. But Shiloh, in the virgin strength of eternal youth, abides at the head of the marching column and the triumphant phalanxes, all dressed in white and panoplied in the robes of truth. But the kingdom of Shiloh is progressive. It is educative and consequently slow in its progress. It is slow to the ideas and conceptions of men, but not slow to God. An educative process must be slow. The universe is a developing universe. Growth and decay, expansion and contraction, struggles of life and death, are universal, perpetual and ceaseless. Nothing essential to this development stands still or falls to the depth of sound sleep or profound quietude. Nothing slumbers through eternal duration. If death comes, life follows in the wake of years, and that which now sleeps will rise again, and at some period in the life of God, assert its right to live again. Nothing comes but by slow degrees. The oak slumbers in the acorn, the tree in the kernel, and the blade of corn in the grain. The rose gradually unfolds its petals, and lilies blush in the eveningtide. Gentle spring comes after the sleep of winter, and the morning succeeds the night. That which once was is not now, but it shall be again. "The war of elements and the crash of worlds" are constant, general and eternal. The glory of systems fades, worlds in conflagration die, and stars from heaven fall, and catastrophes pile their oncoming catastrophes upon the burning decks of waning suns and dying systems, amid the gush of chaos and the death of stars. All is evolution, agitation and change. Like the empire of physical nature, there is a progressive process in spiritual nature, an agitating element, a native force or propulsion that awakes and stirs the properties and engages humanity in the eternal struggles.

Again, it is conflict, labor, and struggle that make a man as well as a world. Nothing can be made perfect without this necessary struggle and conflict with internal and external elements and forces. No conflict is without results and products. Every conflict, whether in the realm of physical nature or of mind, must have results and products; for there is always some end to be attained. A grain cast into the "faithful bosom of the earth" struggles to break its shell, and by the force of natural selection, or elective affinity, throws off its effete properties and gathers and assimilates those things that are needed for its perfect development. The purpose of the struggle is to make a perfect grain of wheat. The oak struggles in the acorn till it breaks its prison walls. It then arrays its friends against its foes in a struggle for survival, until it is crowned with a green wreath of leaves and acquires a sturdy trunk of wood. The waters are purified by their constant ebb and flow, and the germs of disease are killed in the atmosphere by the jarring thunders. Society is purified and humanity is made better by the revolutions and the conflicts of moral and political forces. Corrupt States and depraved municipalities sink beneath the heavy tread and the iron reign of sin; but the innate spirit of a progressive civilization, electrified by religion and virtue, collects its forces, reassembles its agencies, rises from the dead past, gathers the broken threads and continues on the highway of progress. Nothing can be purified and made better without struggle, and no struggle can be without an end.

Struggle implies three things--time, progress and process; but the end is the perfection of character. Everything has all time to be made perfect; and all the time that is necessary for the process, and the changes and accessions toward perfection are progress. The perfection of character is the ultimate end for which time is given, and the process and progress toward perfection cannot cease until the effort is coronated with the brightest gems of nature. The kingdom of Shiloh cannot stand still, because its very life is in its thrift and activity. Israel's God neither sleeps nor slumbers, but watches the forces of the moving spheres, regulates their order, directs their courses, controls their elements, and forces recalcitrant members into orderly lines and harmonious relations. Therefore, every action in the moral and physical worlds has a meaning that may be interpreted at some time in the future, and somewhere in the line of action and of evolution and change. God scatters broadly, but gathers again, and the focal center of all actions is the ultimate will of God, the intricate designs of the

Most High. How, then, can Shiloh's kingdom stand still? How can its propulsive forces, its Godlike energies stand still? Can God sleep, or His Son die? Have the cables of the universal mechanism been broken, its ship stranded and the helm of the universe taken from His hand? Say, ye elements, forces, agencies, natures, and all ye star-crowned immensities and light-begirt intellectualities of heaven, has the King of Saints lost the equilibrium of the spheres, the balances of heaven, or the end of the bright curves? Nay; God reigns as of old, and all the elements are the witnesses of His power and of His presence. He touches the octachord of nature with fingers of fire and hands of power, and at once the thrilling God vibrates the threads, and every part and ramified relation of the universal spheres He fills with His tremendous presence, commands the molecular entities, and the listening sisters and kindred sires to stop to hear and fly at his behests. All things are in His hands. Even the wrath of man, the rebellion of angels, and all the old sinners of the ages are to fulfill some great design or lofty culmination in the executive government of the Most High. Their madness and rage, their hardness of heart and obdurate pride, their lust for place and power, their violent and headlong assaults upon the high castles of heaven's King, and their fierce, demon-like onslaught of the truth and the progress and expansion of Shiloh's empire, are all made to praise the Lord and magnify His wisdom, justice and truth, while unwittingly they are carrying forward the golden threads and silken strands of the Shilohic empire. Fallen devils and wicked men, the devices of hell and whatever spirit, being of character that fights against God and His anointed Shiloh must ultimately fail and sink beneath the direful wrath of "the Thunderer." But the kingdom of Shiloh is to take the place of all others by the process of hybridization, or that smooth and gentle flow of His love, presence and power that is exhibited in the nature, character, work of the ministry of Jesus Christ. "The Son of man came not to be ministered unto, but to minister." His embassy to earth was not in pomp and splendor, nor kingly majesty. He did not come heralded by the sound of trumpets, the blowing of horns, and the metallic clash of loud cymbals and bands of music. No royal robe, nor gem-set crown, nor flash of golden sceptre, nor awaiting throne of ivory marked His coming. No horses and chariots, nor thundering legions of armies, nor tramping hosts of soldiery marked His appearing; but "as a root out of a dry ground" he broke the stony soil of the hearts of men and pushed His way up through the hard and callous surface of human prejudices, hate and depravity, and the meek and lowly Galilean stood forth in the humility of a prophet, the garb of a mendicant and the demeanor of a servant. There was no visible greatness, nor dictatorial air, nor manifestation of earthly power or kingly authority. The silent chambers of the woods were His home, the earth was His bed, the heavens His covering, and His pillow was a stone of the hills. No long-drawn aisles, nor architectural shafts of marble, nor Parian slabs, nor polished flint adorned the temple of His slumbers, nor flashed upon His morning vision; but from the rugged hills and silent plains the divine Master of the ages and the eldest creations, walked into Jerusalem and about Galilee to plant the seeds, and in deeper soil to sow those effervescent germs of truth and nuggets of power and love that were to permeate the nations, cover the hemispheres, ramify the ages, and fill the world with the Shiloh empire.

3. The abstract and concrete empire. "Unto him shall the gathering of the people be." There is something wonderful and

beautiful in the Shiloh empire. It is wonderful both in abstract and in concrete. In abstract there is neither phase nor form nor tangibility of character. It cannot be bought, nor sold, nor bartered in the markets of the world as a commodity in human commerce. It laughs at gold, spurns the diamonds of queens and treads the embossed gems and pearls of kings and millionaires beneath its steady move. Real estate, landed lords, the wealth of dynasties and the gilded splendors of courts and palaces cannot procure it, nor bring it near. But its spiritual dynamos are plenipotent in power, and its strength lay deep in the bosom and nature of Deity. In the abstract, it is the government of God, and has His image and superscription. In every age and phase of civilization it has its magazines of power, its living energies and undying individualism. It is separate and distinct from all other kingdoms that seem to have preceded it, and there are none to follow like it, or comparable to it. In its character, aim and great ends, it stands out in bold relief and incomprehensible individualism. The agencies employed, the elements and principles by which it acts and moves upon the feeling and judgment of men, are absolutely different from and high above the conceptions and calculations of the unaided reason and any discoveries possible for men to make. To "bring forth the headstones" of its expanding empire, with the shoutings of "Grace, grace, unto it," is the sole province of divine revelation. No man can find out God to perfection. He is the ever present, and yet the ever undiscovered, beyond that degree where the mind of man may rise and take hold upon the things of God and know what are those duties and relations that make for the peace of the intelligent creation. All that we know of God and the divine administration is mostly revealed to the sons of men, either through the elements of nature, or by His Word. All along through the ages and the nations of the earth the Lord hath declared His presence, His goodness, and His power to the children of men. He talks to us by day and by night, in the deep resonant tones of a unique empire of thought and action, whose vibrating circuits and electrifying majesty are as deep as human nature, high as heaven and enduring as the years of eternity. Everywhere Shiloh's empire touches the deep chords of human nature and human hearts, moving, stirring, revolutionizing and unifying its forces and agencies, exhibiting those far-reaching plenitudes of power and throbbing energies and plenipotent activites that make up its irresistible character. Every day the empire of Shiloh is making its onslaughts and encroachments upon the ramparts of sin and hell, gathering its forces, collecting its army, disciplining its troops, drilling its agencies and coercing the erratic sons and rebellious daughters into line, and demanding obedience to the sovereign God and His supreme command.

"Unto Him shall the gathering of the people be." All people shall come to Him, and the congregating millions shall gather at His feet and crowd to the sacred shrine and bow before the center of universal power and the majesty of the universal King. Here comes Shiloh, skipping on the mountains and dancing on the hills and filling the plains with the bright halo of His awful presence and the roseate splendors of His power. His voice is resonant, round and full, ringing in seraphic tones through the empire of humanity, calling all his subjects and long-lost children back to their ancient estate, and back to their ancient God. Shiloh is coming! Nearer and nearer He approaches. The thunders of music are rattling through the spheres, and the lofty tramping legions and the heavy treading white squadrons are coming down the line spreading through all lands, wrapping the hemispheres with the light of God and the blessing of His presence. He crushes the thrones of kings, demolishes iron empires, breaks asunder republics, subverts monarchies, throws down "the powers that be" and slays the dragon of sin in his ancient isle. Heathen superstitions, rotten philosophy and godless systems of thought and practice fall before His keen, cold steel of "the truth;" and they with their ancient gray-haired sires and grandsires and mitred priests with hoary locks, and all their deluded devotees, sink beneath his wrath and the power of his sovereign rod. Church of God, get ready, stand up; don't be alarmed! Shiloh is coming, he is coming, coming to reign until the stars of God pale their light, "till moons wax and wane no more," and suns lose their flame and planets die on their track and scatter to the utmost poles their incinerated dust. "Hallelujah! 'tis done," our king is on the throne of universal empire

SERMON V.

The Song of Believers.

"I will sing of mercy and judgment: unto thee, O Lord, will I sing."--Ps. 101:1.

Whoever reads the history of man, weighs his sorrows and measures his joy, will read the history of songs and anthems of his days. Indeed, his pilgrimage through life's thorny mazes is a pilgrimage of song inspired by the lights and shadows that ever shine and shade his pathway. Age or nation, clime or condition, cannot take from him this plaintive or joyous melody that permeates his individuality, and fills his moments with this God-given and heavenly flame. There is in man a golden harp of a thousand sympathetic chords whose deep and resonant tones evolve from the golden strings which vibrate to the music of the spheres and the melodies of the heart. Whether plodding the lower walks of tears and sorrow, or on the joyful wing of prosperity, or hearing the dull thud of the funeral dirge, the carol of the sweetest note will stir the soul, revolutionize the heart and lift the drooping spirit to the altitude of God and the sunny plains of heaven. Song is an antidote of the burdened heart, the laboring soul and the broken spirit. But the song of redemption is preeminently "the song." It is the song of songs. It is the sweetest note on angels' lips, and the sweetest anthem of the skies. Indeed, the song of redemption is the thrilling cry that has stirred the ages, ramified the centuries, filled the decades, inspired the prophets, fired the tongues of bards, poets and seers and cheered the millions with the music of God and of his Christ. Touched by the omnificent finger of God's love, and set to the dulcet strains of joy, the song of redemption shall go ringing through the nations, down the declivities of time, thread the centers of civilizations, cross the howling sea of death, and ring on up to God and heaven through countless ages and evolving cycles of endless duration.

1. But what is song?

Song is the music of the soul, the harmonious vibrations of the deep chords of the heart and the melodies of the spirit life. It involves the elevation of the affections and the utterances of the lips by which some theme, doctrine, or topic is proclaimed aloud and exultingly in the presence of others. In a broader sense, it is the vibration of the musical harmonies of the empire of God, agitated and active. It is the effort of a kindred spark to return to its native sun, and be rehabilitated in its native clime. It is the divinity in man rising to God its source and parent head from whom it came to earth. It is the better and higher nature of man springing forward and leaping heavenward. It is the soul flying through the deep blue ether upon its fiery pinions in search after God its "maker who giveth songs in the night." Song implies harmony in sentiment and strain. Strain is the vehicle--the chariot wheels of song, but sentiment and doctrine are the life and spirit. But song is more. It is a spiritual animation, a flame that stimulates, revives and quickens the moral, mental and spiritual manhood. It is true, song, like speech, may be greatly improved by the processes of culture and practice, and should be cultivated by the whole human race; for no system of training can be complete without it. Yet there is in man an innate attribute of song, an attribute which when touched by the hand of sorrow or joy makes the chambers of the soul resonant with the symphonies of angels and the euphonies of heaven. It is an essential quality of his spiritual and religious instinct--a part of his organic spiritual constituency. It is organic and God-given. It is a part of his individual and indestructible selfhood. Music is harmonies expressed, song is the vehement act of expression. This attribute of song in man has its counterpart in creation. Creation is a system of musical harmonies combining in a common unity, and that common unity is the unit of all units--God. He is the grand total of all the totalities in the universe. All the threads and lines of days and years, of events, acts, facts, natures, beings, agencies, entities, and things, center in his will and power, glory and majesty. The millenniums, with their creative acts and facts, with their mighty ponderable and imponderable realities, are yoked and linked together by the indissoluble bands and bonds of his high and majestic authority. At his command, angels fly, devils fall, comets flash, suns burn, stars twinkle, and systems live. Around him, all things dance and fly in the inimitable beauties of magnificent harmony, or dash their splintered shafts and shattered spears at his feet, and tremble at his voice. Man is most in harmony with the universe and the music of the spheres when the deep and dulcet tones of the octachords of the soul are attuned and set to the music of God "and of his Christ" by the Holy Spirit. The innate principle of song in man is the gift of God in a like sense as speech is the gift of God. When God made man, he placed within his duplex nature certain elements and faculties that compose his indestructible selfhood, and that are essential parts of him. These elements and faculties were in perfect harmony the one with all the others. There was no clashing, nor discord, nor want of harmony in the diapason, but the octaves of man's being were filled and thrilled through and through with the seraphic flame of love and the music of God. It is true, some of the faculties of his nature were more prominent than others, nevertheless, they all were there. They existed, and will exist as long as man is man. Place or condition, age or state, cannot destroy or annihilate these elements of his being. Man is finished in the fact of his being. He is fully man in all those powers and principles that imply a finished work of God. No new property nor attribute is to be added in this or any other state, because his being is finished in all its parts. It is true, there may be deep and latent powers of the soul of which we are not conscious, and which are yet to be developed in a future state; there may be possibilities of endless progression, development and expansion that await us in the great beyond. Our time in this life is too short, and the hemispheres of earth too narrow, for the excursions and expatriations of the soul--the vital flame of life. Yet these facts do not imply that new faculties and elements are to be added to the manhood of man, but imply progression, thrift, go and indefinite development. Indeed, man is but imperfectly known in the present state. He knows but little of himself and his fellow pilgrims, because this is the twilight of his being, the infancy of his life, and the morning of the primal day of his years. The strongest are weak and the wisest sons of men are ignorant. Therefore, the difference is in the extent of his faculties in expansion, application and development, and not that new faculties are to be added in another and future state. The canon was closed in the first act of his creation. True, there is to be, and must be a change, but only such a change as implies physical, mental and spiritual renovation. This renovation does not take in any new constituency, but is a purification and readjustment of that which was put there in the day of his creation. Yet, it seems true that those faculties and agencies that are best fitted for his immediate uses are most developed, and exhibit a grace and prominence that seem to obliterate, or at least to greatly crowd and overshadow the others, and there is an apparent want of harmony in the extent of their uses. But this does not prove that any new principle is necessary to complete his nature. Speech, knowledge, volition, memory, taste, appetite, and all the faculties come in the totality of his inherent and native selfhood. Every constructive element, every fiber and line of his nature is necessary for the ultimate end and completion of the whole. To extract one of these parts or faculties of his nature would unbalance the unity of his being and destroy its harmonious relations; therefore, man has a whole and completely defined status in the fact of his being. But in this nature there must be an association of each of its parts with each and all of those other parts that compose his being. There must be an elective affinity to penetrate and join together the several parts, and give grace, beauty and symmetry to the finished man. Thus song is the golden sunlight that gilds the horizon of the ages with the gladness of the day of Christ, making every flower of hope bloom, the hills smile, and every lily, rose and violet blush in maiden sweetness amid the universal gush of joys.

But song is old. It is older than our physical earth, and was used in heaven before used on earth. Long anterior to the heavens and the earth that rose out of chaos, it was pressed into the service of the eldest children of eternity who tuned their golden lutes in the empyrean of the heavens and sang glorious anthems to the all powerful and all glorious God. Long before a ray of light had pierced the primeval darkness that covered earth and sky, when, as yet, the morning star had not been hung as a pendant lamp in the orient, nor the silvery goddess of the evening had snuffed her candle on the occident's setting sun, eternal beings were singing the praises of God. Yea, there was song when as yet our earth and heavens were held by the iron grip and sable bands of king Darkness who had reigned for myriads of millenniums, but was finally exiled by the Almighty's irrevocable fiat of his power.

> "Ye shades dispel, the Eternal said,
> At once the involving darkness fled,
> And nature sprung to light."

Darkness fled "and nature sprung to light," while mighty and majestic systems rushed on the immortal paths of their burning orbits as if blazing around the throne of God. Where once all was dark and void, there were glory and beauty and the displays of almighty power and everlasting joy. Then it was that "The morning stars sang together and all the sons of God shouted for joy."

But song is universal and is inherent in nature.

Creation is God's great harp of countless living strings that join the universal harmonies in one grand chorus. Creation sings of God, the Creator--the ages sing of his eternity, the heavens sing of his glory, the earth of his power, and hell of his justice. From the burning lips of the lost to the enchanting melodies of blazing seraphs, song rises to God without stint or limit from every part of creation. All nature sings, especially when its golden chords are struck and vibrated by the plenipotent finger of God. There is music around us, above us, and beneath us. The mighty orchestra with rocking chimes sends its thrills through the ages, stirs and stimulates the nations with hope, joy and faith. But man must die. The doleful song of death lulls the nations to long and sound repose, only to be broken by the funeral dirge of time, when the stentorian lays of the archangel in measured verse and solemn strains shall revivify all that have fallen in sleep. Go, take your stand upon some high rocky promontory by the raging sea, and listen to the great bass drum of God--the winds blowing, the sea roaring and spitting froth of its anger into the murky clouds above, and agitating its own deep and pebbly bed as if stirred by the fiery blasts of hell. The plenipotent finger of the omnipotent God strikes the combustible elements of the air, and his red lightnings flash along on their burning cables, sending their soprano anthems to hiss and howl and join the bass strains from the sea below. High above all the sounds just mentioned are the screaking, hissing and crashing of the angry storm, with, as it were, its mottled, scarred and dusky-faced triumphant King rolling upon wheels of torrid amber mixed with fire and blood, and in his wake lay the shattered greatness of nature's might and virgin strength. His thundering chariot rolls in the clouds, while from his burning brazen car incandescent forked tongues leap out. A thousand golden cymbals are being simultaneously struck by the hands of a thousand archangels in heaven's aerial sea. The bosom of the clouds are recharged with electricity--the subtle vitality of nature--and their sable bands yield and in sunder break, baptizing herb, sea and land with the blessing of heaven. When the harsher notes of the storm have flown away upon the wings of the cloud, then nature, in sweeter and softer music of praise and joyful lays, is still heard striking the silver strings of her golden lute, emitting harmonious melodies which dance through the multiplex octaves of the spheres. Blow, ye heavenly zephyrs, blow, agitate, oscillate and vibrate your grand old octachords until oceanic isles and rock-ribbed hills and smiling plains join in the mighty chorus and the gush of thrilling joys. But song is sentiment and doctrine, and has its heroes. The song of creation has God for its hero, and the song of redemption has Christ for its hero, the charming embodiment of all melodies. In creation the harmonies of the spheres sing of God, the Hero of its preservation and the Master of its magnificent parts, forces, properties and powers. Every part is filled with God and instinct with music. "The whole earth is crammed with heaven, and every common bush afire with God." "The heavens declare his glory, and the firmament his power." "All thy works shall praise thee, O Lord," says the sweet singer of Israel. Again, he says, "Praise the Lord from the earth, ye dragons, and all deeps: Fire, and hail; snow, and vapors; stormy winds fulfilling his word: Mountains, and all hills; fruitful trees, and all cedars; Beasts, and all cattle; creeping things, and flying fowl; Kings of the earth, and all people; princes, and all judges of the earth; Both young men, and maidens; old men and children; Let them praise the name of the Lord:" Here God is the Hero of creation's song, the vital Center in which all of creation's melodies, anthems and choruses meet in eternal celebration and forever pour their orchestral thunders at his feet. Christianity is the ethical system, the high moral code of the universe and has Christ for its Head, its Song and its Hero. He is the ransoming and heroic "prince of peace" of which the ages have sung. The song is old and long, but sweet, soft, inspiring and thrilling. "Of him who did salvation bring," the first archangels sang. Living coals of heavenly fire dropped from the golden censers of angels, and started David's harp afresh with deeper notes and softer tunes descriptive of Messiah and his triumphs. Indeed, the Old Testament Scriptures were largely written in verse, the whole of which was a part of the mighty anthem of redemption. The Christ of the prophets is the Christ of the ages. He is the life and subject of all their song and the joy of our salvation. He cheered the hearts, fired the tongues of bards and poets, and dwelt in sweetest strains upon the lips of priest and prophet, prince and king, while the rough seers and shepherds in the wild and weird desert took up the thrilling cry, and sent it back to the walled city, its gleeful notes up to heaven and its joys on to God. While the ages were pouring their verses on the templed hills of God angels heard and awaited "the day star from on high." It is night. Shepherds are in the plains watching their flocks. An angelic legate from heaven's high arch appears. A halo of splendor encircles his dazzling face and his voice, wrapped in the soft accents of peace and love, was thrown out upon the wing of a heavenly carol. His theme is the culmination of the long and hoary decades of waiting. And the angel said unto them, "Fear not, for behold I bring you good tidings of great joy, which shall be to all people." . . . "And suddenly there was with the angel a multitude of the heavenly hosts, praising God, and saying, 'Glory to God in the highest, and on earth peace, and good will toward men.'" How glorious is this song. What impulses does it awaken in the heart of man! "Glory to God in the highest, and on earth peace, and good will toward men."

But the text says, "I will sing of mercy and judgment; unto thee, O Lord, will I sing."

But what is mercy? Mercy is a compound of goodness, patience and kindness to a lost and sinning race, to whom it is extended as a method of escape. God is good to all, to men, angels and inferior creatures. But to man his goodness is extended until it becomes more than mere goodness--it is mercy. It is melting pity borne away from God on the wings of his love and goodness to all the sinning race of Adam. It is an invention of Deity to reach and rescue that which could not be reached and saved by other methods. It presents to the world of man the only gateway of redemption from punishment and eternal "banishment from the presence of the Lord and the Glory of his power." Mercy has no existence except in its exercise, and therefore is not an attribute or perfection of Deity. Now, an attribute is an essential quality or part of the eternal mind of God without which God would not be God. Eternity, self-existence, all-power, all-knowledge, immortality, foreknowledge, infinite wisdom, etc., are attributes of God, because they are essential parts and elements of his character. Without these, or any one of them, he could not be what he is--the only and eternal Jehovah. We can conceive of God without the existence of mercy, but we cannot conceive him to be the Eternal Mind without those natural perfections that we call attributes. Could his power be taken away, he would cease to be God. Take away his wisdom, or goodness, or his eternity, and he ceases to be what he is, what he always was, and what he always will be--the eternal Jehovah. But take away his mercy and he is still "the same yesterday and to-day and forever." Adam before the fall was morally pure and perfectly holy, and therefore, in that state, was not a subject of divine mercy. He was not in a state to need mercy, and, therefore, none was exercised toward him. The same principle applies to all the tribes of holy angels that maintained their original state of purity and integrity of character. But all creatures, whether men or angels, or other intelligences of the universe, needed the existence of the attributes and were dependent upon them for their own being, perpetuity and happiness. They needed his mighty power to perpetuate their days and supply their wants. They needed his love, his goodness, his wisdom, justice, omnipotence, and all the attributes, even while they were in a state of perfect purity and happiness. But in such a state they did not need any mercy, because that could only be extended to a fallen and sinning race of beings. Mere power could create, preserve, or annihilate, but could not save the sinning race. Justice could condemn but could not forgive, justify and purify. These were necessary for the redemption of the fallen race. The province of justice is to condemn the guilty as well as to clear the innocent. The province of power is to execute the dreadful sentence upon the former, and execute and announce the happy acquittal of the latter. And thus might we reason concerning all the perfections of Deity. The attributes of God hold their respective functions and operate their several and wonderful offices, but none of them, and all of them could not, and do not save one guilty sinner. No; the complex government of God needed a provision of softer terms to reach and save the sinning and the lost. It needed the invention of Deity, and an assemblage and combination of attributes so adjusted and balanced as to harmonize with the nature, plan and the whole government of God. Man is to be saved. How shall it be done? All the attributes of God were silent, and profound muteness sat on every tongue. All the wheels of divine government stood still amid the dying echoes of receding centuries, as if the clattering machinery of the universe had unhinged its spindles and ungeared its pulleys and stopped every rolling belt and whizzing wheel, and had broken every bar and bolt that united them together in one harmonious whole. But Mercy, like an archangel, wrapped in the seven colors of the rainbow, stood before God with pacification written on her brow. A tablet of solid carbuncle fringed with purest gold covered her heart, and in bold letters set with diamonds and engraved with the signet of love, was written, "Melting Pity." Around her golden-crowned head flashed a halo of heavenly light, as if the graces of a thousand queens had gathered about her to beautify her glorious self. Her feet were covered with amber sandals as if electrified by the affinity of powers that continued to move while she stood. Her wings of fire were outspread, ready to fly at God's command. The thunders of wrath are hushed. Justice half sheathes her bloody sword. Angels and all the ranks and files of the heavenly world crowd about her to wonder and admire. There stood Mercy. Who is she? She is the queen of heaven, the gift of God to man, the grandest contrivance and the crowning conception of Deity. Slowly, but surely, through all the sinful ages of man she has gathered up the tears, the woes and sighs of men, and carries them to heaven, and to God. The whole earth with its crowded intelligences once cried and travailed in pain to be delivered and saved. Through all the arteries of the human heart and soul, death, eternal death, pulsated in every flowing current, played on every string, gnawed asunder every silver cable and golden thread that ramified and cemented the entities and eternity of man with God. The night of the world was long, dreary and dark. A heavy leaden cloud in which the slow, dull mutterings of wrath were heard threw its dark shade of death and ashy penumbra athwart the space in which revolved the mental and moral hemisphered globe. Now and then, a red current of flame would leap from the darker center and flash across the leaden zones only to exhibit the stronger and sabler bands that held in

awful solitude the pent-up wrath of the angry storm. Should God touch one wire, or send a flash of fire through the whole, like a cloudburst, his wrath would deluge the moral sphere and sink the sinning race to ruin. But Mercy stands before the throne of God and waves the white flag of peace and a truce intervenes. Then stretching her golden pinions she views the leaden cloud of wrath and death, as with steeds of flame and chariots of fire, she sweeps on and down from the throne of the great king. But in mid-air she seems to pause for a moment to survey the continents and islands, to count the slain millions and the dying thousands, to measure the depths of sorrows, and the exceeding sinfulness of sin. Her chariot wheels roll along the defiles of blood and death, where the prisoner dragged his chain, where mothers wept for their slain sons
 and daughters, and starving children cried for bread because their fathers and brothers fell in battle. She stands by dying man and his ruined race. Over his bleeding corpse she spreads her mantle of grace, recovers him from his sins, and establishes him in the Eternal, reconciled, sanctified and saved.

SERMON VI.

The Rich and the Poor.

"The rich and the poor meet together: the Lord is the maker of them all."--Prov. 22:2.

In all ages of the world, mankind has been divided into two distinct classes, "the rich and the poor." While these distinctions are merely artificial, yet the wisdom and intelligence of the masses have always regarded them as permanent and enduring. Even the Father of mercies has recognized these differences that exist between man and man. These distinctions or differences are not fundamental, but conditional. They grow out of the state of society, and those environments that always accompany every age and phase of civilization. So far as science and revelation go, there has not been found any remedy to equalize wealth, or those belongings and personal achievements that have lifted one man above another in those things that add to their happiness. But in spite of all the precaution, the wisdom, and the foresight of the best and wisest of men, the great majority of the human race will be poor in this world's goods; it seems a matter of impossibility to prevent suffering arising from a state of want, and establish any universal rule by which all men may become equal in the comfort and common distribution of wealth. Hence, there is always room for charity, and the exercise of those noble virtues that not only help the poor, but also add to the greatness of human character and the expansion and development of the noblest faculties of human nature. We need not now argue the fundamental causes of these differences. It is enough for the present purpose to recognize the fact of their existence and possible permanence, at least, until the triumphs of the gospel system shall change the heart of man to that degree where the truth shall force his erratic nature to obey its teaching in the fullest sense of its letter and spirit. It is convenient to be rich, but not sinful to be poor. Nor is it sinful to be rich. Solomon says, "Give me neither riches nor poverty," and he further says, "If riches increase, set not thy heart upon them." Both riches and poverty have their advantages, the one in this life, the other in the life to come. Here it may be said that "the rich and the poor" do not "meet together," though the Lord is still "the maker of them all."

1. The commonness of origin and character.

The phrase, "the rich and the poor," refers to our common origin in the creation and construction of our mental and physical character. Man is a genus and not a species. All are made alike in all the constituent elements of their nature. The basic principles upon which character rests are always the same in kind, but different in degree, according to the respective conditions under which they may have lived. The outward appearance and even the varied civil aspects do not affect the mental and moral standing, nor the real fundamentals of character. All have the same number of faculties, or attributes of mind, and the differences we see in mankind are not in the fundamentals of their being, but in degrees of culture and development. If there were any real differences in the nature of humanity as regards the mental ability, then there must have been different laws of both God and man to suit the different capacities. There must have been one law for the naturally superior and another for the naturally inferior.

Otherwise, the ends of justice would be defeated, and rewards and punishments could not take place on equitable grounds. But as there is one God and one moral code by which all are to be governed, there is a single and a one humanity standing upon one moral foundation and with one moral responsibility. There is a difference in mental accomplishments and achievements, but this is in degrees, and not in kind. One is as much a man as the other in the facts of his being, but not in the facts of development. Hence, "the rich and the poor meet together" in a common humanity. But "they also meet together" in the common wants and needs of life. Everywhere man is man, and according to the history, practices and experiences of the life of man, he is one and the same in the substantial realities of his nature. Human nature is always the same, no matter in what part of the globe man lives. The various forms of his civilization, or those improvements that come to him by means of his own efforts, are born of the same principles and the same aspirations, and have always the same end in view, namely, the betterment of his earthly state. "The rich and the poor" are conceived and are born alike. Childhood, youth and growth, manhood, old age and death, come alike to all. They have the same tastes, feelings, appetite, passions, desires, pains and sorrows, and are perfectly the same in their physical and natural propensities. In all these things, "the rich and the poor meet together."

2. But the rich and the poor meet together in a common religion.

They have not only a common fatherhood, and consequently a common brotherhood, but they have a unitary religion. The great thoughts, the high moral ideas, and the lofty conceptions that permeate and pervade the spiritual nature of man, had their germs and inception in the ancient revelations of God, assisted by sober deductions from nature. It is hard to investigate nature without seeing its Creator, or that energy by which all things move and have their being. In some sense, nature reflects God. Creation is the material image of the immaterial God. The universe is a reflector in which the majesty, glory and power of the invisible spirit are displayed. Everywhere an active presence is near, filling the infinite operations with intelligence and the highest ideals of perfections and demonstrations of wisdom. Everywhere the mind is overwhelmed with wonder and amazement, until the living manhood is instinct, ramified and baptized with the spiritual essence. Creation and Revelation tell the same story, and "the invisible things of him from the creation of the world are clearly seen, being understood by the things that are made, even his eternal power and Godhead." The very personality of our manhood takes in and assimilates the universal "Godhood," and the life of man is but the product of another and a higher life, and can but reflect its "image and superscription."

The ancient revelations of God run parallel with the ever-present testimony of creation. So far as they go, both are chapters in the eternal economy, and are the witnesses and loud proclaimers of an unbroken line of control and a unitary system of government. In sentiment and doctrine, the corner-stone of religion is always the same. As there is but one God and Father, there is one government, and consequently, one great religion. As this one government has been perverted by men, so this one religion has been corrupted and perverted by the same power. But its great pillars of truths remain. Idolatry itself is only a fearful perversion of original religion, or ancient Christianity; but as a false coin proves the existence of a true coin, so false religion proves that there is a true religion. The coin may have lost its image and superscription, but the solid metal remains. Here "the rich and the poor meet together," because on the spiritual plane they are compelled to meet in a common religion.

3. The solemn doom will make them meet.

But Solomon intended more especially to emphasize the solemn doom that awaits all the sons and daughters of men--that awful and tremendous catastrophe that involves the dissolution of the body, the flight of the spirit to another clime, and the silent chamber of the grave. What is more serious? What is death? And why must I die? There is nothing in the mere physical change that we call death, but the issues involved, or consequent upon it, are momentous, tremendous, and far-reaching in their effects. Death changes the estate of man, decides the issues of life's conflict, transports, exports, and dissolves relations and dispatches the spirit as a swift courier to the seat of God, the center of universal power. Death involves a mysterious transition between the spheres, since it takes us from one place to another, or from this to another world. Millions have passed over life's boundary line and made the mysterious exit, but not one has returned to describe the way or the place to which he has gone. No voice comes back to us from that far off country, or that unseen realm where God and angels dwell.

No man has, as yet, discovered any remedy or method to stay the hand of death, or stop his fearful ravage and devastating march through the ages. But step by step, and day by day the grim monster encroaches upon the children of men in every clime, kindred, and people. Triumphantly he reigned from Adam to Moses, and claimed those children of men who had not sinned after the similitude of Adam's transgression. He marched captive an unbroken line across the flood, ravaged the postdiluvian ages, swept through the rising generations, crushed the empires of the Mediæval dispensations, corrupted the streams and broke the trend of modern civilization, and ever defies the discoveries of materia medica and the deep ken of modern sciences. All the sons of men quail before him, bow at his command, and fall beneath his fitful rage and outstretched rod. Solomon descanted upon the science of life, and the wise men of the east fled from him. David sang of him, and the prophets of God heard his voice. Job felt his keen cold lance. The struggling millions obey his behests, grandsires submit to his edicts, queens lay their jewels at his feet, kings lay their scepters in his path, and monarchs pile the ashes of their shattered thrones and the dust of their empires upon his calcinated highway. He stops the reign of empire, numbers the days of the mighty, breaks the oppressing dynasties, strips the beggar of his rags, the rich of his riches, silences the lyric of the enchanter, and hushes the noise of battles and the tocsins of war. His bow is of steel, his arrows are adamantine javelins sharper than the fangs of serpents, and more poisonous than if covered with the blood and filled with the venom of asps. Always his "sword is bathed in heaven," by whose double-edged blade, tears are drawn and mingled with human blood. His deadly work goes on always, his havoc is universal, and his reign eternal. No king is like this king, no reign so long, no dominion so wide, no lord so cruel, and no ruler of the nations so exacting. All who owe him must pay in full principal and interest in the awful crisis. Every cent must be paid at the time of maturity, every bond liquidated, and every obligation met. There is no forgiveness nor mercy nor long suffering. He is deaf to progress and to the resonant eloquence of song and the golden strains of instrumental music. No bars of iron, nor gates of steel, nor triple-plated armor, nor barricaded palace, though rock-bound and defended by the frowning artillery of all the nations, can stay his awful hand. He is the relentless enemy of all the living, and plants his waving colors of eternal sleep over all the dead. He proclaims no armistice, nor lifts the white flag of truce. Eloquent orators have proclaimed against him; philosophers, sages, scientists and sanitarian councils have fought against him with all their main and might; but as steadily as the flow of time or the roll of the ages, the haughty monarch rides in victory, whitens the bones of the nations in his dreadful wake, and shouts in triumph over the fallen millions. Onward he ever comes crushing the diamond centers of human greatness and laughing at the wailings and bitter cries of the children of men. O death, how dreadful is thy reign! What terrors follow in thy path! Here "the rich and the poor meet together." In the cities of the dead they shall dwell together until the judgment day. But we are told by the Word of inspiration, "the day of the Lord will come as a thief in the night; in the which the heavens shall pass away with a great noise, and the elements shall melt with fervent heat, the earth also and the works that are therein shall be burned up." But there is a great center to which all things move, and a focal point where all things meet. It is the judgment day, the culmination of all days. Jesus Christ is the supreme

Judge, and God the Father, is the eternal Usher. All that move in heaven, earth and "the deep track of hell" are hastening to that day. Every day with its contents, every age with its thought and action, and the centuries with their chapters of blood, violence and death, shall crowd to the awful assize, "For --evil." "For God shall bring every work into judgment, with every secret thing, whether it be good, or whether it be evil." Every age has its history, every people its records, every man his thoughts and acts. All of these are written in the day-book of time and recorded in the ledger of eternity. Earthly records may disappear, annalists may perish "with their inkhorns dry and their golden styli bereft of their artful touches," and the dusty leaves of their fading folios may be forgotten, or yield to the ravage of years; but all things come to the judgment, "the day of the Lord." All the toiling elements, all the groaning factors, and all the faculties of mind and matter, are the servants of God, and the instruments of his executions. His Word must be fulfilled, and the eternal plan of government must meet all the requirements of his ultimate designs. All the universal propellent and repellent agencies, all forces, contingencies, activities and powers of the infinite spheres of being are but the obedient servants of the Most High to bring all things into judgment at the last day. All the high powers of heaven, all the low powers of hell, and all the creatures of space and time are traveling to the judgment. While they sleep, and while they are awake, whether they rest, roll, wabble, or soar, or move on lightning wings, or dart on electric threads, they move on to the great day with irresistible momentum and exact precision. There are no broken tendencies, nor severed relations, nor shivered bonds, nor lost motion in the wondrous whole. Every star, every sun, every shining system and brilliant orb, and every broken planet and burnt-out world, with their flying fragments of hissing lava, with their dying satellites and perishing kings of the deep and "the lost sisters of the erstwhile seas," shall terminate the long courses of their mighty rounds, fold their wings of flame, stop the flight of their ethereal chariots, break their contracting zones, lose their orbits and plunge into the universal holocaust in sight of the throne of God. Here their forces die, their forms change and their equipoise is lost amid "the wreck of matter and the crush of worlds." Here suns set to rise no more, moons pale their silver faces, stars leap from their sockets, comets take off their sheeny robes, and the trooping steeds of "the milky way" roll up to the end of their long courses, bow at the throne of God, fall in death and leap into the infinite chasm of chaos, and amid the rumbling thunders and howling elements, they sink into the darkness and death of eternal night. Hence, the Savior says, "Immediately after the tribulation of those days shall the sun be darkened, and the moon shall not give her light, and the stars shall fall from heaven, and the powers of the heavens shall be shaken: And then shall appear the sign of the Son of man in heaven: and then shall all the tribes of the earth mourn, and they shall see the Son of man coming in the clouds of heaven with power and great glory. And he shall send his angels with a great sound of a trumpet, and they shall gather together his elect from the four winds, from one end of heaven to the other." But the judgment is coming and its approach is to be heralded forth by "a shout" and with the voice of the archangel, and with the trump of God, and "we shall all stand before the judgment seat of Christ." The circumstances attending his appearing, and the awful signals of his approach are wonderful beyond the power of human description, and are worthy of the great occasion. Ten thousand thunders rolling and filling the spheres with awful tremors, and the heavy tramp of the martial tread of the judgment millions engage the attention of universal humanity. The universal summons sends its deep thrilling sensations along all the depths and heights of the living and of the dead, and all that sleep in their graves shall hear the voice of the Son of God. "Behold, he cometh with clouds; and every eye shall see him, and they also which pierced him: and all kindreds of the earth shall wail because of him. Even so, Amen."

High above the ancient tracks of planets and the burning paths of melting worlds and incinerated systems, the great white throne of Jesus, the Christ of God, appears. Around him bright conclaves and concatinated files of the unbroken ranks of the eldest children of eternity glitter as if colored by the lightning's flash. Millions of angelic golden leagues, like threads of fiery currents and tongues of liquid flame, girdle the throne of the eternal with the congregated citizenry of heaven. Around him cherubic legions and the ever deepening trains of seraphic files radiate the circles and cover the widespread seething seas of living spirits with the scintillations of their wings and the beamy splendors of heaven. The deep rolling thunders shake the mansions of the dead, stir the sleeping millions, and "from the center to the utmost poles," universal humanity, both living and dead, breaks the adamantine links of its long slumber and rises to the judgment bar. No names will be forgotten, nor lost sight of, but every dead son of Adam's race shall be there. The lost thought and the scattered memory of the whole circle of all humanity shall come up with the precise characters and individuals to which they belong, and every man, woman and child shall still be a real conscious self, an eternal moral personality. "All things" shall be brought into judgment. Kings shall bring their crowns, monarchs the histories of their reigns, conquerors their bloody swords, and annalists the records of their people. All the works of the human race, both public and private, shall be brought into judgment and weighed in the balances of truth and equity, and judged by the justice of God and the inexorable law of righteousness. Oh wondrous day! It is the day of days, the culmination of all days, the center where all things meet, the place and date of all final decisions, and the destiny of all men.

> "He comes! he comes! the Judge severe!
> The seventh trumpet speaks him near;
> His lightnings flash, his thunders roll;
> How welcome to the faithful soul!
> From heaven angelic voices sound;
> See the Almighty Jesus crowned!
> Girt with omnipotence and grace,
> And glory decks the Saviour's face.

> "Descending on his azure throne,
> He claims the kingdoms for his own;
> The kingdoms all obey his word,
> And hail him their triumphant Lord!
> Shout, all ye people of the sky,
> And all the saints of the Most High:
> Our Lord, who now his right obtains,
> Forever and forever reigns."

SERMON VII.

The Perpetuity of the Name of Christ.

"I will make thy name to be remembered in all generations: therefore shall the people praise thee forever and ever."--Ps. 45:17.

Originally, this Psalm has reference to king Solomon, the great son of great David, because the kingdom of Solomon, as well as Solomon himself, represented the spiritual and physical empire of Messiah. Solomon in his glory was a fit anticipation and prefiguration of the Christian system in its progressive development and universal sway. Though Solomon was great, yet a greater than Solomon is here spoken of. The name to be perpetuated through all the coming ages is not the name of Solomon, but the great name of Jesus Christ. As the sun, with its piercing and brilliant rays gilds the horizon with its bright light, and fills the world with his golden splendors, so Messiah has arisen upon the dark sphere of human depravity. Though slowly and gradually, yet steadily he will climb the ecliptic of the world's civilizations until a halo of saving grace shall electrify, purify and save the millions from sin and ruin.

It is said of Christ that "on his head were many crowns" and "that he had a name written that no man knew but himself. And he was clothed with a vesture dipped in blood; and his name is called the word of God." So he is distinguished by sublime titles, indicative of his nature, work, and character. Like the stars of heaven, they beset and bestud the oracles of truth, and will forever shine and glitter through all the ages of the nations until every tribe of man shall be bedecked with the gems of truth, and every lip and tongue shall glow with his praise. How wonderful is his name! In Genesis he is said to be "the seed of the woman." He is called also "Shiloh." In Job he is called the Redeemer. In Isaiah he is called the "child born," "son given," "and his name shall be called, Wonderful Counsellor, The mighty God, The everlasting Father, The Prince of Peace. (Is. 9:6.) In Zechariah he is "The Branch," for, says the prophet, "Behold the man whose name is the Branch; and he shall grow up out of his place, and he shall build the temple of the Lord: Even he shall build the temple of the Lord; and he shall bear the glory and shall sit and rule upon his throne; and he shall be a priest upon his throne, and the counsel of peace shall be between them both." (Zech. 6:12, 13.) In the prophecies of Haggai he is called "the Captain of our salvation." In Daniel he is called "the most Holy." (9:24.) In Jeremiah he is called "the Lord our Righteousness." In Hosea he is called "David their king." In Matthew he is called "Christ." In Luke he is called "the Day Spring from on High." In John he is called "the Lamb of God." In Acts he is called "Lord of all," and "Prince of life." In Hebrews he is called "the Captain of our salvation." In Romans "the Deliverer." He is called "the Alpha and Omega," "the beginning of the creation of God," "the faithful witness," "the root and offspring of David," and "the lion of the tribe of Judah." But the especial and preeminent name of the Redeemer, is Jesus, and in connection with this, is "Christ," the anointed of God. He is appointed of God to fill a great office. He is a Priest to offer up sacrifices for us--for all the sinning nations of the ages. He is a King, for, says the prophet, "Behold a king shall reign in righteousness, and princes shall rule in judgment." He is the

Prophet of God to man, to teach him the deep things of God and the mystery of salvation.

    I. His name is great because it is significant of a great character. "What think ye of Christ?" Who is he? and whence did he come? For what did he come? His word records the work of human redemption. He came to seek and save that which was lost. He came as the God-sent, the heavenly Legate, with the instrument of peace written by the finger of the King of heaven. He came to bind up the broken-hearted, and to cheer the millions with the music of God and the message of love. He gave sight to the two blind men at Capernaum by the word of his power, and at the same place the dumb demoniac was healed. At Gadara he made the deaf and dumb man hear the sweet accents of love and speak the praise of the Most High in Decapolis. At Nain he gave life to the widow's son and joy to a mother's heart. At Samaria ten lepers were cleansed of the most loathsome of all diseases. At Gadara the legion of devils fled at his command and plunged headlong into the sea. The raging storm upon the sea of Galilee heard his invincible fiat, and the waters ceased to dance to the music of the winds. At Jericho blind Bartimeus saw the bright light of heaven for the first time by the healing power of Messiah. At Bethesda five thousand were fed by the incarnate Son of God. He raised Lazarus from the grave, expelled the palsy, scattered fevers, dried up issues of blood, and restored the withered hand. But his name is to be perpetuated because of the doctrines he taught, "for he taught them as one having authority, and not as the Scribes and Pharisees." It is said that "he spake as never man spake," but no man knew the truth as he knew it. He taught the truth--preeminently the truth of God. His doctrines dropped "as the rain," and his "speech" distilled "as the dew, as the small rain upon the tender herb, and as the showers upon the grass, because he published the name of the Lord; ascribe ye greatness unto our God." What would we do without the words of Christ? To what school of science and law should we go to learn what we have learned from the blessed words of Jesus? Can human wisdom find out God to perfection? The world without a Christ! How dark and desolate! "Thou hast the words of eternal life, unto whom shall we go?" Nay, the world belongs to Jesus Christ. It is his by redemption: "Ye are bought with a price," and that price was the blood and tears and sorrows of the Son of God; "being rich, he became poor, that through his poverty ye might be made rich." He is at work to-day for you and for me--for every child of man. His doctrine is being distilled as the dew upon the delicate violet, the fragrant lily, the blushing rose, the lofty pine, and towering cedar. His sweet words of truth and love still play on the harp of life, and ring out and spread over the world, crossing seas, oceans, islands, piercing continents, sweeping through the gates of kingdoms, and the melodies of his name are chanted in palace halls and ivory temples. On his name flies as if winged with the zephyrs of Ceylon's isle, laden with the breath of flowers and the melodies of the spheres. The name which angels adore and worship, the name so full of consolation to the sinning and lost race of Adam is Jesus, the Christ of God.

"I will make thy name to be remembered in all generations, because all great events are connected with it." "The Lord possessed me in the beginning of his way, before his works of old. I was set up from everlasting, from the beginning, or ever the earth was. When there were no depths, I was brought forth;

when there were no fountains abounding with water . . . . . When he prepared the heavens, I was there; when he set a compass upon the face of the depth: when he established the clouds above: when he strengthened the fountains of the deep: when he gave to the sea his decree, that the waters should not pass his commandment: when he appointed the foundations of the earth: then I was by him, as one brought up with him: and I was daily his delight, rejoicing always before him; rejoicing in the habitable part of his earth; and my delights were with the sons of men." (Prov. 8.) The Apostle, in Hebrews says, "By whom also he made the worlds." Thus he is identified with the creation of the world. In Revelation he is styled, "The beginning of the creation of God," and "the first born of every creature." He is the Lamb slain from the foundation of the world. He was with God the Father when he said, "Let us make man in our own image." He is the Angel of the covenant which appeared to Moses in the burning bush in the wilderness, and said, "I am that I am." He it was who smote the first born of Egypt's rebellious sons and overwhelmed her haughty king and his hosts in the Red Sea, He was the rock smitten in the wilderness which gave the sons of Israel drink; for says the Apostle, "That rock was Christ." He was the fourth one that looked like the Son of God in the fiery furnace with three Hebrew children, and by his power he quenched the violence of the fire, so that they came out without the smell of fire upon their garments.

As the Great Redeemer, he "cometh from Edom, with dyed garments from Bozrah." He "is glorious in his apparel, travelling in the greatness of his strength" and hath trodden in the winefat alone. As the Redeemer, he came to establish his church by organizing its spiritual forces, uniting its energies and inspiring the millions with hope, causing them to call him blessed. Onward he drives his chariot wheels. They are thundering and rumbling along every commercial channel, darting into every little trading cave, and rolling through the streets of the great cities, while rural plains and flowery dells rejoice at the sound of his coming. He is the Hope of the world, the Light of the nations. He is moving and stirring the public heart and changing sentiment and thought. Ancient superstitions and modern infidelity are trembling at his approach, while the evolutions of society are moving upward to the mount of a purer faith and a higher standard of morality. The lightning carries his word, and winds transport his name across the seas, and ocean cables quiver with his truth and dance with his praise. But the remembrance of his name cannot be blotted out. It cannot be lost or forgotten among the vast assemblage of great names. He stands not as a star in the zenith that bestuds the "Milky Way," but as a great shining sun superlatively luminous and alone flying along in his own glorious orbit, and with an undimmed lustre he shall shine on through endless days. But few names have outlived the centuries and none have been so universal as Christ's. Many whose names have been remembered by posterity have been remembered because of their wickedness, monstrous crimes and diabolical acts, as Nero, Antiochus, Domitian and Herod. Others have their names kept alive because of military prowess and warlike achievements, as Cæsar, Hannibal, Alexander and Napoleon. Some are remembered on account of discoveries in science and art, or because of their philosophical and literary productions; others on account of their virtues and philanthropy. The nations extol their heroes and praise their greatness in verse, song, and national airs. They celebrate their birth and death, and perpetuate their memories in shafts of marble, pillars of stone and monuments of bronze. The mother endeavors to perpetuate the memory of her darling child by wreathing its grave with garlands of flowers and softening of the sod by showers of tears. The children of dead fathers carve in solid marble, enduring epitaphs of love and esteem. But verse and national air shall cease amid the clash of nations and the wreck of kingdoms. Shafts of marble, pillars of stone and monuments of bronze shall tumble and crumble and perish under the heavy tramp of the ages. The graves of parent and child though wreathed in flowers and wet with tears, shall be forgotten, yet the name of Christ shall be remembered in all generations. It shall be remembered because of his personal purity, his gracious words, his wonderful miracles, his unbounded love, his sufferings and vicarious passion and death, his glorious triumph over men, devils, earth and hell. He will be remembered as the Founder of Christianity, the universal Savior, and the ever reigning King. His name cannot be blotted out by any earthly power. Earth and hell have conspired against his name. Kings and rulers have covenanted against him. Learning, philosophy, power, wealth, influence and the arms of nations have all been employed against him, but all in vain.

But says the text: "Therefore shall the people praise thee forever and ever."

Some men have said in effect the time will come when the name of Christ shall be forgotten! This cannot be. God has said, "His name shall endure forever." Again he says, "Thy throne, O God, is forever and ever, a sceptre of righteousness is the sceptre of thy kingdom, therefore God, even thy God, hath anointed thee with the oil of gladness above thy fellows." How can his name be forgotten, when "the people shall praise him forever and ever?" Can the sun be forgotten while he pours his burning rays on the earth? Indeed, his name is the sympathetic chord in the octachord of the ages and nations. His praise vibrates all the fibres of the heart, plays on every string, flashes on every nerve, quivers on every golden thread and fills every chamber of the soul with his love. He has been praised by prophets, lawgivers, priests and kings, by shepherds, seers and bards. From the temple hill of God, his praise rang out from the hosts of Israel, and thrilled Judah with the music of his name. Solomon calls him "the rose of Sharon, and the lily of the valley." David said of him, "Thou art fairer than the children of men; grace is poured into thy lips; therefore hath God blessed thee forever." The celebration of his name began of old. Each generation will continue to praise his name. The fathers will die with his praise upon their tongues, but his praise will not cease. Where the fathers may leave off, their sons and daughters will come forth with youth's enlivening fire and chant his blessed name to the next generation; and then that generation will swell the high sounding chorus until at the base of the imperial throne of the judgment day, all the choruses of the ages, though old and gray with the weight of centuries, will fall upon the ear of an assembled universe. Nay, more, they shall go ringing on through the cycles over the mountains of God, and over the hills and wide extended plains of heaven, until again all the morning stars shall sing together, and all the sons of God shall shout for joy. Where will the celebration of his name stop? Who can set bounds to it? "Sirs, if these hold their peace, the very stones would cry out." Sweet carols would spring from the earth, and songs of praises from the rocks of the hills. The rivers would murmur it, the rills would dance it, the seas would hum it, the storm would howl it, and the winds would whistle among the trees of the wood, until leaf, bud, flower, and trunk would quiver with the melodies of his name and the joys of his salvation. Before his name should cease to be praised by "the people," Jehovah, his Father, would evoke all the powers of the universe, because he hath declared that "the people shall praise thee forever and ever." Yea, he would raise to life every dead prophet and sleeping saint, gather the broken strings of every harp, reassemble every choir, call up from the dead past every lost song, and revive afresh all the melodies of the centuries and the anthems of the ages. He would touch all the golden strings of nature's great harp and fill them with the music of his name and the praises of his great Son. Think what it would require to erase his name. Every Bible must be burned. Every book, page, and tract that contains his name must be destroyed. Every church must be torn down. The tongue of every Christian must be hushed in death. Every Sunday-school must be banished and its songs annihilated. All the harps of heaven must be broken and all the angels destroyed. All the saints in heaven must be silenced in eternal muteness and the heavenly tabernacle of the most high left without a note of praise. David and Asoph, the sweet singers in Israel, must be brought up from their long repose, their hymns and songs gathered and burnt to ashes. What will you do with Milton and Watts, Toplady and Charles Wesley? Their songs will outlast the ages, and are to-day ringing around the globe, warming the hearts of believers, inspiring the laboring sons of God, and filling the world with joy and gladness. What will you do with the Te Deums of the ages and the melodies of the spheres? Before the name of Christ can cease to be praised, seraphs must lose their joys, angels their songs, and all the symphonies of the redeemed in heaven and on earth must be struck dumb with silence of the grave. Bards and prophets, philosophers and sages, must all be annihilated, and their names and songs and melodies wiped off the face of creation and erased from the annals of the ages. But man is a harp of a thousand strings. In his redeemed state this harp, with all its strings and scales, vibrates the name of Jesus Christ. His name fills all the sympathetic chords in the octaves of his soul and in the octachord of the nations and ages. We are taught in the Scriptures, that if men are repressed from praising the name of the great Redeemer, the stones would cry out. The idea is, Christ's name must be praised, for the word and promises of God must be fulfilled, and therefore, before his word is allowed to fail, he will make the stones praise the name of his great Son. Yea, my friends, before the promises of God can fail, he would give every rock a harp, every tree a song, every flower a melody, every hill a verse, every breath of ether a symphony, every sunbeam a carol, and every streamlet, river, sea, bay and gulf an anthem. He would fill heaven and earth with hymns whose choruses would praise the name of Jesus Christ. Stirred by the breath of God, the saints would arise from the dead, take up afresh the name of Jesus and thunder it through the vaulted mansions of the skies. The stars would hand it down, the moon would kiss it, and the sun would shine it through all the planets, while ethereal currents would waft it away, until "Arcturus, Orion, Pleiades and the Chambers of the South" would start all the celestial inhabitants of the "Milky Way" to the celebration in sublimest strains of the name of Jesus Christ.

But his name is to be remembered in all generations, in the sense of including all the nations of the earth. His name is to be as widespread as the human race itself. The millions of earth's inhabitants are to join in the universal jubilee and know the universal salvation. The wheels of commerce are to roll it along their iron highways. The steel-clad "grayhounds" of the seas, dancing on the foam-crested paths of interoceanic traffic, must bear his name to millions who have not yet learned all the verses of the mighty chorus. Cables that sleep on the pebbly bottom of the deep must hum the syllables of his name to China, Japan, Africa, Australasia, to the "Latin States" and the great islands of the seas. Telegraphy and Telepathy are his winged messengers that stand ready to do his biddings. These fly and dart at his command and quiver with the celebration of his name. Shall the praises of his name stop here? Nay, my friends, in heaven it shall be continued, while the millenniums shall roll on their eternal cycles. Moons may wane, suns change, stars perish, and the centuries burdened with the weight of events, may die, but his precious name will still be the theme of angels and all the redeemed children of God.

SERMON VIII.

From Repentance to Final Restitution.

"Repent ye therefore, and be converted, that your sins may be blotted out, when the times of refreshing shall come from the presence of the Lord; and He shall send Jesus Christ, which before was preached unto you: whom the heaven must receive until the times of restitution of all things."--Acts 3:19-21.

The text is designed to cover all those periods and dispensations of time through which and over which the Gospel kingdom should extend, and to cover those ages and arenas that compose its fields and areas of activity. In its organized capacity and character, the heavenly kingdom has its external and visible coalition of forces and its confederation of progressive and active entities and elements, as any other kingdom. Consecrated manhood with its wisdom, experience and achievements, makes up a great part of those factors that must always be an essential part of the visible body of the church of Christ. In one sense the church is a kingdom of men, since men must constitute its subject and present that plan of operation in which the splendid rule and power of the living Christ is manifest. But this part of the heavenly kingdom in which man is the active subject is but a part of the invisible and far-extended empire that covers the deep steps of the Infinite and that lives and acts upon the broader planes and the boundless spheres of being. On earth we only see and comprehend a diminutive phase of the power and majesty of that glory that lies in the beyond. It is only in the ages to come and in those wonderful transitions of power; goodness and grace that the whole kingdom of the Most High can be revealed. As creation rose by the touches and successive wonders of the hand of God, so His spiritual and visible empire must rise until the evolutions and relays of His hand "make all things new." As creation had its incipiency--its first step and its first day--so the expanding "kingdom of heaven" has its beginning in the bosom of the children of men. Rising from the darkness of the past, like the first morning star of the oldest creation, it began its upward climb upon the ecliptic of the world's humanity in the shadows and mists of mental night. Though apparently slow, yet upward amid the din and roar, the hiss and clash of displaced elements of reigning sin and triumphant hell, the Son of God piles stone upon stone, arch upon arch, until golden turret and flaming spire gild the universal horizon with light and truth, and the majesty of His love. As all the stones in a building are cut, polished and fitted, so every one who becomes a member in this heavenly kingdom, must be changed by the operations of His grace, love and power, and made to fit his place in the heavenly temple. There must be a perfect harmony of parts with parts, and a perfect harmony of relations. There must be a homogenizing of heterogeneous parts, principles, natures and agencies with divine equanimity and the invisible fullness of Deity. There must be that plenitude of power and cohesiveness of elements to solidify all parts and immortalize the whole. This kingdom must be God-made and God-given. It must be like God.

But the text says: "Repent ye, therefore, and be converted."

1. Repentance and conversion. In what do they consist? And why are they necessary? In the very nature of the laws of God, and in the very nature of man, repentance is absolutely and indispensably requisite. The illustrations in the above show the reasons why there must be a change in human nature before entering the kingdom of God. Not only do the Scriptures declare, but history, fact and experience declare, man to be a sinner, a woeful sinner, and therefore needs repentance and conversion that there may be a peace-offering and reconciliation between him and his God. Nothing can be done for human redemption and the peace and happiness of mankind unless there is some way, means, or plan by which man and God call be brought on terms of reconciliation. We are taught in the holy Scriptures, that "sin is the transgression of the law," the violation of God's command, and the natural consequence is the punishment of death, "for the soul that sinneth shall die." And this applies to all the intelligences of the universal empire of God, whether they be men or angels or any other rational creatures. If angels sin, they are cast down to hell and overwhelmed by the burning floods of death and darkness to await the judgment day of Almighty God. If man sins, then he also must be punishcd, bccause for every transgression and disobedience there must be a penalty attached, and as surely as there is a law to be obeyed or violated, there is of necessity, a penalty, a sure penalty, that will fall where it belongs, unless through mercy there is made a way for forgiveness. Mercy, therefore, is the gateway of man's escape from death or that punishment due his sins. Now, mercy is not an attribute of Deity. It is not a single inherent quality or part of God, but it is rather a combination or mingling of some of the attributes of Deity. It is an invention of God, to reach and save the lost. Wisdom, power,

love, goodness and pity united and formed the splendid scheme of redemption, and selected the Son of God as the living embodiment of the divine combination. Hence, mercy is a harmonious combination of deistical elements so attuned and balanced that the universal diapason plays in unison in the government of God without friction. Every wheel and cord, every band and cog, with all the listening elements and obedient forces conspired to reach the ends of government, save the sinner, and "justify the way of God to man." Therefore, the plan of salvation, is a plan ofmercy, the best of schemes, the crowning work of God, and the divine ultimatum in the skill of government and the loftiest and the sublimest executive wisdom. Power was infinite and stood ready to create worlds or to execute the vengeance of God and spread his wrath upon the heads of the rebel compact, but power could not save the sinner. Love, the sweetest, the softest, the superlative attribute of God had no power to save the sinner. It had the will, the wish and desire, but had no means to reach the sinking culprit. The will of God was chained by the dictates of Justice who clamored for the death of the sinner. Omniscience, on his speedy wing of flame, swept the spheres, sounded the depths of space, weighed the elements in the balances of judgment, but could not reach the sinner. The Eternity of God, robed in the belted splendors of the cycles, with the dead centuries and the broken wheels and severed cables of the decades piled at his feet, spoke and said, "Nay." But Love called a council of all the Attributes of God, and Wisdom said, "Let us form Mercy," and at once all the splendid qualities, faculties and harmonies of Deity glittered around the shining center of Love and Goodness, and gave birth to divine Mercy, and then crowned her the Darling of God, the Queen of heaven and the conquering Mistress of the centuries. "Repent ye, therefore, and be converted," that you may obtain this mercy, that is, be sorry for your sins, forsake them, "and do work of righteousness."

2. But what is conversion? It is regeneration. The making of a new creature in Christ Jesus. It is a reformation or a work done in us by the Holy Spirit. It is the impartation of the divine nature to that of the human, and is instantaneous. Man repents, but God regenerates. The work of regeneration or conversion is, therefore, divine and superhuman. No man can regenerate, or recreate, or pardon sin. This is the work of God alone. Every pardoned soul must be conscious of it, he must know what the Lord hath done for him, otherwise he would be devoid of that knowledge that is essential to his keeping the law of God and living obedient to his commandments. This is the groundwork of salvation, the beginning of the kingdom of God in the hearts and lives of men. It is the essential badge and seal by which we enter the kingdom of God, both in earth and heaven. Sin expatriated man from the family of God, regeneration matriculates him, and brings him into naturalization with the government of God and the family of heaven. Hence, the Savior says, "Ye must be born again," that is, "born" from above, so as to reflect the perfect image of the invisible God. "If any man be in Christ Jesus, he is a new creature," or a new creation.

3. Each regenerated soul is an image of God. This is "the restitution of all things" mentioned in the text. The declarations of God must be fulfilled. His word cannot return unto him void, but it must accomplish that whereunto he hath sent it. Every knee shall bow, and every tongue shall confess. Now, "the restitution of

all things" is a process. It is the outgoing of the divine power, the manifestations of the truth of God in human life and in the ages of humanity. The ultimate design of the gospel system is the radical reconstruction of human nature, and consequently the predominant reign of the truth by organized Christianity. The things to be restored are the things lost. Christ came to save the world, to regain the long lost ones, and to reestablish God's ancient authority over the children of men.

"The restitution of all things" is to put man back in favor with God and in harmony with the laws of God, both in his spiritual relation and in his personal and physical conditions. God "made him a little lower than the angels," "crowned him with glory and honor," placed his image upon him, and made him lord of creation. In the ascending chain of creation man stood next to angels. The first links in the chain of creation were the formless and insensitive elements that slumbered in crudest shapes and deadest chaos. Darkest forms swept the bosom of the deep. Black squadrons of burning clouds and howling thunders hissed and roared and sported in gyrated rills, and rose in splintered shafts and broken spars and threw billions of their liquid tongues across the highest empyrean and died in writhing agonies hard by the throne of God. The eternal seas, impregnated with ancient night and unpenetrated by angelic wing, or thought, covered all the unmeasured spaces and distances from naught to God. The oldest eternity left the oldest creation without a zone or a hemisphere, and played about its own shifting centers, unconscious of order, and unconscious of its God. No sun shone, no star twinkled, no comet with fiery tail and burning disc flashed across the mighty deep, nor cut the ambient rims of darkness by its majestic sweep or godlike steps through the fields of night.

But the second link of creation's chain began. God touches the elements with omnificent finger. Material for the second link is laid upon the anvil of almighty power. The trip-hammer of wisdom plays on the burning material while ten thousand worlds, and ten thousand more, fly out into space, seek the golden threads of their orbital rounds, and like battalions of blazing seraphs, crowned and robed in the splendors of omnipotence and the power of the eternal, they dance on in space to the command of God, the song of the cycles, the chime of the ages, and the music of the spheres. The oldest children of eternity, the tall archangels, and the heavenly princes and "morning stars that sang together," stepped out from their places in the lofty house of God, and with golden cymbals and high-keyed organs all the thundering orchestra of heaven touched the deepest chords and dug from the spheres the sweetest melodies and the ascending scales of the euphonious vibrations of all the ages known to immortal spirits and immortal singers.

Thus the second link of creation rose from the sparkling anvil of God to the crowned melodies of heaven and the jubilees of angels.

The third link in creation was man. Creation rose from the insensitive to the sensitive--from the non-thinking elements to the conscious, thinking man. He was made "in the image of God." He was made like God in the faculties of his moral and spiritual nature. Like God, he was endowed with a mental constitution that should always reflect the image and nature of his Creator. And this part of his being is its most essential characteristic, and is the real fundamental elements of his individual character. We cannot conceive the idea of some, that man is like God in his physical personality. God is not flesh and blood and bones and sinews, like the children of men. He has neither body nor parts after a physical sense. "God is a spirit, and they that worship him, must worship him in spirit and in truth." He is the incomprehensible Deity in his substance or in the mode of his existence, as well as in the grandeur of his power and sublime perfection of his being. How, then, is "man made in his image?" Evidently, "man is made in the image of" his Creator in the mental and spiritual faculties of his being. As God is a spirit, man is a spirit, and as He is a mental character, so man is a mental character. As God cannot cease to be, neither can man cease to be. As God will live forever, so will man; for he is eternal in the fact of his being. He is an entity, and never can be a non-entity. He is an existence that cannot become a non-existence. His conscious humanity is incapable of decay, and incapable of annihilation. "The heavens shall pass away with a great noise, and the elements shall melt with fervent heat," but "the new heavens and the new earth, wherein dwelleth righteousness" shall find the mental humanity of man unharmed and indestructible. Age upon age, cycle upon cycle, century upon century, may flow on in their streams through the shoreless ocean of eternity; but man will live on in his conscious existence, and rise above all the changing scenes and diversified elements, conditions and powers that may come upon the plane of being in the spheres of the universe. Man may be lost in hell, or saved in heaven, but in neither place can he die the death of annihilation, or fail to be himself in all the power, fullness and plenitude of his Godlike personality.

4. "The restitution of all things." Creation is a system of harmonies, as well as a system of melodies. Though one star differs from another star in altitude, magnitude, power and glory, yet each and all work in harmony with the God-made plan of creation, fulfilling His will and His pleasure. The imperceptible and incohesive elements that swim the airy seas, or sleep in their gulfs, or linger in space, are in harmony with the plan of God and the scope of creation. The small dust of crushed worlds, the scattered cinders of burnt out suns and dead planets, the broken stars and groaning systems writhing beneath the heavy steps of centuries, the massive tread of cycles and the grinding hand of Omnipotence, are yet in harmony with the eternal decrees and the immortal fiats of the immortal King. They play on their own pivots, dance on their burning curves, keep their eternal chronologies, thread their long lines with angelic precision, coerce erratic forces into line, belt their splendid onflow to the throne of God, and weave in mysterious webs their incomprehensible transitions around the seat and center of universal power. Every floating molecule, every winged atom, every breath that glides on sea and air, or leaps the mighty channels of space, is in harmony with the Creator, God. Every string, cord, thread and silken fibre of the universal mechanism is in place. Every spindle, wheel, piston-rod and cylinder moves on in splendid flight and Jehovic harmony, and all is well, and all obey the high behests of the imperial mandates. The centuries, as the crowned kings of the cycles, and the decades as the crowned queens of the centuries, tabulate their chronologies upon the mind of God, and write their

feats upon the eternal ledger of the eternities, and every system is in its place, and ultimately reaches its great ends and wonderful designs. Our earth is the servant of God. It is a spark from the anvil of his omnipotence and practical mandates. God made it and threw it upon its belted rim of fire and told it to play on its orbit and sing on its winged track around the King of day. He covered its continents and islands and towering hills, with trees, flowers and, grassy landscapes, and said to its flora and fauna, "Bud and bloom and blush on forever." The billowing waves of the seas, the thundering torrents leaping and screaming over the shoulders and giant bones of the eternal rocks, roll on in their majesty and splendid trim as if impelled by the presence of God. Night and day, winter and summer, spring and autumn, and the windy blasts of the seasons, move at his command, keep his law, and sleep upon their dusky pillows at his will. All the elements, forces and agencies are held as golden strings in his hands, and every part of the universal mechanism is filled with his power and plethoric with the music of his great name and the melodies of his love. He "maketh his angels spirits and his ministers a flame of fire." The beasts of the field, the birds of the air, with all the finny nations of the deep, and the billions of the insect tribes that rest, creep or soar, sing in their sportive glee, and in sweet obedience chant the name of God in the forest and on the high keys of the air. Every winged lightning, every breath of ether that fans sea or land, and every ray of light that dances the plains, and all the trooping wonders of the ethereal ways, run and return at God's command, covering the hemispheres with his smile, yoking the moving caravans to their centers of action and their dynamic thrones. The centuries and cycles, stepping through geological chronologies and the genealogies of worlds, have faithfully kept the ways of

God, and in the sealed book of fates have recorded their acts in the annals of his providence and have written the history of their life, work and character, in the eternal ledger. The name of every dead child, and of every living spirit, the recorded birth of worlds and the death of planets, and the funeral dirge of sinking systems that have lived and finished their mighty rounds in awful space, have been piled at his throne, and laid at his feet in obedience to his word. He speaks, and all the elements, agencies, and the living and erratic forces of eternal duration crowd to their places, re-gather their threads of construction, take up their appropriate rounds, and crown the whole law of God with the silent splendors of perfect obedience, fulfilling his will and pleasure.

But who, then, are sinners? What vile hand or puny arm has been lifted up against the law of God and the omipotence of the Most High? What rebel in the vast domain of being has risen up and assaulted the ramparts of heaven and defied the King of saints? Let creation answer! Standing on the rocky promontory, at the flinty base of a mountain, where the emerald lips of the foamy seas kiss its bony feet, and where the dashing currents from every island, land and shore bring back the tidings of nations, and hum the music of the spheres, I ask them the story of their being, and in loud acclaim, accentuated with the harmonies of God, and the dictates of his love, they reply that we have all kept "thy law" from youth to hoary years, and from their natal day, when God "set bars and doors" to the seas, and said, "Hitherto shalt thou come, but no farther, and here shall thy proud waves be stayed." I ask the winds whence they came, and with united breath they whistle the name of God, thunder his commandments over earth, air and seas, and hide beneath the sable bands of death. Walking down the azure paths of the seasons, roseate spring with bursting bud and blushing flowers is seen breaking the icy fetters of winter, expelling the hoar frost and crowning creation with a wreath of flowers, and wrapping her in silken robes of queenly trim and dazzling beauty. This is "the unity of nature and the reign of law."

On the outside of this "unity and reign of law," there is a discordant element, and an inharmonious string in the common diapason, composed of a rebel host, a sin-smitten earth and a perverse humanity. Great was the fall of man, because it involved the fundamentals of government, the moral harmony of the universe, and affected the physical spheres. It affected the spiritual, moral and indestructible nature of man to an extent that changed his relations to God, and the regular order of his divine administration. A new combination of elements, including the federation of great totalities, must be evoked, and brought upon the drama of government, and operated on those planes and lines in total and strict accordance with truth and righteousness. The great God could not do wrong, but he could have mercy and send it to earth in the person of his Son. Hence, Christ came not to destroy, but to restore; not to condemn, but to save; not to bring hell, but to bring heaven; not darkness, but light; not disease, but health; not death, but life; therefore, he came to "restore all things." He came to recast and set up the fallen temple of a broken humanity, reassemble its scattered parts and thrill its entirety with the ancient Shekinah. Humanity is to be restored, but how? "Not by might, nor by power," but by Jesus Christ--the living-vital Christ--who is to take charge of the forces of nature, the elements, agencies and all the powers, natures, combinations, federations, fraternities, leagues, societies, constitutions, and all the active potentialities and grand totalities that operate upon the expanding horizon of universal humanity. God said to his Son, "Ask of me, and I will give thee the heathen for thine inheritance, and the uttermost parts of the earth for thy possessions." Again, "Behold, a king shall reign in righteousness, and princes shall rule in judgment. And a man shall be as a hiding place from the wind and a covert from the tempest; as rivers of water in a dry place, as the shadow of a great rock in a weary land. And the eyes of them that see shall not be dim, and the ears of them that hear shall hearken." All things shall hearken to his voice, dance at the touches of his fingers, and vibrate at the majesty of his power. Every element, quantity, faculty and quality in the intricate mechanism of the universal order will be manipulated, wrought into beauty and harmony and made to assume its ancient relations by the coercive hand of the Eternal.

"The restitution of all things" includes the suspension of war, the nullification of corrupting institutions, and the overthrow of the massive conclaves of sin and infidelity that have poisoned the nations, slain their millions and left their writhing bodies, broken bones and bleeding carcasses in their track of death. It means the close of the saloon, the overthrow of drunkenness, the destruction of the opium traffic, the fall of slavery in every form, the purification of human society, the breaking of the prisoner's chains, and the freedom of the long-bound captive. It means the destruction and the total overthrow of all the forms, codes, teachings and ungodly practices of heathen priests and their superstitious systems of ill-founded theories and false religions. It means the fall of empires, the dissolution of kingdoms, the disintegration of states, and the perishing of municipalities, and the obliteration of every opposing foe and antagonizing power. Who can stand before the power of the Eternal, stay his hand and stop his kingdom? Look up, ye sons and daughters of God, get ready for the coming of the bridegroom. Fill your vessels with the oil of his truth, "trim the golden flame," buckle on your sandals, girt your habit and march out to the music of his voice, and the choruses of his love. Look up, he is coming! I hear the tramp of horses, the hum of chariots, the blasts of bugles, bands of music and the thunders of a moving army. Swift-running feet skip lightly along the horizon, and wings of majesty flash on the zones, and inflame their parallels with his presence and the light of his countenance. The throne of earth's new King is set "on Zion's hill." Around him flash the crowned princes, the dignitaries of state, the majesties of empires, the governors of provinces, and the mayors of cities. These bring up the threads of government, make them fast to Jehovah's chair and bind them to the foot of his throne. "The earth is the Lord's and the fullness thereof." Hallelujah! the Lord God omnipotent reigneth.

SERMON IX.

Deep Concern for the Welfare of Zion.

"For Zion's sake will I not hold my peace, and for Jerusalem's sake I will not rest, until the righteousness thereof go forth as brightness, and the salvation thereof as a lamp that burneth."--Isaiah 62:1.

The language of the prophet involves a deep concern respecting the Zion of God, the spread of the truth and the extension of an organized Christianity. Every true believer in the gospel of Christ, and especially every minister, should feel the same impulse and burning desire for the extension of the kingdom of Christ that glowed in the prophet's heart and flamed upon the prophet's tongue. It is a most healthy and significant fact that characterizes all the true children of God, that they have an ardent desire and a consuming zeal to spread the truth and make others feel, hope, and live as they do. The first impulse of the young Christian is to tell others that he has found the Christ of whom the prophets wrote, and who, in subsequent years died upon the cross to demonstrate and seal the truth of his mission and doctrine by his death. "Zion" and "Jerusalem," are used as representative of the earthly city of God--the capital and metropolis of the Jewish theocratical kingdom. It was Jewish, because its subjects and inhabitants were of that race. It was theocratic because God was the only and legal King thereof. As a capital and metropolis, it represented more than its mere own existence and form of government. In the highest and fullest sense it represented a kingdom yet to come--a spiritual empire that should fill the whole earth with the glory of God in the triumph over sin and the salvation of universal man. "Zion" is the templed hill from which the divine word and laws should be issued for the government of man and the propagation of those edicts and stern decrees that claim the allegiance and obedience of all intelligent beings. For says the Scriptures, "The law shall go forth of Zion, and the word of the Lord from Jerusalem."

1. Let us consider the spiritual "Zion" with Christ its reigning King.

We must repeat here the fact that Christ is the reigning and true king of Zion, though not reigning in a human or physical sense. In this sense, he does not appear in regal splendor and as dictator over the earthly affairs of men. As yet, he has neither throne, nor crown, nor earthly dominion. These are to come in his glorious future. For the physical earth and heavens, with all the elements and resources of endless nature, belong to Christ in as true a sense as the spiritual and invisible. The seen and the unseen, and even the unseeable, with all their tangible and intangible entities, are in the range of his touch and his controlling power. But for the present, and a specific time measured by centuries, his operative forces are those that lie in the field of spiritual power and that divine energy by whose formative and mysterious operations creation sprang into being and man into light and life. How long his reign is to continue spiritual and invisible as it is at present is a great and profound question that the great future alone can fully answer. But according to the Scriptures, he is to reign until "he hath put all enemies under his feet." "Then shall the Son also himself be subject unto him that put all things under him, that

God may be all in all." Again, says the Apostle, "Then cometh the end, when he shall have delivered up the kingdom to God, even the Father; when he shall have put down all rule and all authority and power." So that from the Word of God we learn that the spiritual reign of Christ is restricted to the length of certain periods or centuries, when in some vital form the phase of his kingship shall be changed, or, in other words, "He shall deliver up the kingdom to God, even the Father," "that God may be all in all." Christ will not cease to reign, no matter what may be the change or peculiar transformation of his spiritual and physical empire. Evidently, the Scriptures present to us at least two forms of his reign. The first form is purely spiritual and invisible, and is the formulative and transforming period of the human church state. This is the state in which we now live, familiarly known as "the gospel dispensation." This gospel dispensation was fully developed on the day of Pentecost, when an organized Christianity became intensive and extensive by being endued with power from on high. This is the beginning of the mediatorial reign of Christ in the shape and capacity of a redeemer. This mediatorial reign is to continue to "the end" of the restricted period when he shall have finished the work of human redemption, in the destruction and overthrow of every foe and every opposing element and power that hinders the spread and success of the gospel system. Now, Christ is the Apostle and High Priest of our salvation under whose direction is the organized church, with its living ministry, with the silent, yet powerful spirit operating in the world, reproving "the world of sin, and of righteousness, and of judgment." The processes of the redemptive scheme to human conception seem slow, creeping along the paths and highways of the ages and the civilizations of man, contending with perverse human nature, and the obstructive forces of sin and Satan. Yet gradually and surely "the end" cometh when he shall put down all rule and authority -- all organized forces, powers and elements--of wicked men and devils, and at "the end" of the prolonged struggle, Christ shall present to his Father the world redeemed and the finished church as a chaste virgin without spot or wrinkle.

2. Christianity is first intensive and then extensive.

Intensive because it involves the greatest interest of man, and plays upon the deepest chords of his being, and thrills the resonant depths of his soul with God and heaven and an endless salvation. In the text it is called "brightness" and "a lamp that burneth." Says "the sweet singer of Israel," "Thy word is a lamp unto my feet, and a light unto my path." The blessed Savior says, "I am the light of the world." The prophets wrote of the gospel age as "light." "The people which sat in darkness saw great light; and to them which sat in the region and shadow of death light is sprung up." He is a light for the Gentiles; "to open the blind eyes, to bring out the prisoners from the prison, and them that sit in darkness out of the prison house." "And the Gentiles shall come to thy light, and kings to the brightness of thy rising." All these passages adumbrate the intensive forces of a nascent Christianity. Entering the arena of thought and action, it glows, sparkles, and flames as "a lamp that burneth." From the intensive elements of Christianity, from its heat and flame, throwing its bright light along the centers of social and civil life, comes that force and spiritual power by which the church is extended, and the gospel of truth is sent to the remotest parts of the habitable earth. As light and heat are the greatest forces in physical nature--the creators of energy--so spiritual light and the heat of God's love are the greatest forces in spiritual nature--the creators of thrift and go, bringing into active service all the latent powers of the church and ministry, to extend its influence and its saving grace to all the race of Adam. Man needs an intensive or forceful Christianity. Any religion that is benificent and calculated to elevate and save the human race, must be forceful and capable of adaptation to all the ages and conditions of men. It must be commensurate with their spiritual needs and ethical requirements. It must be accessible to the poor and unlearned as well as to the learned, the rich, and the powerful. The very fact that the Christian religion has all the needed elements in richest profusion, demonstrates its divine origin, and proves it to be of heavenly extraction. The goodness, the wisdom, the love, and the power of God are thereby exhibited in the system.

But why should it be forceful and glow with intensive fire? Because it proposes to do what nothing else can do. It proposes to save man from all of his foes, such as sin and Satan and his own crooked and perverse nature. It proposes to renovate and restore the human kind to God's favor, enable man to regain his lost prestige, purify, and give chastity and dignity to human nature and the civilizations of the world. And this is a more wonderful work which Christianity proposes to do, when we consider the vileness, the hardness, the deep depravity and perverseness of the human race. Man is a sinner. His race is the sinning race. He rebels against the laws of God and nature because he wills to rebel. It is not within the range of possibilities for him to cure and restore his fallen and depraved self. Intelligence and personal culture, with all the accomplishments and possibilities of his own efforts cannot reach the deep-seated malady that dwells within and contaminates the fountain of his being, corrupting every stream and poisoning every spring of life. Is not man a sinner? Man is a sinner. Misery is the proof of sin. "If thou doest not well, sin lieth at the door," is the declaration of the oracles of God. If there is misery, such as sickness, pain, sorrow, poverty, want, suffering and death, it is the evidence that some law of God has been violated, and these come to the violater as a righteous penalty from the jealous and sin-avenging God. Who then can say there is no misery in the earth? Yea, there is no end to the suffering of mankind in the world.

Every page of history and the annalist of every age, tell of the horrors of wars and the mighty death-roll of those who have fallen upon the field of sanguinary strife. Every battle of warriors is with confused noise and garments rolled in blood. Religious persecution and strong drink count their victims by the millions, crowding the open gates of death with the pale caravans of nations. The fever, the plague, the epidemics, sweep from the surface of the earth the great and the small alike. A mighty stream of the dead forever rolls on in silent rush to the unseen and "the great beyond." It is the business of the human race to come and play its part upon the stage of life but for a few short days, and then make its exit by death along the downward plain into the grave and dissolution. Great rivers may be diverted from their courses, lakes may be drained and despoiled of their waters, isthmuses may be cut asunder, and peninsulas may rise from their submarine recesses and assume the grandeur and proportions of a continent upon whose ashy face and bony structure a thousand cities with their mighty civilizations may exist; but none can change the awful course of the mighty phalanxes of those millions that traverse the moribund ways of human life. It is the irrevocable fiat of the great God, and the changeless edict of nature, that all who live must die. Who can tell what is in the great beyond where spirits live and move? Who can describe the place and topography of that land covered with deepest shades and wrapped in the dark bosom of mystery? Who can photograph its mountains and landscapes, measure its rivers and sound the profundity of its oceanic depths? What are the distinctive features of its social life and civilization, if civilization there be? Yea, my friends, "the gates of death" are "open" to all the living for their ingress, but closed against the egress of the millions of the dead. These are awful questions full of interest to every living man upon the face of the earth, and without the solution of the revelations of God are a productive source of misery and distress to the sober and contemplative mind. But there is hope. The power of the gospel stretches beyond the shady land, and pierces its deep gorges of night, sounds its oceanic depths, plows up its submarine caverns, breaks up its bony structure, and thrills its valleys with the song of the resurrection, covers its dark mountains with light, shatters the kingdom of the dead, breaks the bands of the sleeping millions and lifts them up to God and his Christ. Let us sing then,

> Hope looks beyond the bounds of time,
> When what we now deplore,
> Shall rise in full immortal prime,
> And bloom to fade no more.

2. Organized Christianity is diffusive and extensive.

This is expressed in the phrase: "Salvation thereof as a lamp that burneth."

Christianity is not designed to be the religion of the few, but of the many, indeed of all. The author of man's being is the author of Christianity. Man is made, but Christianity is not made in the sense that man is. Man had a beginning, and is an organized intelligence; Christianity is a native truth founded upon the divine nature of God. The fashion of its ministration and its external organizations may change in its phases, and its forms of worship in one country way differ from that of another. It is the state-church in one country, and the non-state-church in another. It may cause peace in one country and civil revolution in another, but everywhere it is the same in nature, origin, spirit and effect. The same great fundamental principles and truths lie at its base and support its indestructible superstructure. The central and unifying principle is the Christ of God, and its adaptability to all the spiritual and religious needs and conditions of men is proof of its divinity. As such, it cannot stand still. It cannot live domiciled or nationalized in one country while other countries and nations are in the darkness of ignorance and heathenism. It lives by propagation and its diffusive elements, and is essentially missionary in its nature. It cannot rest at home. Its home continents and islands are too narrow for its extensive and expansive operations. Its life is in its activity and agitation. The ways of the world's developments are the high plains of its achievements, and the national lines of progress are its channels. The climates of the world are its inheritance, the mountains are its thrones and the valleys its palace gardens. The high arch of heaven is its temple, and the spacious earth its footstool. Its chariot wheels roll along the arteries of commerce, and its ships plod the veins of ocean trade. It yokes the winged lightnings to its car and whispers the music of its Christ over the steel cables of commerce, and shouts its sweet accents of peace from isle to isle, and from ocean to ocean, and back to its thundering shores. It ticks in telegraphy and hums upon its galvanized threads of iron, calling nations to councils of peace and good will, and staying the bloody hand of war and international conflict. It penetrates the continents, searches the forests, navigates the seas to ameliorate and save the lost and dying sinners of Adam's race. It is the soul of progress, the life of civilization, the quickening power of thought and the guiding star of human judgment. It explains the intricate problems of biological science and those far-reaching and important spiritual relations that exist between God and man, and that exist between man and his fellow-intelligences. It explains man to himself, leading him through himself to God, his Maker, and on through all those subtle questions and profound inquiries that have agitated and perplexed the thoughtful heart of man in the ages of the past. It directs his feet along the ways of life, and develops his mentality and spiritual manhood as nothing else can do.

3. Organized Christianity appeals to all men for the consecration of themselves and their wealth as a means of saving the world.

"I will not rest until the righteousness thereof go forth as brightness, and the salvation thereof as a lamp that burneth."

This is an appeal to the church and the living ministry for perfect and thorough consecration of themselves and all that they are for the spread and universal diffusion of Christianity. Nothing but such a consecration and such a ministry will do or can do the great work assigned to it by the Author of our salvation. As instruments in the hand of God, the ministry of the Word and the propaganda of his truth must be adapted to the ends in view. As instrument, the ministry must partake of the spirit and nature of the message which it is to declare. Ministers must know Christ to preach him successfully to the nations and peoples of the earth. They must know him in the fullness of his love and in the fullness of his power and grace. As such, they must know him historically, philosophically and in his redeeming grace and functions. They must know him by personal experience and spiritual commission. They must know him in his power to save from all sin in a deeper, profounder, and more practical sense than they know him in his mere historical life and character. They must know him in a higher and broader sense than mere philosophical sylogisms and premises evolved from systems of thought and reason. To them he--the Christ of God--must be more than a mythical character or allegorical hero without body or parts. To them he must be more than Moses to the Israelites, more than David to the Jews, and more than Solomon to the house of David. To them he must be more than Alexander to Macedonia, more than Cæsar to Rome, and more than Napoleon to France. To them he must be higher and greater than the princes and kings of the earth, and greater than the angels in heaven, and all the universe besides. They must know him as he is--the full and plenipotent Son of God, in whom "all the fullness of the Godhead" dwells "bodily," and as the Lamb of God that taketh away the sin of the world. The living ministry must know him as the dying Savior, as the risen God, the ascended Prince, the reigning King, and the officiating High Priest of our salvation.

    The work of the ministry and the operation of organized Christianity requires not only personal consecration, but the setting apart of a large share of the wealth and material interest of man. God's plan of human redemption is largely dependent upon second causes, such as the expenditure of money, the devotion of talent, bodily labor, and physical exertion. Nothing can be done unless there is an effort made by those who are in charge of the affairs of the church. The law of labor and activity is the law of nature, and applies to physical and mental achievements alike. The systems of nature and grace are in perpetual agitation that arise from, and out of their own innate elements. The ebb and flow of the oceans purify the waters of the seas, and give life, vitality, glory, and beauty to the face of the earth, crowning the mountains with the trees of God and the smiling valleys with the blushing rose and the blooming lily. Let the ocean stand still; let its bosom be smooth as glass and cease to lash its tide into madness, the world would soon be denuded of its people, and vegetation would droop and die. The howling winds would no longer whistle across the plains to carry the fresh ozone to the nations and living tribes of beasts, birds, buds, and flowers. The chariot of the clouds would cease to roll along the skies with terrific clangor and with passive, repulsive obedience fall back on the placid bosom of a dead sea, from which would arise a vapor of poisonous breath unendurable by any living thing. The great sea is the breath of the world, the respiratory organs of the globe. By its living breath and dancing spray, the parallels and zones breathe the breath of life and stir the febrile torridity of earth's Saharas. Every respiration that expands our lungs and fills the blood with oxygen is a flying wave of living air from the mighty deep, chanting as it comes the music of the seas and the melodies of God. "O, the depth of the riches, both of the wisdom and knowledge of God! how unsearchable are his judgments and his ways past finding out."

> God moves in a mysterious way,
> His wonders to perform,
> He plants his footsteps in the sea,
> And rides upon the storm.
> Deep in the unfathomable mind,
> With never failing skill,
> He treasures up his bright designs,
> And works his sovereign will.

"Work out your own salvation with fear and trembling, for it is God which worketh in you both to will and do of his good pleasure." This, then, is the law of creation--work. Organized Christianity comes to work. It is the soul of labor and the sun of evolution. What the sea is to the physical earth, the religion of Jesus is to the moral and spiritual world. Its influence is felt in every civilization, and is building its temples and lifting its blood-stained cross in every land. Already its golden anthem flashes along upon its silvern threads of truth, begirting the globe with the sunbeams of his love. "Ask of me," says the great Father to the great Son, "and I will give thee the heathen for thine inheritance, and the uttermost parts of the earth for thy possession." "Thou shalt break them with a rod of iron, thou shalt dash them in pieces like a potter's vessel."

"Awake, awake, put on thy strength, O, Zion, put on thy beautiful garments, O, Jerusalem." Now thrilling is this cry from the hill of Zion! Let the church awake, and stand up for Jesus. Let the rich pile their wealth at his feet. Let kings bring their crowns, their broken scepters, their hoarded wealth, and coffers of gold and silver, and lay them down at the cross of king Messiah. He has use for them all. "Oh, that men would praise the Lord for his goodness, and for his wonderful works to the children of men!"

SERMON X.

Life and Death.

"Who hath abolished death, and hath brought life and immortality to light through the Gospel."--2 Tim. 1:10.

In the wide realm of human thought there cannot be any questions of profounder concern than those involving the great and absorbing themes of life and death, and their fearful consequences. Life and death are the antipodes of our existence upon the face of the earth, and constantly appeal to our consideration of their great moment and awful concern. The tongue of man, the pen of the philosophic scientist, the rapt visions of seers, the songs of the Muses, and the anthems of angels cannot bring to the contemplation of man a greater theme, more engrossing or charming than that involved in the text. Indeed, it is not possible for the mind of man to dwell upon matters of more interest and deeper importance than that of life and death. Like a shock of electricity it flashes on every wire, plays upon everything and ramifies all the deep gorges and labyrynthian chambers of the moral, physical and mental man. It directs the thoughts and mind to those solemn realities, and those fascinating conditions and relations that meet him in the present, and await him in the endless future. It is worse than useless for man to attempt to reject those premonitory thoughts that open to his view the stern decrees of God, the Irresistible, the Inevitable. Life is the normal condition of man, death is the abnormal. Man was made for life, and not for death. He was made to live and not to die. Death is the result of sin and disobedience. It is condign punishment for crime committed against the majesty of heaven and the law of God. A state of perpetual felicity, with the faculty of progression and development is the law of his being and the object of his creation. This view is anticipated by the wonderful construction of his physical constitution. The upright bearing of his body, its symmetrical beauty and enchanting charms, the radiance of the sparkling eye and beauty of the glowing cheek, the wonders of the human foot, and the greater wonders of the human hand; the astounding miracles of the voice, the communication of thought and feeling by word, the towering mind, the massive, expansive, and versatile intellect, all present man as the masterpiece, the highest ideal of God's conception of all his earthly creations. Indeed he is the crowning architrave of heaven's architectural skill. By these high attributes of greatness he stands at the head of all earthly creations and sublunary wonders.

But the dignity of man is augmented and multiplied many times when we consider that ethereal spark and diviner subtle force which we call the soul. And this soul is the master of sovereign man.

Whatsoever the soul of man may be, as to its nature and functions and those peculiar powers enabling it to subsist apart from the body, it is the source, the foundation and spring of life. While the soul is not life itself, yet there can be no life without it. Thus the soul of man is the precious gem, the indestructible jewel "that keeps two worlds at strife"--the world of hell and the world of heaven. In fact, there is a constant and perpetual struggle between heaven and hell for this precious gem, this substantial, yet spiritual entity. Two spiritual powers --antipodal and antagonistic--assemble their aggressive and gigantic hosts in battle array upon the broad arena of every man's existence, and with jarring tread and heavy tramp of war, seek to lift the soul to heaven or cast it down to hell.

But there are many theories as to what the soul of man is, in its nature, attributes and origin. The materialistic theory is, that the soul of man is not a substance or reality, but a mere result of the combination of matter so attuned and refined as to produce results, and therefore, is not a thing with sensible properties in the sense that matter has properties. The manistic theory is substantially the same, in the final logical results, both denying the existence of spiritual substances in the Scripture sense. But the Scriptures declare that "the Lord God formed man of the dust of the ground, and breathed into his nostrils the breath of life; and man became a living soul." This "living soul" in man, was created by the breath of God, a flame kindled within by the power of the Creator. We observe, too, that it is a distinct creation from that of the body, the two creations being distinguished by two separate fiat acts of power. He first made his body "of the dust of the ground," and made his soul by "the breath of his lips," so that both body and soul are creations proper, and not the mere result of any peculiar combinations of matter, so adjusted as to produce all the phenomena and wonders of the human mind. Then man has two parts, the mind or the soul, and the body. This makes man an ideality, in eternal entity. He cannot be more than he is, he will never be less as to the nature and number of his faculties. Time or eternity, condition or place, can never change the nature of man so as to make him anything other than he is--man.

The abolition of death is the hope of man.

This is the work of Christ; and Christ alone. He has abolished death, in the sense that death can do the believer no real harm. It is the abolition of that death that involves the punishment for sin and transgressions committed against God and the moral code of the universe. This abolition of death involves the forgiveness of sins, the reconciliation of God and man, and the redemption and salvation of all who come to Jesus Christ as the Savior of the world. Christ came as God's Interpreter, a heavenly Legate with plenipotentiary powers to make plain the will and laws of God to sinful and rebellious man. He uncovers the mystery of God that could not be explained by the wisdom, research, and learning of man so as to annul the power of death and take away its terrors. He does not come to destroy natural or corporeal death, but to remove the sting of death, and release us from punishment eternal, and give us joys everlasting. Hence, "he taught them as one having authority and not as the Scribes." Death, then, is the first great foe to be overcome or destroyed. This was a work that all humanity combined could not do. It was not in the capacity of the dying to remove or destroy a power greater than itself, and there was no process or method known to mankind to remedy the defect or evade the results of sin. The sinner cannot heal himself of a spiritual malady that requires more skill and power than was in the sinner. Again, Christ has a complete knowledge of the state of man. He had the most perfect and minute comprehension of all those principles and elements that existed in man, and which had been disjointed and confused by transgressions and sins. Being man himself as well as God, he comprehends the remedy as well as the disease. To destroy death he must die himself, and to raise the dead, he himself must rise, and to break the force of the grave, he must enter its dark and cold precincts and tread the dark "valley of the shadow of death." To save man, he must become man with all his pains, his sorrows, his tears and all those death agonies through which every man must pass. "For as much then as the children are partakers of flesh and blood, he also himself likewise took part of the same, that through death, he might destroy him that had the power of death, that is, the devil; and deliver those who through fear of death were all their lifetime subject to bondage."

But what is death?

Death is the antithesis of life, the removal of the spirit from the body, the extraction of the moving and animating principle from the material machinery. It is a profound quietism and the disintegration of all of the bodily parts. This is natural death, pure and simple, This, Christ did not come to abolish in the immediate sense. But spiritual death is the death of the soul--the punishment of the spiritual and mental man, in a state of consciousness and personal identity. There is no death in the sense of annihilation. Dead men are not annihilated. Their bodies are disintegrated, and their souls are in the spirit world, but they still retain all the faculties of their being. Indeed, death cannot shake off human character or personal identity, or utterly obliterate those distinguishing features that characterize intelligent existence. Even man himself cannot devise any means to destroy himself in the sense of annihilation, because he is a stern entity, whose eternal decrees forbid his nonentity. Could an intelligent creature thus make his place a blank in creation, the will of God would be defeated, and his moral government could not be maintained. No, when the sinner lands in the state of punishment, he will still be all that he was in life and character. He will carry with him all the consciousness and vividness of memory that he ever had in this state of trial and probation. State or condition cannot change character nor mental personality. He will be himself in spite of himself, and in spite of all the efforts he may make to become nothing. He may treasure up unto himself "wrath against the day of wrath, and revelation of the righteous judgment of God," yet he cannot remove himself from the Creator, and thus evade "the day of wrath" and those awful responsibilities that belong to him as a moral being, because of his free moral agency. The elements and properties of man's being make him an everlasting entirety as a part of the permanent fixture of the universe, a real part of the most real elements-- the mental part. No other being can fill his place in the eternal series and concatenations of the endless creations of God. He is an essential part of the moral universe that cannot be extracted or separated from it, and every single individual of the race must fill his own place in the mighty series of responsibility. There is a personal responsibility and moral obligation involved in human existence that cannot be escaped or evaded by shifting it upon the shoulders of others, or by sinking it in some deep and unknown part of the universe. We cannot hide our obligations any more than we can hide our sins and crimes which are written upon the tablets of the heart and wrapped up in the convolutions of the soul. Man cannot hide from God any more than he can hide from himself, and he can as soon flee from himself as he can flee from God or the moral universe of which he forms an essential part and an inextricable force. He makes one in the vast number intelligent individuals, and is a link in the great chain of being that threads the fiat acts of God, making each man a part of every other in the most minute and mutual relation. Because of the high dignity, spirituality and indestructible individualism of man his annihilation (if such were possible) would unbalance the moral sphere, and throw out of harmony the moral government of God, affecting every interest and part of moral and intelligent existence. The great chains of creation's symphonetic links would become disorganized and stripped of those consonant and responsive octachords that have for interminable ages made the universal diapason a system of wonderful and amazing harmonies, transcending the comprehension of men and angels and all the towering intellects of the universe. How, then, can man be annihilated any more than the universe can be? Is he not an important part of the great whole, made in the image of God? Nay, nay, friends, the stars may fall, and heaven and earth may pass away as they must in the coming ages, but man, the offspring of God, will hold his place in the economy of God, and the native eternity of his being. Since he has begun to be, and since he does exist, creation would be without its crown and the preponderating element in the absence of man. Man, then, is an important element in the creations of God, comprehending in his being the physical, spiritual and mental parts that belong in common to all the kingdoms and dominions of God. And because of these relations in his origin and nature, he must be an interesting object to all other intelligent creatures of the worlds of the universe.

But man is immortal. He shall live forever in some place in the universe. In the onflow of his days, four great facts surround his being. These are, place, state, development and his service or religion. These are the main and central facts of his future. The place that he shall occupy in the potency of his being is designated under the relative terms of heaven and hell--the two extremes of the moral pole. Whosoever is in heaven is not in hell, and whosoever is not in heaven is in hell. At the end of every man's physical life stands the open gate of heaven or the open gate of hell, and nothing can divert his rapid course to one or to the other. Propelled by his eternal destiny, and forced on by inexorable decrees, he traverses the dark and cold territory of death, and enters his everlasting habitation. His home is found, and his place is fixed, and he begins his eternal rounds in the infinite domains of place and space. Man may not be confined to a small hemisphere, either in heaven, or in hell. Wide, deep and high may be the prison house of the lost--a world of darkness where no suns burn, no stars twinkle, no comets flash, no meteors blaze, and no "pale empress of the night" smiles on a darkened world --a world where no orb of fire ever sent a rippling rill of flame across its dark mountains, nor plowed those abysmal depths of interminable night. The place may be a house with steel gates and adamantine floors, with rock-ribbed mountains of impassable heights, from whose fiery summits sentinels of towering blasts forever play upon angry floods and burning seas--a place where every man is against every other man, and where envy, anger, hatred, malice, lust and pride fill every heart, and falsehood and slander ride supreme on every tongue--a place of perpetual strife and endless war, endless in duration and endless in the depth of its vileness and infamy--a place where spirits bold and daring meet in dreadful conflict and battle array with clashing sabres playing upon the bosom of the deep in the plenitude of power and the darkness of the night. But hear it, prison house of the lost, with your gates of steel and adamantine floors, where no suns burn, nor stars twinkle, where no comets flash nor meteors blaze, no "pale empress of the night" smile on a darkened world, where no orb of fire has sent a rippling rill of flame across thy dark mountains, nor plowed those abysmal depths of interminable night. Hear it, ye spirits bold and daring, with your clashing sabres playing upon the bosom of the deep in the plenitude of power and in the darkness of hell. Man is immortal, and has endless development and endless progression, whether he is in heaven or in hell. Man, then, is a gem. He belongs to those bright stars in the galaxy of God whose unfading lustre and brilliant coruscation will shine on through endless days. Christ came all the way from heaven to seek and save him. He is lost. His place is vacant in the twinkling galaxy of heaven. His value is measured by the price paid, and that price is the blood and tears and the death of the Son of God.

But death is a conqueror. He is the proud and haughty king of the ages. He reigneth over the kingdoms of the earth. His hand is on the land, and his arm is in the seas. His triumphant chariot rolls along on the declivities of the ages and through the cities and rural plains of all the people, breaking the bones of the nations, crushing out the life and vital powers and spattering the blood of the dead and dying millions on his own garments amid the shrieks and cries of weeping thousands and the lamentations of the people. His track along the ages is marked by painted sepulchres, mausoleums, sarcophagi and widespread cities of the dead. Cruel and relentless, he invades the sacred precincts of every family, greedily plucking the blooming infant from the mother's breast, and the darling child from the downy lap of ease, transporting them to the eternal city of ineffable brightness far beyond its narrow sea. Before him, thrones topple, crowned heads fall, empires quiver, sceptres break, kingdoms disintegrate, and States crumble into dust. At his command warriors bow, armies flee, swords are sheathed, and belching cannon cease to play on the bloody arena of death. His quivers are filled with arrows poisoned with the venom of serpents and the pangs of asps that fly thick and fast from his bow. The winds are his horses, the zephyr his chariots, and the blushing rose and smiling lilies of the plains his boudoir. He "lurks in every flower," ripples in the curling flood, whistles in the winds, screaks in the storm, thunders in the air, and bellows in the earthquake, sweeping the zones and parallels of earth with the dense shades of Hades and the smoke and fumes of Tartarus. He has plucked crowns from kings, jewels from queens, gold plate from emperors and gems from princes and rulers. Who can stand before him and resist his power? "Who can open the doors of his face?" "He esteemeth iron as straw and brass as rotten wood." "The arrow cannot make him flee; sling-stones are turned with him unto stubble; darts are counted as stubble; he laugheth at the shaking of a spear."

See, see, he cometh over the hills, over the mountains,

over the plains, through the streets, and his heavy tramp is heard on the door-sill. The latch flies, the bolts roll back and whisper sadly to the affrighted inmates, saying,

> Arise, my love, make haste away,
> Go get thee up and die.

But death, the conqueror is conquered by Jesus Christ. He opens "the doors of his face" and unhorses the proud rider, for he "hath abolished death," broken his long reign, taken away his terrors, demolished his throne, scattered his kingdom and rent his empire into pieces, and set the captives free. "If the Son therefore shall make you free, ye shall be free indeed." "Death hath no dominion over" the believer. But the abolition of death means that all the children of God shall be beyond the reach or possibility of death in that blessed place and future home. We know it is a future, and according to the Scriptures of truth it must be a place, a place of all the realities, perfections, splendors, glories and magnificences that are befitting in its wonders and elaborate arrangements for the throne of Christ, with all the equipages, powers and necessities that belong to a city of the greatest of all kings. "There God the Son forever reigns, and scatters night away." There are no "cities of the dead," nor grave-diggers, nor coffin-makers, nor black hearses, nor mournful wails of the funeral train; for death is absent--slain by "the Prince of life"--his kingdom dissolved, his scepter broken, and heaven shouts on through the ages, and fills the rolling cycles with the anthems of redemption and the glories of Messiah's triumphs. Amen! Amen!

SERMON XI.

The Insufficiency of the Wisdom of Man.

"That your faith should not stand in the wisdom of men, but in the power of God."--1 Cor. II:5.

The author of this epistle is the Apostle Paul, who was, at that time, in the great city of Ephesus. He had spent nearly two years of his apostolic life in Corinth, at which place he had planted that important church, to whom this first epistle was addressed. Having lived in Corinth for nearly two years, and having become familiar with the people, he was peculiarly prepared to instruct them in all the doctrines, principles, and practices of the Christian religion. There was much in the church that was contrary to the plainest principles, doctrines, and precepts of Christ. Under these conditions, it became the imperative duty of the Apostle to correct those errors which were then prevalent in the Corinthian church. Parties and divisions had grown up among them, and schism and discord began to do great damage to them as followers of the meek and lowly Jesus. For those who recommended to the unbelievers the great truths of Christianity which they professed, should themselves show it by their well-ordered conduct. "Every one of you" says the Apostle, "saith, I am of Paul, and I of Apollos, and I of Cephas, and I of Christ." Here we have four distinct parties in the Corinthian church. The first party was made up of those Christians that had been converted from Paganism. This was the St. Paul party. The second party or division was that of Apollos. These were made up of those who wanted to mix religion with Grecian philosophy, and engraft upon the Christian system those philosophical tendencies that then prevailed in Greece and Alexandria. The third party was for Peter. They favored the mixing of Judaism with Christianity. They thought that a little sprinkling of Judaism over Christianity would make the doctrine and precepts of Christ more acceptable to the unbelieving Jew. How much like our modern ritualistics. They are blind to the substance, but grasp at the shadow, and are content to live in the mere shade of the tree of Christianity without enjoying its wholesome fruits. The fourth party was for Christ. They wanted no leader but Christ. They seemed to have thought that Paul, Apollos, and Cephas had transcended the powers delegated to them by Christ, and, therefore, it would seem best to them to throw off and discard their authority. Some of our modern religious partisans still retain this fourth party spirit. Extremes are dangerous, especially when driven by the storms of partisan interests. When we follow men, we should follow them only as they follow Christ. When they cease to follow Christ it is the part of wisdom, and will add to our happiness and peace to leave them to themselves. Paul, Apollos and Cephas were all servants-- ministers of the word. They could sow and plant, and they could dig the soil and cast in the seed, and water, but Christ alone must give the increase. How different is this from the Corinthian idea of propriety! Corinth was a place noted for its learning, wisdom, and erudition, but it was "the wisdom of men." It consisted in philosophizing upon those wonderful and profound subjects that belong alone in the province of Revelation, into whose mysterious precincts none but God can enter. The city was renowned for its wealth, luxury and refinement, as well as for its learning and the ingenuity of its citizens. Equally noted and attractive was the magnificence of its buildings. Splendid palaces, theaters, elegant temples, and other public buildings, beautified and adorned with the greatest architectural skill, rose to the height of sublime altitudes in every part of the city. Statues, columns, capitals, and bases, were the pride of the inhabitants, and the admiration of strangers. The citadel was built upon a mountain which overlooked the city, and was called "Acro-Corinthus." The temple of Neptune, celebrated for having a thousand slaves, or prostitutes, devoted to licentiousness and the lewdness of the people, had its influence upon the morals of the Christian Church, and gave it lax ideas respecting the true spirit, nature, and practice of the precepts of Christianity. As Corinth was celebrated for its marvelous schools of philosophy and rhetoric, it was easy for the church to suppose that the great truths of the gospel should at least be clothed in the magnificent paraphernalia of philosophical and rhetorical diction. The sciences and the arts were carried to such great perfection, that Cicero terms it, "The light of all Greece." Florus called it "The adornment of all Greece." When we take a survey along the centuries of Grecian life and civilization, taking in the city of Corinth as the best specimen of that civilization, we form some conceptions of the true character of its being and life. While looking into the social, civic, and religious life, two things are particularly prominent, and that is, that learning and licentiousness, both great in degree and kind, should be so closely wedded, and go hand in hand, amid great learning and social refinement. In other words, it is remarkable, how, under the influence of so much learning, that there should continue to exist so much debauchery among its learned and intelligent inhabitants. The temple of Neptune, situated in the central part of the city, with its thousand vile prostitutes, threw its dreadful and polluting contagion over the whole of that populous and proud city, contaminating the entire social state. Strangers from all parts came to her as to a mart of science, law, and art, and likewise fell under the moral plague that was then destroying their great civilization. Splendid orators, magnificent public speakers, made the great halls of the theaters ring with powerful eloquence upon theories of science, law and art. Symphonious notes of the muses and melodies of the spheres, throbbed and thrilled the enchanted souls of the spectators, and wrapped and ravished their spirits in visions of pleasure and ecstasies of delight. Situated on an isthmus between two seas, she became a great commercial emporium, and in consequence of which her merchants became princes, and her people opulent, while luxuries poured in and held universal sway, bringing with them that ease and fullness of bread which accompany a debased, profligate, and declining civilization. Taking this view of the subject, how reasonable and appropriate it was for St. Paul, being fully acquainted with Grecian life and the errors and the weakness of Grecian philosophy, to exhort: "Your faith should not stand in the wisdom of men, but in the power of God."

    1. The wisdom here spoken of is called "the wisdom of this world," "the wisdom of men." This wisdom consists in the theories and the philosophical reasonings that obtained in the Grecian schools respecting those things that can be only subjects of Revelation. The rules that govern it, the subjects discussed and the conclusions reached by the unaided faculties of man, are "of this world" in contradistinction to the wisdom of God set forth in the Scriptures of truth. The mere term, wisdom, is of great latitude, and includes the wise application of knowledge so used as to reach and accomplish the best ends. Wisdom and knowledge

are often used interchangeably, when, in truth, they are two distinct things. Knowledge is to know, or understand the relation of things, while it is the province of wisdom to select the best means to accomplish the best ends. In the Scriptures it often means "right judgment and feeling" respecting "religion and moral truth." "Behold, the fear of the Lord, that is wisdom; and to depart from evil is understanding." (Job XXVIII. :28.) A man may have a great deal of knowledge and yet be imprudent, impractical, and unwise. He may see the ends to be reached, but how to reach them he cannot tell. Knowledge hews the rough stones for the building, wisdom piles the whole into a majestic temple of beauty and symmetrical proportions. Knowledge is the prepared materials, wisdom is the house built and made ready for habitation. But "the wisdom of men" here spoken of may mean any system or code of ethics, or moral philosophy, taught by "the wise and prudent" of this world, and in this particular case, has reference to the systems of religion and philosophy that then prevailed in Alexandria and the Grecian cities.

2. There is a profuse religious tendency existing in the moral nature of man that cannot be smothered or eradicated. Its voice is stentorian, continuous and electrifying in spite of the wickedness of his heart. It is a part of him--an element of his moral stamina. It is natural for him to be religious, and unnatural for him to be irreligious, and he comes nearest to occupying his original and ancient relation with his Creator, when he is worshiping God in spirit and in truth. Since the fall of man, this relation can only be attained by the atonement of Christ and the plan of reconciliation instituted by him. Since man is a sinner, and has departed from God by his own chosen way, he must, if ever he does, return to

God according to God's plan, for except God directs his return, he can never get back again to enjoy the smiles of his countenance and the warm sunshine of his love. He is a worshiping being, and an adoring servant. He will seek and give his affections and esteem to some real or supposed supernatural being, whether such be real or imaginary. He has adoration to give; to whom shall he give it? He has petitions to be presented; to whom shall he present them? He has sorrows, pains, and grievances to be redressed; to what power or authority shall he present them? He has a heart and a whole nature to give; to whom shall he give them? He has an eternity to spend; with whom shall he spend it? Some one has the property right in man, and it is the design of revelation to direct him through the meshes and labyrinthian windings to his rightful Lord and legitimate Master--God.

The insufficiency of human wisdom to make the world wise unto salvation, appears in its efforts and nature, and in the fact that it has always proved a failure to supply the moral and spiritual necessities of the human kind. We are taught that "the world by wisdom knew not God." It could not attain unto the Most High. Such wisdom was too great for the world to discover and digest to the satiety and satisfaction of the hungry soul of man. Nothing can be more important to man than his eternal destiny and spiritual interests. The philosophy of the schools and the wisdom of the wise and prudent utterly incapable of managing the moral and spiritual interests of the human race, and in such things the wisest of men have made the greatest blunders. In the midst of so many religious proclivities, it would amount to the greatest catastrophe to commit the world's spiritual, moral, and religious interests to the vague, subtle and unreliable theories of human devices and philosophical calculations; besides there are a thousand reasons why our "faith should not stand," or depend upon "the wisdom of men, but in the power" or capacity "of God," "who is able to save to the uttermost" every sinning and repenting child of Adam.

3. Religion is man's avocation. It is his chief work on earth, and there is nothing for him to do in the great world to which he must go, but to worship and adore that Supreme Being who is the author of his existence, and by whose power and will he will be perpetuated through the endless cycles of his being. The highest designs of his creation, the inspiring and noblest ends of his personal entity and eneffaceable identity, fit him for the place of eternal service in the ever expanding phalanxes of the worshiping and the adoring hosts. His nature--the attributes and faculties of his being-- cannot fulfill their functions and operate in their legitimate sphere if he is otherwise engaged. He is made for, and suited to worship, and when in true devotion to God alone, it is the only possible relation which he may sustain to the Creator and the universe for the development and highest evolutions and possibilities of his being. Time and place, and even the mode of his existence cannot nullify these natural, organic, God-given and eternal relations between the Creator and the created. The modes and methods of his service to God do not touch the indissoluble bands that hold him in eternal relation to his Maker and preserver. Lost spirits with changed state and conditions are still the servants of God in the sense that they still belong to him, and are a part of his kingdom and dominion; because, in a high and important sense, they still glorify the great Creator by demonstrating to the universe the justness of their punishment and the equity of his government. Even in their state of sin and rebellion they not only

feel the power and wrath of God, but they must admire, if not adore, that inexorable fiat of justice and equity that sent the rebel hosts pell-mell into hell. His justice is as great as his goodness. He is infinite in both. And the goodness of God is as wonderfully demonstrated in the punishment of the finally disobedient as it is in the saving and the protection of the obedient; for when the sinner --be he man or spirit--is punished for crime, the interests of the intelligent universe are protected thereby and the executive God is vindicated in himself and by the judgment of his moral creatures. The great end of creation is the glorification of its creator, and this object can best be attained when the physical and moral elements are coerced into line and made to reach their original designs. Of course God loves all his creatures. He takes no pleasure even in the death and punishment of the wicked. But since they are wicked and disobedient to the laws of God, his own love of order and righteousness demands that force and restraining power be exercised to preserve the union and peace of his empire. This is to be done at all hazards and in any sphere of the universe where there are sins and outbreaks against the laws of God. All intelligent beings are necessarily and constitutionally religious, because wherever such creatures or beings exist, their existence is dependent upon a higher and pre-existent being. Since their existence depends upon a pre-existent being, they must be under certain laws known to them as the product of a higher power. Intellect carries with it the conceptions of the rule of actions and its author as the giver of that rule of action. None can live in absolute ignorance of God since they are in contact with tangible objects and mental conceptions, both of which can only lead up to the Creator, in a greater or less degree. The heavens declare his glory, and his invisible parts are seen in the creation of the world;

yet the wisdom of man, unaided by the light of the Bible, cannot find out God to perfection, or in those details and degrees of his will and nature to that extent that is necessary to approach him in a manner that is most conducive to his glory and the happiness of man.

4. "That your faith should not stand in the wisdom of men, but in the power of God." That is, we must not rest our hope of salvation upon the philosophy, the theories and conclusions of men, no matter how wise, learned, or erudite they may be, because after all they would be certain to be in error respecting the most important things that can possibly enter the mind and being of man. In short, in the very nature of things, if we would be saved, we can only be saved by a reliance and trust in the atonement of Christ and the mercy of God.

Christianity begins and reaches its ends in faith, because "it is impossible to please God" without faith, for "he that cometh to God must believe that he is, and that he is a rewarder of them that diligently seek him." Again, says the Apostle, "Faith is the substance of things hoped for, the evidence of things not seen." Faith is that belief and trust which brings us to God, and causes us to live according to the precepts of Christ and his Apostles. It implies: (1) That the teachings and doctrines of Christ are true; (2) That since they are true a reliance or a trust in them for salvation, through Christ, as the atoning Savior of men, is true faith, or that faith that saves. The fruits of faith are the inner consecration of man to Christ and his teachings, and a consistent life in the world. "By their fruits ye shall know them," says the Savior; for if there be no fruits there cannot be any true faith, or that faith that saves.

Faith, then, is necessary to human salvation, since, say the Scriptures, without it, "it is impossible to please God." The grounds and reasons for faith are in the very nature of man and God. God is necessarily a spirit--an incomprehensible and indivisible substance. He is intangible in spirit and essence, and consequently cannot be grasped by the human mind in any possible state or condition in which the mind of man may be placed. He always was, and is, and always will be the incomprehensible Jehovah, and when the disembodied spirits of men shall ascend the scales of a thousand billions of rolling cycles in their advancive and serial development, they--the mind of man or angels--will never reach that stage in their intellectual evolutions where they might become familiar with the Infinite. He is the intangible, the unknowable, the immeasurable essence of all space and time. He is so near, yet he dwells in an infinity so vast, deep and broad, that no lofty creature's thought has ever descended to his depth, measured to his height, or crossed the seat of his high and holy place. To what degrees the intelligent mind of a creature may know the Creator in the onward wake of mental progression, is an unknown quantity in the cycles of endless ages. The question itself is astounding and overpowering. It is the unthinkable part of eternal progression. Its endless threads of evolutions and translations are ungatherable and hide in the unzoned and nameless future. How then shall men or angels or any, draw near to God? How shall they reach the unreachable and know the unknowable? How shall they approach unto the dwelling-place of the Most High? "Not by might nor by power, but by" faith. On its bright pinions we can soar along the great outlines of his ineffable parts, cut through the clouds of darkness and doubt and sit down under "his banner of love" in his bright abode.

But man himself needs faith. What is impossible to knowledge, wisdom, and philosophy, is possible to faith. Human wisdom is what we do for ourselves, but faith does for us, through God, what we cannot do for ourselves.

5. This faith must stand "in the power of God," and not "in the wisdom of men." "The power of God" is his ability or capacity to do, and to execute his will, and fulfill his pleasure. Nothing is of greater pleasure to the Almighty than the salvation of sinners, and the redemption of that part of his intelligent offsprings that have violated his laws and rebelled against the government of heaven. The moral "power of God," (or those convincing and persuasive methods which he has adopted) shows that man has the power of choice, the ability to accept or reject any proposition laid down by the Almighty. This, of course, makes man largely responsible for his own salvation, since he cannot be saved unless he does as God commands, and comply with those requirements set forth in the gospel system. In the nature and fitness of things, the gospel system presents for man's acceptance the only possible plan of salvation, and to stand aloof, or go outside of that plan, leaves him in a state and condition where divine mercy cannot reach him. Christ is the only Savior of men, the only gateway to God, to heaven, and reconciliation, and all must come through or by this way if they be saved at all. Hence "he tasted death for every man;" that is, he has prepared the way for the salvation of all whether they accept it or not. Not only has he made provision for the salvation of all men, but has made it most ample, full, and

free. And in the wisdom and plenitude of this provision, the worst of rebels and "the chief of sinners" can be saved.

"The power of God" here spoken of, is not mere physical, arbitrary force, that acts upon the material world with propellent and repellent forces, but is that capacity that inheres in the Divine Being by which he sustains those of his offsprings that obey his law and "keep his commandments." When we "keep his commandments," then he engages his infinite and exhaustless resources to "save to the uttermost" all who "call on the name of the Lord." "The power of God," then is the foundation upon which the man of God hangs the cable of hope and the threads of his salvation. These are strong, uniting God and man together in the strong bands of his love and power, forming a spiritual compact of harmonious relations, unanticipated by the wisdom of man and unknown to the philosophical research of the schools and the keenest conception of the wise men of the ages.

Many have established themselves upon their own wrought systems of religious thought, while ignoring the truth of God, that great system of Divine Revelation which presents to men the only solution of the mighty problems of life and death, of the present and the future. Everywhere, the power of God is exhibited in his works as the wonderful and all-resourceful governing creator. "The Lord hath prepared his throne in the heavens, and his kingdom ruleth over all;" over all things in the visible, invisible, and the spiritual divisions of the universe, from the highest heaven to the deepest hell. Creation in its marvelous amplitude, with its contending and extending forces of precipitant elements, is held in space and place by "the word of the Lord," and the invincible fiat of his power. He is the coercive God that throws around rebellious planets, broken systems, and sinking suns, his golden arm of power, and adamantine peripheries of hardest and unyielding bands of steel, triple-decked and serrated with mountains of flint and valleys of flame. At his command, shattered suns, corroding orbs, and dead planets mount from their "funeral pyre on wings of flame" and sing on their eternal rounds as fiery arrows from the bow strings of God. From his hand a thousand moons, the pale princesses of a thousand worlds, dazzle into space, kiss the hem of burning circumferences and fly on their cold silver tracks in the unfathomable bosom of space. God speaks again, they hear, skip, leap, and move along their bright curves forever, the maid-servants of radiant orbs, the sisters of kings and the daughters of God. But this is a changing universe with an unchanging God. Eternal ages corrode and melt the hardest bands of steel, break asunder every cable, shatter every cog and bolt, take off the rim of every wheel, destroy every connecting link, crush in the keel of every floating world, blow out the fires of every orb, unhinge every star, dim the lustre of every sun, cut the wings of every comet, cast down every moon from her silver track, put out the fires of heaven, and take the lights from every soaring beamy car, and every sparkling gem from heaven's high dome, and every glittering pearl from the unmeasured palace of God. Yet he is king over all.

> "Star after star from heaven's high arch shall rush,
> Suns sink on suns, systems systems crush,
> Headlong extinct to one dark center fall,
> And night and death and chaos mingle all,

> Till o'er the wreck emerging from the storm,
> Immortal nature lifts her changeful form,
> Mounts from her funeral pyre on wings of flame,
> And soars and shines another and the same."

But high above the crash of "the wreck of matter and the crush of worlds," the mighty God, whose "kingdom ruleth over all," maintains his power, keeps his own in perfect peace in his bright abode, in a clime whose elements and entities and component properties are incapable of dissolution and decay. Amid the transition of matter and the clashing of diverse elements and forces "the power of God" is pledged to keep him in perfect peace whose mind is staid on him. "Let not your heart be troubled; ye believe in God, believe also in me. In my Father's house are many mansions; if it were not so, I would have told you." These are the blessed words of the Christ. Oh! brethren, your faith should stand, not in "the wisdom of men, but in the power of God."

SERMON XII.

Why We Should Love God.

"On these two commandments hang all the law and the prophets."--Matt. 22:40.

The gospel of Christ is a system of divine ethics. Its philosophic and fundamental principles are few and simple, and it has its claims upon the attention and consideration of mankind, because it affects his happiness in the present and for all time to come. It is a system reared upon few pillars, yet these are but the stronger and more enduring and far-reaching because of their foundation and simplicity. It is not a mass of unintelligible enigmas whose intricacies cannot be understood or explained; but it is simple, convincing, comprehensive teaching, fitted to instruct, elevate and save the race of man. Its scope embraces the moral code of the universe in its governmental theory and practice, and is a transcript and photograph of its moral phases. The system, as such, is presented to our judgment, and appeals to our reason, and then demands our faith in its Author and in its doctrines. Faith is essential to its acceptance and fair consideration, for "without faith it is impossible to please God." It is a system that breathes "the spirit of life from God," and quickens and brings into lively play all its parts, spirit and elements of that life. It defines the moral faculties, and locates God and man in their native and true relations. As a code of morals, it is best understood when we examine its separate parts and primary principles, and observe those results that flow from its practice. It has three great properties-- morals, doctrines, and faith. We can have no proper conception of any ethical code without its elements and primary principles. These compose the bone and framework upon which sinew, flesh and skin are laid, and then the purple current of life is seen to ramify, vivify and dance through every part, diffusing light and activity and filling its spheres with God. If we would be the devotees of any system of religion, we must first partake of its spirit, become imbued with its life, learn its idioms, dogmas, and demands. The life and power of the one must be infused into the life of the other, and then the outlines of our life and character must accord with the spirit and teachings of the same, otherwise we cannot be true disciples of the system. To meet the spiritual necessities of the devotees, the system must not only be true as to its real existence, but must be true within itself. Its promises, doctrines, and predictions must rest upon truth in such a manner as to bring sure and certain realization to its followers and adherents, and thereby verify itself as true. If there is a failure here, all else is failure, intrigue and irreparable loss. This position is more apparent when we think of the stupenduous fact that it may promise more than it can verify. That is, it may promise us heaven and give us hell. It may promise us life and give us death; promise good, and give us evil instead. It may pierce the heart with a thousand pangs of demons, and pour into the soul the poison of asps and the venom of serpents, and leave the soul with blasted hope and withered spirit. For instance, Mohammedanism is a system of error mixed with truth and gilded with glittering promises that it cannot fulfil; yet it is a fact that such a thing as the system of Mohammedanism does exist, but its existence or power to be does not prove that its doctrines, dogmas and idioms are true. Yet it has the same persuasive effect upon the mind, life and civilization of its millions of votaries as the system of Christianity has upon its followers. Both obtain their hold and power over their respective followers upon the same principles of faith, theory and practice. The one is as conscious that his religion is true as the other, notwithstanding the one is false and the other true. Because of these conditions the followers of Mohammed are as devoted to their religion as the followers of Christ are devoted to theirs. If a man believes a thing to be true, when at the same time it is false, the same devotion and earnest faith is given to it as if it were true. Therefore, a system of religion does not destroy the faith and devotion of its candid believers, whether true or false within itself. How important then it is that a system of religion, presented to the world of man for his faith and practice, should be true in itself, and true in its promises, predictions and realizations. We need not enter here upon the divine originality, truth and authenticity of the Christian system. Its reasonableness, its powers, nature, and adaptations to meet the spiritual needs and the practical necessities of mankind in all ages and conditions, are a sufficient refutation of the infidel and those who doubt its truth. Mankind will seek only that that they believe to be, and such exertion depends upon faith and hope and realization. Faith is the connecting link between God and man, between heaven and earth, between the visible and invisible, between the finite and infinite. By this we see the unseen, and approach the unapproachable. It brings us to God; it brings God to us. It humanizes God without making him less God, and deifies man without making him more than man. Christianity then is more than a name, more than a theory, more and greater than even faith and practice. It is a revolution, a transformation, and a process of redemptive restoration, by which man is evolved from and out of himself, to, and into God. This redemptive restorative process not only changes the moral status between man and God, but imparts to man a new life, a new nature, and the infusion of the Deity himself. If, then, we would be Christians, we must go farther than a mere profession, a mere assent to and practice of the formulas of the religion of Jesus. My friends, without the work of God in the soul, there can be no true, vital, spiritual and soul-saving Christianity on earth. True, we may read its history, memorize its language, repeat its dogmas, and chant its melodies and shout with its heroes, yet there are depths and heights, lengths and breadths, still farther on in the great redemptive, restorative process, which by mere formalities can never be attained. Still farther on, beyond sky-blue tops of the cloud-covered mountains and the deep gorges of repentance, are the sacred precincts of a perfect salvation. We cannot be half Christian and half alien. We must be the one or the other. In the shining phalanx of the living God, there are no mongrel progeny, half-breeds and cross-bloods, but all are shaped in the same heavenly mold, and healed by the same cleansing blood. In this earthly pilgrimage of song, there are no mutes, no unstrung harps, or silent choristers. You must sing the enchanting melodies of heaven, or the bacchanalian songs of sin, moving up to heaven, or moving down to death. There are no neutral grounds in this great warfare, but fight you must. And you must fight for God, and against the devil, or fight for the devil and against God. Two kings cannot reign upon one throne; neither can God and Satan reign in the same heart, for they are antagonistic and antipodal principles. If ever in the onward wake of the ages the world shall ever be redeemed from the thraldom of sin and darkness, it can only be accomplished by the gospel of system. Christ alone supplies all the wants and necessities of man in this and in the future state.

The Jewish people are a standing miracle and living attestation to the truth and Divine authenticity of the holy Scriptures. They are the most peculiar and most remarkable people that have ever lived upon the face of the earth. God selected them from all the idolatrous nations of the earth to serve him, and to preserve the oracles of truth as delivered to them from time to time. Amid the moral and mental darkness that covered the earth, the Israel of God had light from heaven to guide them in the way of truth and moral rectitude, and in this respect the Jew served a great end in the salvation of mankind, though this "peculiar people" has been scattered, and its polity broken into a thousand fragmentary parts. Their kings reign no longer. Their temple hill is desecrated by the Mosque of Omar and the abomination of the Mohammedans. They have been driven by the storms of persecution into every land and clime, from the cold north to the torrid south, and from the orient to the occident. The Jew lives with every nation, but mixes with none; and under all the varied conditions that have tried him through the ages, he maintains his identity and is still what he was three thousand years ago--a Jew. Though his people have been despised, rejected and slain by the hundreds and thousands, and their blood has flowed down the declivities of the ages; though aspersions, calumnies, and vile indignities have been poured in fury upon their heads, still he lives amid them all--a Jew. The Jew can trace his historical pedigree through the fleeing circles of the ages and the dispensations of the past. The storms and howling tempests have rained hailstones upon his quivering bark for three thousand years. Empires have arisen, kings have reigned, states have grown up, towered and fallen, hoary dynasties have been broken upon the wheel of time, great rivers have changed their beds and have cut their pathway through the hardest rocks, filling seas and gulfs with their drifting matter. In the wake of the ages and the march of time, the bodies of the millions have fallen, and their bleaching bones and "cities of the dead" tell the sad story of death. The tall cedars of Lebanon, and proud oaks of Bashan, have withered by the blight of age; still the Jew is the same. He has outlived the ages, outlived the ravages of war and persecutions. He has lived through flood and flame, through famines, pestilences, endemics and epidemics. Like the Gulf Stream, he flows on in his own channel without mixing with contacting elements, whether they be Japhetic or Hamitic. They are God's ancient people--the repository of the oracles of truth--and he will punish the world for the slain of his chosen Israel. In the economy of Providence he stands as a gigantic tower of strength to attest the truth and the Divine authority of Revelation. This is the standing memorial of Christianity and the miracle of the ages. Infidelity may rage and vent its keen shafts of spleen against the ramparts of God, but here is a truth whose impregnable parts stand the rage of the enemy and the assaults of hell.

"Then, one of them, which was a lawyer, asked him a question, tempting him, and saying, Master, which is the great commandment in the law? Jesus said unto him, Thou shalt love the Lord thy God with all thy heart, and with all thy soul, and with all thy mind. This is the first and great commandment. And the second is like unto it, Thou shalt love thy neighbor as thyself. On these two commandments hang all the law and the prophets."

Let us observe then, three reasons why we should love God: (1) Because he commands us to love him. (2) Because we cannot be happy without loving him. (3) Because he first loved us.

We should love God (1) Because he commands us to love him.

God is a sovereign. He has the undivided authority to command all creatures in earth, heaven and hell to do his biddings--to do or not to do certain things. He possesses the unquestionable right to dictate to the consciences of men and all intelligent beings. It does not affect the case whether we understand the reasons why or not. These may be given, or they may not be given. They may be positive moral commands or mere edicts of the king immortal, yet if they are from him and apply to us, we cannot disregard them without condign punishment and destruction to our happiness. As a Father, Master and Ruler, he commands. As a Father, we are his children; as a Master, we are his servants, and as a Ruler we are his subjects. Whether he speaks to us as Father, Master or Ruler we are his subjects and are bound to obey. We may not know at all times why he commands this, that, or the other. To know this is the province of the sovereign God, and not the province of his subjects. With consequences and results we have nothing to do; these belong to God alone. Christianity is a temple of truth of sublime proportion and changeless principles, whose stones have been hewn and polished by the hands of God, and placed in glorious beauty and symmetry one upon another in ascending scales and eternal harmony. "Thou shalt love the Lord thy God" is the changeless and faultless command--changeless because founded upon the equity, the justice and will of the Creator. "The law of the Lord is perfect." Nothing can be added to it or subtracted from it. There can be no review, supplement, nor second edition, nor amendments. It "is perfect" in all its parts, parcels, and ramifications. His "statutes are right" in their native and constitutional inherent qualities. True, they are the dictations of a Sovereign, yet they are none the less righteous and equitable within themselves, since they involve the "eternal fitness of things." Thus we should love God--(2) Because we cannot be happy without loving him. This is axiomatic. We have every evidence that the race of man was made to be happy, that the Creator originally designed that all his intelligent offspring should remain in such a state, and pursue those lines of avocation that would redound to his glory and the greatest degree of their perpetual well-being. Consequently, happiness is the natural and universal desire of the human race. This also applies to all sentient and intelligent creatures, whether they be men or angels, and it may not be going too far, when we assert that even devils and lost spirits would repent and regain their lost estate and revert to bliss, if they could. Misery and pain must be utterly at war with the feelings and desires of all intelligences, no matter in what part of the universal dominion they may live. Even the lower animals and the non-intelligent parts of creation, give evidence that show that they have the instinct of happiness impressed upon their nature. The worm of the dust wriggles beneath our tread; the wild beasts of the forest flee at the approach of man, and the finny tribes of the deep elude his presence; all have some natural means of defense and exercise a vigilance that shows their apprehension of danger. They fear death because of the pain and misery that is connected with it. If this is true respecting the non-intelligent, it is so in a larger degree among those who are "made in the image of

God." Man desires happiness. It is the natural prompting of his heart and the proclivity of his being. The Creator made him to live, and not to die; he made him to be happy, and not to be miserable. The faculties of the mind, the attributes of the soul, the construction and ease and grace of the operations of the physical and perceptive attributes are splendidly fitted to promote his peace, ease and comfort upon the plane of his being. It has been very properly said, that "death is a foreign foe," an alien and an unlawful invader into the kingdom of life, except as man forfeited the protection of God by his rebellion and the violation of those laws and uncompromising principles upon which alone his continued prosperity depends. If we would be happy and fulfil the natural proclivities of our nature--as it was originally intended--we must obey the laws of God, "and keep his commandments." If the subjects of earthly governments cannot be happy without obedience to the laws under which they live, much less can we be happy without obedience to those laws and changeless rules that the all-wise and supreme Creator has prescribed as the norm of action laid down for us. The end of law, therefore, is the glory of God in the happiness of his creatures. One of the plainest things in the world is the fact that no intelligent being can be happy when he is violating the principles in the universe by which alone it is possible to reach the goal of bliss. The Christian system presents to the world the only foundation of substantial peace and enduring bliss, because there can be no such thing without reconciliation with God. Whether in heaven, on earth, or in any other place in illimitable space, the same principles and facts must apply with undiminishing and equal force to all localities and beings. God is God, truth is truth, love is love, and fear is fear. Time or place or conditions cannot alter or change these. Truth on earth is truth in heaven and in hell. Christianity, therefore, is not the religion of men on earth only, but is the only true God-serving and God-adoring system that can exist, because it absorbs all those great underlying principles of love, obedience, and truth upon which the government of the Almighty is founded. No, my friends, there is but one remedy in all the wide domain of God for human misery and human recovery from sin and death, and that is, "Thou shalt love the Lord thy God, with all thy heart, and with all thy soul, and with all thy mind." It is not possible for any intelligent creature to be happy without Christianity. Let a man be placed in the most propitious condition possible in this life, yet he would be unhappy without the love of God and man. He may recline upon couches of down with ivory posts, studded and bedecked with rarest gems and precious jewels and hung with the richest damasks of the east, while frescoed walls and fluted columns ascend in awful grandeur, covered with gold and glinted with silver. Let him eat the lambs of the flock and feed upon the fat of stall-fed beasts. Let his steeps be washed in butter, and his teeth be white with milk. Let his maidens sing, and with sweetest voice and dulcet strains of harp and organ lull their enchanted lord to soft slumbers. Let him be a king upon a royal throne whose empire covers a continent with teeming millions to do his biddings. Let him be secure from fear and danger and the ramparts of his rocky castle be defended by the invincible legions of the Cæsars and the Napoleons. Let his granaries be filled, his wealth boundless, and his cattle cover a thousand hills, feeding upon the living green, richer in beauty than all the productions of the Persian looms. Let him in the splendors of courts quaff to uttermost satiety the cup of pleasure. Let obsequious millions bow the knee to honor and admire their great Lord and master. Let annalists with pen in hand and ink horn by their sides stand to record the words of wisdom and the mighty acts of the king. Yet with all this, and more, he cannot be happy without the love of God, and the power of the religion of Jesus. For amid all this marvelous wealth, honor and greatness, there is an accusing or excusing monitor--conscience--within that tells him that he is a sinner going to death and to hell. "The wicked fleeth when no man pursueth" and "are like the rough sea when it cannot rest, whose waves cast up mire and dirt." Nay, there is no place, no real substantial happiness and peace without God in the soul, Christ in the heart and life, and the whole man converted, changed, and thoroughly consecrated to God, and separated from the pollutions of the flesh, and the contaminations of the world. How can you escape or set at naught these obligations? How can you or I throw off the yoke of God and evade the momentous issues? Go, take the flight of the eagle to his lofty aerie, and build your secret chamber in the highest cleft of the granite peak, and dwell solitary and alone out of the reach of your fellows. Leave your feet in the cloud and stand upon the celestial pyramid with careless indifference as to human affairs, yet without Christ in the soul there is a burning hell within that is incompatible with peace and ease of conscience. Even in heaven, were it possible for the sinner to be carried there, he could not be happy without the love of God, because he could not enjoy the glory and pleasures of the redeemed and sanctified. There congenial spirits meet in the raptures of redeeming love to celebrate in lofty anthems the praises of God and the Lamb, saying, "Amen." Blessing and glory and wisdom and thanksgiving and honor and power and might be unto our God forever and ever, amen. And one of the elders answered, saying unto me, "What are these which are arrayed in white robes? and whence came they?" And I said unto him, "Sir, thou knowest." And he said unto me, "These are they which came out of great tribulations and have washed their robes, and made them white in the blood of the Lamb." Here are the congregated millions of congenial spirits. They "have washed their robes and made them white in the blood of the Lamb." They have passed through "great tribulations," swept through the zones of life's fiery trials, entered the city of the great king, wrapped in the shining robes of beauty and clothed in the bright habiliments of eternal salvation.

(3) We should love God because he first loved us.

"Behold what manner of love the Father hath bestowed upon us, that we should be called the sons of God." What a lofty title is this, and yet it is true--"The sons of God!" John says, "Hereby perceive we the love of God, because he laid down his life for us." But "In this was manifested the love of God toward us, because that God sent his only begotten Son into the world, that we might live through him." "For God so loved the world that he gave his only begotten Son, that whosoever believeth in him, should not perish but have everlasting life." "He first loved us," with that love that stirred his heart and moved his arm of power. But man is a sinner. He is wretched, vile and polluted, lost, ruined and broken by the fall. An outcast alien under just condemnation. A smiling heaven and a laughing paradise receded from his vision, since God, the gracious Father, was offended. Epochs and dispensations rolled on, chronicling the rise, growth and death of ages and nations. Darker and blacker grew the mental and moral night of the world, and as man multiplied sin did much more abound. Now and then a meteor flashed across the dark hemispheres, and here and there altars glowed and priests officiated. The ages, old and gray, traveled slowly down the declivities of time and space until the dying Jacob heard the rumbling of Messiah's chariot wheels, caught the whispers of his coming and the flash of his eye. When he said, "I have waited for thy salvation, O Lord," he spoke the sentiment of universal humanity. But the law must be given and the foundation of the Jewish polity of types and shadows must be laid, and its superstructure reared, and the blood of sprinkling must antedate the blood of cleansing. Jehovah descended from heaven in clouds and flaming fire. The trumpet's awful blasts and the jarring appeals of thunder announce the awful presence of God in his kingly majesty. Onward, in appaling grandeur descends his chariot of flame. Louder, longer, and louder still, swells the high trump of God. Israel looks up and the heavens are dark with sable bands and thick clouds. Lightning sparkles in fantastic and vivid glare, and play upon the burning waves of the air, as if the atmosphere in chaos trembled under the mighty tread of Deity. The legislative God descends, the earth quakes and an empire of solid granite dances beneath his feet, while wreathing columns of smoke mingled with flame are the curtains of his sanctuary. The walls of the royal sanctuary were amber flames, fanned by the swift moving wings of mighty seraphs and great archangels, attending the royal presence. And so terrible was the sight that Moses said, "I exceedingly fear and quake." "The law was given by Moses, but grace and truth came by Jesus Christ." The law could not save. Jesus alone can do that. He loved us first and pointed out his soul unto death. See him as he lays aside his crown, his kingly scepter, his robe, and the glory of heaven for you, for me, and for all the sinning race of Adam. O, come to

Jesus and be saved. Why not? Hath he not loved you? Did he not give himself for you? O, ye sons of Adam, arise, stand up and flee the coming wrath of God. O, praise his name, ye his saints!

SERMON XIII.

The Work of an Enemy.

"And he said unto them, An enemy hath done this."-- Matt. 13:28.

When we contemplate the history of man and view him in his physical, moral and spiritual relations and conditions, and then compare his nature and career with the dealings of Divine Providence and the requirements of Revelation, we must admit that there is "an enemy" strong and mighty, cosmopolitan, universal and profound in his operations, affecting every age, people, and individual. Whether we stem the tide of the rolling ages and ascend the stream of time, or take our stand upon some lofty eminence of the present dispensation, and view the whole circle of earth's teeming humanity, the same verdict will be reached by the impartial mind in regard to the existence and work of an enemy in human society. His name is carved on every brow, his hand hath touched every heart, his image is stamped on every soul, and his footprint is in every land, and his blood-curdling banner floats over every stream and on the rolling waves of every sea. All along through the ages, malevolence, destruction and the utter subversion of human happiness have characterized his diabolical designs and distinguished his mighty operations. He it is who hath sowed tares among the wheat and corrupted the whole field of the moral spheres. Who can count the millions slain by him, or number the carcasses of the bleeding victims and the fallen tribes? What stream can contain the tears of the heart-broken and sorrow-stricken? Behold! men count the stars, number the planets, measure the sidereal heavens, traverse the wilderness, pierce the profundities of earth's deep bosom and weigh the mountains in scales, but they fail to compute the misery of man and the number of the dead slain by our great foe. On a thousand battle-fields, in the political arena, in the palaces of great kings, in the revolutions and evolutions of human society, and on the broad fields of false religion, of investigation and discovery everywhere, the great foe is active, wise, astute, and sways the hearts and consciences of the nations. Let us beware of his artful hand, of his nimble power and widespread and all-permeating influence. Let us contemplate the great foe under the following divisions:

- I. The origin and advent of the enemy.
- II. His nature and powers.
- III. The ends designed.
- IV. The agencies employed.

I. The origin and advent of the enemy; that is, of Satan or the devil. 1st. He is a being, a living creature, because he was created by the Almighty. 2d. He was in heaven, in a state of bliss and happiness, but in a state of probation and trial, and consequently the perpetuation of his happiness was contingent upon his obedience to the divine command. 3d. Being in this state or condition, it was possible for him to sin, which he did, and thus he lost his place in heaven among the sons of the Most High, and by the Almighty power was cast down to hell, and with him legions of other mighty flaming spirits were cast out; for, says St. Peter, "God spared not the angels that sinned, but cast them down to hell and delivered them unto chains of darkness, to be reserved unto judgment."--II Pet. 2:4. Jude makes substantially the same statement. The time of his fall and advent is not known, but the fact of both his advent and fall is a stern reality, demonstrated by all his dreadful and terrific acts and mighty doings upon the face of the earth.

II. His nature and power. 1. He is spirit, incapable of decay and dissolution, of course. The Father of spirits can dissolve and annihilate any and all organized beings, whether they be men, angels, mighty spirits, or powers; thrones, dominions, principalities, or all things in heaven, earth and hell. But God's methods are otherwise ordained. However, Apollyon's power is great--that is, his capacity to do, to perform wonders, to execute mighty deeds. Though fallen and cast down to hell and restricted to certain limits in the divine arrangements, yet to an astonishing degree he is still in the possession of mighty power. Smitten by the omnificent hand from the fair fields of the paradise of God, hear him cry as he flies like a mighty scintillating spark struck off from its native sun, as Milton describes:

> "Farewell, happy fields, where joys forever dwell;
> Hail horrors! Hail, Infernal world! and thou
>   profoundest hell:
> Receive thy new possessor; one who brings
> A mind not to be changed by place or time."

But he is a spirit, though he may be possessed with an ethereal, corporeal frame, suited to the spirituality of his nature. He must be gigantic in stature, magnificent in person, and possessing much of his original comely proportions.

The fact that he fell from his high estate does not necessarily imply that he lost all of the might of his strength and the glory of his power. Since he is the chief of devils, a leader of a mighty flock, and the governor of dethroned powers, dominions and principalities, it is fair to infer that he is possessed of many of those noble traits of character and appearances which distinguish him as a great leader among the millions of fallen spirits. Lifting his lofty crest in the councils and assemblies of the mighty in arms, he is at once the center of attraction and action, and leader of rebellious millions. His power, though limited and restricted within certain degrees, is yet very great. The essential elements of durability, versatility, accompanied with a capacious mind and varied accomplishments, makes him a most remarkable and wonderful creature. It is true there may be somewhere in the universe of God mighty spirits more gigantic in form, more comely in symmetrical proportions, possessing a higher range of knowledge and greater powers of activity and alertness; yet we have not been informed in regard to them. But we know Satan. "We are not ignorant of his devices." His history is written in the annals of the nations and upon the world's civilizations. He is great in power, mighty in strength, wonderful in knowledge, profound in wisdom, exhaustless in the ability to plan and endowed with a marvelous capacity to execute the desires of his heart. He is a great scholar, with ripe experience. He is acquainted with the history of the nations, the sciences of the ages, the philosophies of the schools and the great men of the world. His power of locomotion and celerity of flight are most remarkable. The Savior says, "I beheld Satan fall from heaven like lightning." He walks up and down the earth, traverses the zones and hemispheres, and plows the briny main, bent on high-handed mischief, seeking his victims in every clime, seeming to be almost ubiquitous. Let us watch the manoeuverings of the great foe, the mendacious leader of hell, sin and death.

III. The ends designed. His aim is to defeat the glory of God in the happiness of man. And since the Almighty is Invulnerable and flanked about with infinite power, he knows that it is impossible to do Him harm. This would be a hopeless undertaking and incompatible with wisdom and the skilled tactics of a wise and sagacious leader.

Having no hope of success here, Satan turns his multiform machinations and operations against man, the intelligent creature of God. If happiness could dwell in his hell-stirred heart, he would enjoy the greatest proportion of happiness when he has rendered man the most miserable. The desire to render others miserable because he is miserable is the quintessence and climax of wickedness and diabolical abominations too intricate for the human mind to conceive of. If such procedure would add one single item to his own well-being, or in any way lessen his sorrow and ease his pain, or if it were possible to gain anything thereby, there might be some palliating circumstances in the case. But there are none. Yet the natural proclivities of his wicked heart urge him on with uncontrollable momentum to do his black and cruel deeds of violence, crime and shame. His object is to rob God of his glory, man of his happiness, heaven of its wreathed victors, and populate hell with the slain millions. How cruel is our great foe! How obdurate and callous is his heart! How foul is his spirit! And how has he succeeded? Would you know? Go view his tracks from the Garden of Eden down the steep of ages. Go read his history of the peoples of all realms, of every clime, of every tongue. Go count the kingdoms broken, the empires destroyed. Go count the wars and battle-fields, and measure the tears and blood of the dead and dying. Go count the groans and sighings of the widow and orphan, the friendless, the naked and the poor. Go number the debauched hordes and superstitious ranks that crowd heathen temples and pay their homage to gods that are no gods. Go follow the blood-stained track of this great Moloch, crested with fiery plume and direful hate, into the courtrooms, the jails, penitentiaries, and gallowses. Go, traverse the burning track of hell, and number the black millions of the lost, and then consider the eternity of their damnation and their banishment from the presence of the Lord and the glory of his power. Over these slain the heart shudders, the blood curdles, and trembling takes hold upon the frame. Oh, what hath this enemy done? Who, oh who, can compute the lost of these thousands of years of the long reign of sin and Satan?

IV. The agencies employed. These are varied, extensive and exhaustless. In his selections the fittest are chosen to accomplish the ruin, the marvelous work of human destruction and the subversion of every institution whose aims and designs are to soften and ameliorate the conditions and rugged circumstances of suffering humanity. All the instruments, ways and means of human happiness and man's promotion from a lower to a higher state of morality, religion and social refinement, are eagerly sought, and when obtained, are polluted and diverted from their proper channels, and made to do what they were not designed to do. Let us briefly note some of these. Diplomacy and war, from the most remote ages, have been employed by the great enemy of

God and man to destroy the peace and break the harmony of all the families, tribes and nations of the earth. No instrument employed by him has done more to hinder the progress and civilization of the world than war. Goaded on by the powers of darkness and lead by the prince of the aliens, it takes but a little to fire the public heart and kindle the nations into strife and carnage that cover the earth with blood and the broken bodies of the slain and dying. Indeed, the world has often appeared as one great battle-field, sinking billions of money, exhausting the flower and strength of the people, bankrupting governments and destroying the resources of the public revenue. Ambition, the lust of power, the love of display and wealth along with hatred. and malice have characterized the great kings and conquerors of the nations. In diplomacy, what treachery, perfidy and deception! In war, what cruelties and human butchery have been displayed by the conquerors! When we see an Alexander, a Xerxes or a Napoleon making war on surrounding nations, apparently with no other object than to get gain and extend their power and slake their greed for human destruction, we must conclude that there is a power behind the agent that engages in such hideous deeds of death and horror. In their track of destruction, what a train of evils follow! Kings are dethroned, dynasties destroyed, states and kingdoms subverted and disintegrated, cities, towns, villages, hamlets and the rural plains filled with the broken ruins and the smoking débris of houses, mansions, palaces, forests; weeping widows, sighing orphans and those institutions of learning and science that have been put on foot to promote the happiness of man and lift him to a higher plane in the civil state, are overwhelmed in ruins. The ingenuity of man has been wrought up to its highest pitch to invent missiles and diabolical machines for the wholesale murder and destruction of the humankind. What a black train of evils follows war! Society is upheaved, the wicked and the base are brought to prominence, and all the worst elements of depravity are put into active and lively play upon the stage of life. Famine, pestilence, disease, poverty, the stagnation of every branch of industry, and ten thousand other ills too numerous to mention follow. Surely "an enemy hath done this."

Learned, capacious minds have been perverted in the hands of this foe. "God hath made man upright; but they have sought out many inventions." The human intellect has often been prostituted to unholy and unsavory ends. It has been so darkened by the enemy, that they have put truth for falsehood, and falsehood for truth, light for darkness and darkness for light. It has made heaven hell, and hell heaven. One of the first things done by the perverted learning of man is to seek to disprove the truth, the authenticity, divine inspiration and originality of the Bible. At all hazard, and at any cost, the unsanctified mind strives to uproot the oracles of God and thus increase unbelief and destroy the devotees of truth, religion, and virtue, and ruin the eternal well-being of man. The God of nature is made to contradict the God of the Bible. "The fool hath said in his heart, There is no God." False religion has always been a powerful instrument in the hands of Satan to blind and obscure the mental vision, to corrupt the heart and to vitiate the moral and social tastes of mankind. Half truths are the most insinuating and deceptive form of falsehoods. A little truth mixed in with a great deal of error is more palatable to the vile and sinful heart of man. To establish a falsehood, therefore, there must be put into the otherwise untoothsome bait some truth. Hence all false religions are a mixture of truth and untruth, and the shades of light and darkness, of life and death, of hell and heaven are so blended that the unpracticed mind and heart unhesitatingly take in the deadly venom. All false religions, therefore, are the counterfeit pieces of one great and only true religion--Christianity. Nowhere in the history of sin has Satan succeeded more admirably and universally than here. Here, in error's chains the millions of blind and deaf votaries soundly sleep and have slept for ages. Here is the smooth road and the wide gateway of death.

Song, the music of the soul, and the melody of heaven has been perverted and used to rally the forces of hell and inflame the basest passions of wicked men, and stimulate the blind votaries of superstition and diabolical intrigue. On her swift pinions of gold she has been the herald, the grand messenger to waft the mandates of hell around the globe into all the nooks and corners of human society. The flute, the harp, the bagpipe, the horn, the trumpet, the pianoforte, the soft notes of the organ and the trained voice have for many an age made up the minstrelsy of hell. Man will sing, though he sing going hellward. Oh, stop! hush the loud mouth of the bacchanalian!

Learning, money, influence, precious gems, eloquence and poetry, all have been pressed into the service of Satan and the cause of hell. Master minds, towering and great with their marvelous productions, have worshipped at the shrine of the great deceiver and done homage to the prince of darkness. Millions of money is poured at the base of his throne, and his exchequer is filled with heaps of gold, and yet he clamors for more. The pillars of his temple are embossed with the gems of earth's kingdoms.

The lavished influence of the mighty and noble force the weak and ignoble to follow in their mad dash for death and hell.

But is Satan always thus to reign and triumph over the earth and tyrannize over the sons of men? God forbid. "The kingdom is the Lord's." It belongs to Jesus Christ. It is His by right of His death and sufferings, by His agonies on the cross, by his blood and tears, his groaning and shame, and the multitude of sorrows which He bore for you and me, and for all the dead and living sons of Adam and daughters of Eve. The enemy is great but Christ is greater. He is the "Prince of the kings of the earth," "the bright and morning star," and "the Alpha and Omega." "Oh, that men would praise the Lord for his goodness, and for His wonderful works to the children of men." Oh, that he may come, "whose right it is" to reign forever and ever. Amen!

SERMON XIVI.

Holiness and Peace.

"Follow peace with all men, and holiness, without which no men shall see the Lord."--Heb. 12:14.

Every system of morals and ethical science presented to the judgment and consideration of men has its supposed or real central truths. It matters not whether the doctrines taught be true or false, good or evil, they come, resting their claims upon pillars of brass, blocks of marble, or banks of sand. But it may be asserted, without the fear of contradiction, that every system of religion, philosophy, or science is best known by the effects it has produced upon society and those followers and devotees who obey the mandates and precepts of such a system of doctrines and teachings. This is the rule laid down by our Savior when He says, "Ye shall know them by their fruits." As a good tree cannot bring forth evil fruit, so a good system of religion or philosophy cannot produce evil converts and a corrupt or pestilential progeny, since the religious faith, views and practices make up the moral life of peoples and individuals. A man's theory of morals and religion may be right or wrong, and in results may be destructive to the best ends of society, yet he will follow the theory upon which his faith is founded. So deeply seated are the religious faculties and proclivities in human nature that they demand not only faith and belief, but demand that in their essentials they should be correct and true within themselves. If we look into the history of the past ages, and scan the religions that have existed and contemplate their forms and aspects, we shall find that their theories and practices went hand in hand, and the development of the religious life was a recapitulation or reproduction in tangible form of their faiths and beliefs.

The Gospel of Jesus Christ is a system of revealed religion, presented to us with claims of divine authority and divine originality. It matters very little as to the mere authenticity of the divine Revelation, for a thing may be true, and yet not authentic. As to the essentials of Christianity, it matters not who wrote or compiled the Pentateuch, or who wrote the book of Job or the books of the New Testament; but it is a matter of infinite concern whether the essentials taught therein are true or false, right or wrong, since the life and character of men and nations are to be shaped and governed according to the doctrines and commands therein revealed. On the other hand, if men can shape and form and even reform the essentials of the religion they profess, it shows the falsity and insufficiency of the system to meet the eternal and substantial needs and aspirations of men. No man or set of men, nor school of science, nor of philosophy, no matter how wise, ancient and venerable they may be, has the right or capacity to make a religion and present its claims to men. They could have no authority nor power to dictate the faith and consciences of men. And even if they could go that far, yet their systems would fall short of that high and awful sanctity that God has bestowed upon the divine revelation found in the Scriptures of truth.

As the Gospel of Jesus Christ is a system of divine truth and morals, instituted and revealed to man by the infinite Deity as a standard of faith and conduct, so it has its fundamental and essential truths and principles. As such it comes to enlighten, cheer, strengthen and guide the judgment and tastes of men and nations, and to lift up, sanctify and save. As the sun is the essential force of light and heat in the planetary system, so Jesus Christ, shining in and through the gospel system, is the essential element of force, light and heat by whose bright rays and shining gems of truth and power the whole race of man is stirred and stimulated to seek that life and salvation which He came to make manifest to all the children of men. But, says the text: "Follow peace with all men, and holiness, without which no man shall see the Lord." For convenience we invert the text.

- I. What is implied in the holiness here spoken of?
- II. What is implied in peace?

"The holiness" here spoken of as an essential of the Christian life, "without which no man shall see the Lord," is that moral purity that is absolutely and indispensably requisite for the redemption and salvation of every man. It is that high and holy state of moral purity and sanctification that every man, woman and child, and all the intelligences of the universe must possess, before they can reach or obtain that happiness and peace that make up the present or the future state of bliss. It is the sanctification. The sublime, unique and eminent truth, lifting its lofty cone, as Mount Everest, high and alone, towers in gigantic form and heavenly majesty up above the clouds and storm-line in the serene and clear atmosphere of a happy realization of its spiritual power and vital force. The new translation has it, "Follow peace with all men, and the sanctification." "The sanctification" is the great act in the redemptive process, because moral purity is the only ground upon which it is possible for men ultimately to be saved. A pure life, a pure heart, a thorough consecration of one's self to God and his service, as well as a purification of the heart and soul, must be obtained. Hence sanctification is not a process like the growth of a tree or plant, neither is it the collection or congregating of those accretions of decent acts and amenities that give the life a consistent and anagreeable appearance. But it is the deeper work of the Spirit of God in cleansing of the Adamic soul, or the cleansing of that nature that is imputed, and really given to us because of our descent from Adam, our sinful father, and Eve, our sinful mother. We cannot grow into holiness any more than we can grow into regeneration. Both are acts in the redeeming process, but acts that none can perform but the Holy Spirit. Regeneration or justification is the work that God does for us, but sanctification is the work done in us. The former is the pardon of sins, the latter is the washing out the inbred or Adamic sins. When God pardoned us of sin, he did not pardon us of Adam's sins, or that sinful nature which we have received from him as his children, but God did pardon us of our own sins, those sins which we have committed against His law and against His revealed Word. As to the acts of justification and sanctification, they follow each other as the acts of a judge upon the bench follow the justifying of a prisoner who, having been indicted for crime, was cast into prison by the public authorities. But when the judge pronounced the sentence of "not guilty," that is justification. This is one act. When the sheriff opens the prison doors, takes off the chains and shackles, and lets the prisoner out, this is analogically sanctification. The prisoner is, therefore, free. He is not only pardoned, or justified, but free. Free from natural, inbred or Adamic sin.

> "He breaks the power of cancelled sin,
> He sets the prisoner free;
> His blood can make the foulest clean;
> His blood availed for me."

Thus far the great majority of Methodists are agreed upon this fundamental doctrine of the Bible. But, as to the time between the acts in the process of redemption, there is a great controversy and constant agitation. Some believe a man is both pardoned and justified in the same act, place and time, while others believe that after justification, the act of cleansing, or purifying, must take place; that in the act of justification there was no cleansing or purifying, and therefore, the cleansing, purifying, or the act of sanctification, must be sought after justification. But it seems to me that the truth lies between the two extremes. A man that is converted to-day, or justified, may be sanctified in the next hour, the next day or next year, and, therefore, sanctification is to be sought as we sought regeneration or justification; for he may be justified and not have a perfect and distinct knowledge of it. No man knows that his sins are pardoned until the Spirit "bears witness with his spirit that he is a child of God." The knowledge of our acceptance with God can only reach us by His Spirit informing us that we are sanctified, and, therefore, pardoned. Why do I say this? Because the Holy Spirit of God will not come into the heart or soul when it is unclean or unsanctified. I am not so anxious to prove the method of procedure in the redemptive process as to prove the fact and philosophy of the case, as it is taught in the Bible. We want to know the Word and will of God, so that we may do his will and conform to the requirements of the divine commands.

We might take up the subject and treat philosophically, or from a metaphysical standpoint prove the truth of the Bible doctrine that "without holiness no man shall see the Lord," or enjoy that perfect love and reconciliation with Him and in His holy and divine presence that are the only inherent and fundamentals of happiness. What is demanded of men in respect to moral purity is also demanded of angels and all spiritualities of the universe. The conflict of elements and the war of forces are inharmony, and however that strife or inharmony may come, and no matter whatever else an intelligent being may have, or whatever may be his exalted station in the degree and dignity of being, we cannot see how he can be happy or enjoy God unless he is in harmony with the great "I Am." Hence, holiness, or that moral purity that God demands, is the only ground of harmony, of happiness, and of heaven. There is no place in the universal dominion of being for the unholy, the impure and the unsanctified heart or soul to be happy, neither in this present state of being nor in that which is to come. The wicked and polluted soul could pot be happy, even in heaven; for he would be without those principles and elements of character that are indispensable for his peace and the enjoyment of those pure, holy, and thronging millions that compose the company of heaven, who came "through great tribulations," and had "washed their robes, and made them white (pure) in the blood of the Lamb." We believe that it is possible, and in many cases a fact, that thousands are sanctified without ever having sought for it or having any knowledge of it, since we must suppose that many ignorant and illiterate people are truly Christians, lived and died as such, and went home to heaven. There are thousands to-day, as of all past time, who are incapable, and who have neither time nor opportunity of understanding fully the essentials of Christianity, yet they love God, love their neighbors, belong to the church and are willing, obedient servants of the Most High. They have a vivid experience, if not a perfect knowledge of their conversion; they well remember the struggles, groanings, sorrowings under the heavy load of sin; they well remember the day and place when and where they felt their hearts changed, and their feet plucked out of the mire and the clay and a new song put into their mouths, even praises unto God; but they know nothing of the special

and specific work of the cleansing, or the act of sanctification. They are the children of God as much as the theologian who, because of his calling and superior advantages, understands many of the deep and intricate things of God and the religion of Jesus. Shall we say that these poor, ignorant and uncultured children of God are not saved to the uttermost, because they were unlearned and untutored in the philosophy and fundamentals of Chistianity? No, not all. But since they must be holy before they can enter heaven and enjoy God, they must have been sanctified and made pure, as well as pardoned somewhere and at some time, between the natural birth and the moment of entering the paradise of God. But you say God winks at ignorance, and that when we have the opportunity to seek sanctification and fail to do it, He will hold us responsible for it, and, therefore, we should seek it. That is true. Every word of it is to the spirit and letter of

God's commands; but that does not alter or change the fact that many are sanctified without their having any specific knowledge of either seeking it or having obtained it; yet they have it, because they show all the fruits of the Spirit, and gain heaven in the end. The predominant idea of holiness, or moral cleanness is that it fits us for the awful presence of the Infinite Deity. It is the clean clothes, the pure and "bright raiment" "without spot or wrinkle," that fits all comers to the heavenly tabernacle to enter and to be entertained by Jesus Christ, who is "the Prince of the kings of the earth," and "the bright and morning star." What elaborate preparations are made by the great men of earth to meet their kings, emperors and crowned heads! What studied programs, magnificent pageantry and splendid equipages to meet their earthly masters and human leaders! These are men of state, governors, lawyers, doctors, judges, clothed in the bright ermine of their office, senators, representatives, and statesmen; laborers from field and forest, artisans from shop and forge, the painters from the studios of art, women and children and old men bent under the toils of life and the weight of years; philosophers, scientists, mathematicians and metaphysicians, old and gray with struggling thought, whose souls aflame have "walked the solar paths" and driven their chariots of silken sunbeams over the high domes of the "Milky Way" hard to the universal center. All, all, come to meet their earthly lord and reigning king, and amid booming cannon, and stately cordons of national armies men stand in awful silence, with bated breath and uncovered heads. The king is passing by.

But what is this compared to the infinite and high presence of the King immortal? How weak and insignificant is this earthly grandeur and majestic display of a nation compared with the greatness of the majesty of the court of heaven? If an earthly monarch demands such high and respectful allegiance from his subjects as to awaken the keenest interest and profoundest attention, how is the interest and attention heightened when our moral and mental manhood shall stand in the awful presence of the Infinite Creator, before whose all-discerning eye every heart is open, and all the inner consciousness is discovered in its multiform and intricate actions, relations and conditions! But a clean heart and a pure, blood-washed soul can tread the holy courts of God and dwell in His high, holy and majestic presence.

II. What is implied in peace?

As holiness is the fundamental and the cardinal principle of reconciliation between God and man, so peace is the product or resultant factor in the redemptive scheme. It ushers in that period and brings us into that relationship with God where there is perfect harmony, and that parental relation that is more real, more splendid and beautiful than that of the tender babe and the loving mother. It is the deep and abiding consciousness that there is nothing between God and ourselves but an unclouded vista, wreathed with flowers all fragrant with His love and replete with the bright and beaming sunshine of His face, filling the soul with the radiance of heaven and the music of the angels. This is personal peace, spoken of by the Savior, when He said, "My peace I give unto you, not as the world giveth"--a peace that ramifies the soul, filling all its chambers and deep recesses with an unearthly calm and heavenly assurance that belongs only to the true children of God. Whoever has this peace is a child of God; for none can have such a priceless jewel but the true children of the Most High. But as there was a struggle before personal peace came, so there must be a struggle and a conflict of forces before national, international and world-wide peace shall fully prevail on the earth. There must be a conflict of opposite and diverse elements, agencies of spiritual, mental, civil, social or economic forces. Christ came to stir, agitate, and set in active operation all the attributes, natures, things, principles, and powers that pertain to all the great concerns of the glory of God in human redemption. For he says, "Suppose ye that I am come to give peace on earth? I tell you, nay; but rather division." Again, "I am come to send fire on the earth; and what will I, if it be already kindled?" Again, "There is no peace to the wicked saith my God." That is, there can be no compromise between good and evil, between the forces of Christianity and the forces of sin and the Devil. There must be a struggle, a long and dreadful conflict for the mastery and control of human hearts, human governments, and all the spiritual, moral and mental empire of the children of men. And this struggle for the mastery, in the very nature of the case, is necessary and indispensable. It is a natural consequence of the long and dreadful reign of sin. It is the irrepressible conflict of the centuries, that cannot cease its fearful hostilities until peace is declared in favor of that just and holy administration which Jesus Christ came to establish. This universal peace cannot be established until the Word of God shall have been preached in all the earth; until all the vile and depraved and black squadrons of sin and hell shall have been overthrown, and the beautiful and majestic reign of Messiah shall cover every land and sea, and sit enthroned in every heart, and in every tribe and nation; "for He must reign until He hath put all enemies under His feet." But how? "Not by might, nor by power, but by my Spirit, saith the Lord." Not by the might of nations, nor the concentration of armies, or stringent laws, nor yet by national and international treaties; not by fire, war and blood, nor the arbitrament of the sword, but by the preaching of the Gospel, the conversion of sinners, and the Spirit of God permeating, reforming and sanctifying human hearts and consecrating the mental faculties of intelligent humanity to His service and His love. These may be deemed the spiritual energies and those deep and silent forces that act beneath the surface of society and human tastes and agencies. But as man has a tangible existence as well as an intangible reality, the physical and mental forces and powers must coöperate in the redemption of universal humanity. Not only will the people of God coöperate with His Spirit with this end in view, but the widespread physicalities of nature, under the control of inter-racial and international barter and trade, are to be the able, although not efficient, agencies under real and sentimental Christianity. But the relations of nations, with the interchange of thought, learning, and all the powers of increasing civilization, are to be swift-running couriers to bear to distant lands the glory of His kingdom, the greatness of His truth, the sweetness and melodies of his name.

Let us remember that "the earth is the Lord's and the fullness thereof," and that we are looking for "a new heaven and a new earth, wherein dwelleth righteousness." "Let not your hearts troubled, ye believe in God, believe also in me."

O, ye saints of God, look up, He is coming, he is coming to do justice and judgment in the earth. Hell is great, but Christ is greater. Behold, he cometh skipping over the hills and mountains of broken decades, dying years and dead centuries. Before Him the dead and stupid gods of the nations are falling and the empire of sin upon its ancient base is trembling and rocking. I see Him rising above the surging waves of space and time and ascending the horizon in His chariot of flame, with the greatness and the indescribable majesty of His kingdom following in his train. I see men, women and children, with harps and cymbals, drums and golden lutes, and all stringed instruments of music playing with nimble fingers, and singing the great doxology of triumph. "The Lord God omnipotent reigneth."

SERMON XV.

The Unity of Christianity.

"Therefore let no man glory in men. For all things are yours."-- I Cor. 3:21.

In the second chapter of this epistle the apostle begins it by saying, "And I, brethren, when I came to you, came not with excellency of speech or of wisdom, declaring unto you the testimony of God," etc. Again, he speaks of the wisdom of this world as being "foolishness with God, for it is written, He taketh the wise in their own craftiness," etc. But let it be understood that neither God nor his inspired apostle designed to discourage the culture of the brain nor the pursuit of knowledge or wisdom. But the apostle designs to show the folly, the uncertainty, and the mental darkness under which the ancient schools of science and philosophy labored; and that because of human weakness, and mental depravity, the learning and product of Grecian philosophy then prevalent, could never solve those religious and profound questions that have, in a greater or less degree, stirred and agitated universal humanity. In this sense, "the wisdom of this world," or the old system of Grecian dogma and philosophy, "is foolishness with God." On the other hand, God designs and religion comes not to make men fools or less wise, but it is sent from God to man to enlarge his sphere of knowledge, quicken the mental faculties, clear with the bright sun of righteousness the moral atmosphere, making mankind "wise unto salvation." Indeed, among the forces and agencies of God which he has put into operation on the human plane, none is more essential, befitting and resplendent with the redemptive elements than the mental faculties. Knowledge is an essential element in human salvation, as much as it is an essential element in human progress and the world's civilization. Christianity comes to expand and extend the moral, mental, and physical horizon, to lift the mists and clouds, giving to the honest and true believer an untrammelled highway and an unshaded view in the deep vistas beyond. "This is life eternal, that they might know thee, the only true God, and Jesus Christ, whom thou hast sent." Knowledge is given us to know the right, to comprehend the majestic, and to fathom the ways of God, that we may praise and adore him. Indeed, the universe is his grand temple, the court of his justice, the field of his power, and the gilded empire of his glory. Far, far beyond blazing suns, shining orbs and trembling systems, he rides the winged flame, treads their burning currents, buckles the systems to his belt, wreathes his brow with stars, and chains the sisters of the Milky Way to his feet, and bids them do his will. Also, "he maketh his angels spirits and his ministers a flame of fire." Spirits are his servants, and angels are his messengers. Around him they stand as if hung on threads of silver, play through all parts of the universal mechanism as sunbeams play on the face of the earth. At his command they ramify his wide domains, sweep the studded chambers of the vaulted dome, and chain the swift-running lightnings to their native spheres. Around him, the universal Center, systems play and cast their shivered crafts, and flying boulders, and splintered worlds at his feet, and in awful chaos praise the eternal thunderer "that bids them roll." "Oh, the depth of the riches, both of the wisdom and knowledge of God! How unsearchable are his judgments, and his ways past finding out!" But, says the apostle, "All things are yours; whether Paul, or Apolos, or Cephas, or the world, or life, or death, or things present, or things to come; all are yours, and ye are Christ's, and Christ is God's." That is, the church with its living ministry, its divine oracles of truth, or all the forces, elements, and agencies of organized and unified Christianity, with the physical and civil creations belong to you. They are all your servants and your friends to bring you to God, and perfect your manhood, advance your happiness and give you heaven in the end, while they give humanity glorious perpetuity and resplendent activity throughout the ages to come.

1. The unity of Christianity.

Nothing proves the divine originality of Christianity and the authenticity of its cardinal doctrines more than its unity and perfect harmony with itself and with the ends and aims that it has in view. All through the ages, and all through the nations and the world's greatest civilizations, religion has been the universal and most prominent factor in the tastes, feelings and aspirations of men. The political, national and social forms that have obtained in human progress and developments have circled around its standard of morals, and received their force and propulsion from the germ seeds and grains of truth that have been evolved or brought from the great mine of the world's great religions. Though often mixed with error and covered by the dust of ages, though its symbolisms and external faculties have been perverted, prostituted and made to reach unholy ends, yet these religions carry with them some grains of truth, and in their fundamentals, when properly interpreted, point to God as the great Author and Founder of their central truths and vital principles. They show a unification of nature, intent, and purpose that make up a consistency and harmony in their respective parts which declare themselves to be of the one God. "Hear, O Israel, the Lord thy God is one Lord," and so it might be said, "Hear, all ye religions of the nations and ages, the Lord thy God is one God and one Father." From him all truth must come, since he is "the only true God," and the only One in the universe that can dictate to the will and conscience and moral and religious proclivities of men and angels, and whatever other intelligences may reside in his dominions. All truth is from God, and must lead to God. Every thread and line and living cable that ramifies and thrills the living entities, though sometimes hidden and broken and covered with the débris and scoria of the wear and tear of the centuries, will take us back to God, the great Original, chaining all to the rock-ribbed mountains of the eternal shore. If there were ten thousand religions, and ten times ten thousand forms of worship, to be true and beneficial to mankind, they must all point to God and own him as the true and only proper and rightful object of prayer, praise and adoration. "All things are yours," to lead you to God and plant you on the solid rock of truth and the eternal shore.

2. As there is a unity in Christianity, there must be a unity in the government of God.

As there is but one God, there can be but one universal government, founded upon principles of oneness, uniformity and justice. The eternal form of government is nothing compared to its principles, those fundamentals upon which the kingdom may rest. God's Government is always right, and just, and uniform. In the simple ground-principles upon which it rests, and by which it is perpetuated, there is a complete, full, and perfect conformity. It is a system of universal harmonies, so full and replete with its own Creator, that no true government can exist except the government of God. Human governments, because of their weakness, depravity and sins, are not true governments, but are merely legalized mobs and perversions of the great original--the government of God. As religion becomes corrupt by the additions of men, so human governments become corrupt by a departure from moral rectitude and the administration of justice. There should be no difference between the government of God and the government of men, except in degrees. But in nature and kind both should be the same, and steadily maintain the same ends in view, namely, the happiness of the governed. Now, the government of man is an image or a reflection of the kingdom of God. He is the great ideal, the ne plus ultra of mental, moral, and physical conception. He, with his government, is the highest standard of excellence. No thought, act, being, form, or conception, can go beyond him. He dwells in the loftiest altitudes and the sublimest wonders of the possibilities of being. Manhood is a struggling image of the infinite and triumphant God, and perpetual struggle is the price of eternal life. We reach the immortal fixedness by labor, toil, and the fierce ordeal of death.

3. But the government of God is dictatorial, ministerial, executive.

He dictates, he sends forth his ministers and agencies, and by them he fulfills his will in the armies of heaven, earth and the myriads of the deep. He dictates to all the elements, forces, agencies, and the incomprehensible majesties, both material and immaterial. His will is the law of being and his commands are the immovable statutes of their mode and motions. Whether they roll, rest, or soar; whether they sing, hiss, or sigh--they are his servants and trembling ministers, bent on their eternal rounds to bring to their noble and glorious ends the great designs of his love and power. Every angel in heaven, every man on earth, and all the devils, lost men and fallen spirits in hell, are his ministers, and in some mysterious way fulfill his high behests and his wise commands. Men may rebel, infidels, sceptics and scoffers may swear and oppose the truth, and hate the kingdom of God; they may make war on the Bible, persecute the saints, and seek to destroy the whole of the united forces of Christianity and subvert its organized forms; yet their madness and rage can only intensify the friends of the truth, unite the armies of God, and solidify a nascent and an advancing Christianity. The will and purposes of God cannot be defeated, nor fail to reach the ends which his wisdom, love and goodness have proposed. Hence the government of God is dictatorial, ministerial, and executive.

4. We are in the presence of some great agency, power, or personality.

We are in the presence of an influence and an expanding energy, that are stirring, agitating and moving the forces and elements of nature as never before in the history of the world. The nations are all aglow with the ardent flame of progress, development, and expansion. This age is the culmination of ages. The concentration of centuries is shaping and fashioning universal manhood into a total unity of a personification that is wonderful and unique. This great agency is Christianity, this power is God, and this great personality is Jesus Christ. This triune character or trinity of forces is drawing "all things" toward the center, to a social, civil, political, commercial and interracial manhood, whose empire of brotherhood must and will rule over all. Indeed, we are living in an age of blending interests, when the great capitals of the world are getting nearer and nearer, and by reason of rapid transit and the quick transmission of thought, time is blotted out and space is annihilated. New York, London, Paris, Berlin, St. Petersburg, Pekin, and Canton, the great commercial centers, speak to each other daily and on hidden cables of elastic steel. The lightnings vibrate the sympathies and feelings of the nations, as if universal humanity were hung on one solid nerve cord, or as if there was but one great heart of the world of man. Racial prejudices[,] national hate, tribal distinctions, together with all frivolous conventionalities, must yield to the martial steps and massive tread of a newer and better civilization, quickened and made resplendent by an active and reformative Christianity.

5. "All things are yours," to make you a man.

Men are not made in a day, nor a year, nor a dozen of years. It takes nearly a half of a century to make a man. His physical constitution matures in less time, but the real man, the true, hidden man, is made by slow process and by degrees. As the skilled mechanic frets and belabors a piece of pig iron into a useful and beautiful instrument, or as he makes all the parts of a steam engine or some other mechanism with its delicate and intricate parts, wheels, cylinders, springs, axles, cogs, pulleys, bands, steamchests and piston-rods, and as they are properly adjusted, each working in perfect harmony with all other parts, so all the faculties of humanity must be fretted, belabored and cultured, until the full, matured and perfect man comes from the hands of the master. It is true, man is finished in the fact of his being. He is finished in the nature and number of the mental, moral, and physical faculties. Nothing new in kind can be added to his being in this or in another state. He cannot have two memories, two or more judgments, or have a duality or multiplicity of moral ideals. Neither can he have comprehension or perceptions differing from those that he now has, because this would be to change his being, divert him from his original channel, and throw him out of himself where he becomes another or a different self. If such were possible with the nature and state of a personal, conscious being, moral responsibility would be impossible, and the rebellious and intelligent would escape punishment, and the righteous lose their reward. As, also, the justice of God would be a more sham, the ends of his government would be defeated, moral order subverted, and his kingdom which should rule "over all," a failure. No, the complex mechanism of humanity was completed in the number of its faculties and essential elements in the first fiat act of his creation. Hence, no property, faculty, attribute, or fundamental can be added to his being. Again, he is made in the image of God. His mental and moral manhood is like its great Creator--spiritual, ethical, fixed in its statutes, and dwelling in altitudes and on a plane above all other things and powers that may produce death or bring decay. Hence man, as are all intelligent creatures, is naturally and constitutionally immortal and imperishable. What, then, is culture? Culture is the enlarging and expanding of those faculties and powers already given. It is development and the bringing out and putting into useful activity all that mental manhood that we call mind. The advancements and improvements of the intellect are not the attachments of new essentials or fundamentals achieved by culture, but they are old powers and latent forces put into activity. The intellect, then, is capable of perpetual and indefinite improvements and advancements. Step by step, evolution after evolution, the mental humanity ascends the rounds of the ladder of development, gaining in experience and self-force, until in the galaxy of its own perfect nature and purer light of God, all the powers and faculties will be in perfect balance and in full and endless harmony with all of its self and with its perfect ideal-- God.

6. But "all things are yours," to bring you to a better and higher self.

The world was made for man and God. The Garden of Eden was made for Adam and his sons, and for Eve and her daughters. The universe was made for the temple of God, and a house and dwelling-place for all his children. The vaulted dome, bedecked with gems and cities of stars with the countless "hosts of heaven" that make up "the shining frame," were made for you. They were made to lift your aspirations, inspire your hope, nerve your effort. The rainbow bends over you, and spans the cerulean arch to give you patience and hope, and the lightnings flash to quicken your steps and clear the physical and moral atmosphere of the pestiferous seeds of sickness and death. The thunders remind you of the presence of the awful God, great Jehovah who makes "the clouds his chariot" and the winds his horses. The thunderbolts are his winged arrows from his bow of fire, and his grape and canister from the pent-up magazines of the skies. The dewdrops are gems of blessings and silver crown of glory set in heavenly trim upon leaf, bud, petal and ripening fruit to remind us of the crowns of heaven. Seed time and harvest, spring and summer, the alternating seasons with their refreshing changes, are all yours. The sun shines to warm you and give you light, the winds blow to waft you on to God and make you a perfect man and a perfect woman; the seas roll, and rivers play on their rocky beds, and like cables of gold, tie the mountains to the seashore, that you may know there is an eternal anchorage hard by the throne of God and held by his hand. For you the stars revolve, comets flash and meteors fly in the open skies. "All things are yours." Deep in the bowels of the earth there are mines of richest ores and living veins of gold and silver. There are beds of jewels, sleeping diamonds, and undiscovered urns of brightest gems to crown our queens in brilliant stars, and bedeck the royal insignia of our kings with the beauties and studded grace of angels. There are magazines of oil, empires of iron, and kingdoms of coal to keep us warm in winter, cook our food, move our machinery, turn our wheels and spindles, propel the mighty iron-clad monsters and "swift-running greyhounds" across the surging seas, that we may speak to our sisters and brothers of the islands and continents. There are mountains of stone, with giant bones of granite and massive ledges of unpolished marble to cover our streets, build our houses and temples of honor, and halls of pleasure. At the voice of the thunder and the flashing of the lightning, the melting clouds pace along the skies on the chariot wheels of the wind and play upon the heaving bosom of the air, as if they were the fleecy cars of heaven, drawn by troops of angels, that there may be seed to the sower and bread to the eater. The whole kingdom of nature, with its scenes of beauty and charming embodiments of delight, with its robes of living green, and crowns of brilliant flowers, blushing lilies, and bursting petals of fragrant roses, is for you and for me, to help us on to God, and to the sublime heights of a better, even a perfect self. All the listening elements, the faculties and sleeping propensities of the universal spheres, with their countless billions of molecular entities and atomical relations, unite their forces and combine their energies to make a sinless man, a sinless humanity. Every thread and fibre, every string and wire, every cord and cable, and every golden nerve and silver strand, and all the wheels of the universal mechanism, are our willing servants and God-driven steeds to land us all in heaven and crown us with immortal green and the blushes of eternal youth. Civilization, with its forms, relations, institutions, achievements, and discoveries, is made for you and all the sons of men. Its flourishing cities, its moving millions, its laws and customs, its codes of wisdom, books of learning and folios of experience with the arts and sciences, are the beacon lights and polar stars to catch the radiance of the Sun of righteousness and scatter its warmth and sparkling beams to the utmost length and breadth of the royal highway to the city of God. Organized Christianity, with its living ministry, its temples of song and worship, with millions of consecrated men and women and little children, is your helper and comrade on the highway of light and truth. All things in the heights and depths and the rimless and measureless expansions, with their unknown and infinite capacities, realities and possibilities, and whatever else may exist in the concrete or in the abstract universe, are ready and waiting to gather up the reins and buckle up the habit and yoke on the pinions of flame and cut the belted and burning peripheries of the outermost glories of ethereal currents, that they may crown the royal hosts of Christ with the wreaths of conquerors and the gems of kings.

But Calvary is yours, with its dying Savior, its forsaken Son, its bleeding Victim, its smitten Shepherd, its scattered flock, and the uplifted sword of the executive God. "All things are yours." Amen and amen! So let it be.

ESSAYS; ADDRESSES, ETC.

The Christmas.

No anniversary or celebration of any great event in the history of man contains within its significant parts and high symbolism, greater interests and broader and deeper relationship to the intelligent inhabitants of this earthly sphere than that which Christianity brings to remembrance by the annually returning Christmas. The wheels of ages, the revolution of planets, the flight of comets that spin and dance and wrap their golden trails around sidereal wonders, and carry the news of God from the seat of eternal power to the utmost periphery, bear no greater news in their eternal mail car than the birth of Christ, and the advent of the Son of Mary. In the history of God and man, and all the angels besides, there can take place no event of greater moment, of vaster, deeper, and more infinite import to the Adamic race. What event, era, age, cycle, or dispensation in the history of God and creation can be compared to it? What physical catastrophe, or mental evolution, or spiritual transition in the depth of being, in the wonderful universal mechanism can be compared to it? Far back in the misty deep of the cycles, before Aurora blushed at her halo of the morning flame, or the Polar star kissed her gorgeous trail on the Northern seas, and when as yet Alcyon had not stepped from the deep precincts of her boudoir and chained her burning sisters as sandals on her feet, when as yet the fiery mists rolled, soared, hissed, and in serpentine splendor moved about their own center, our Christianity, of which Christ is the active, forceful embodiment, sat in eternal enthronization in the bosom of God, as the only possible moral principle of His universal empire.

Again, we say there is no event in the history of man and God, whether physical or mental, that can be compared to the advent and birth of the great Messiah. The fall of the great Lucifer from the imperial empyrean, succeeding the great conflict of the loftiest majesties of the spheres and of the towering intellectualities of the universe, was a great event. It was the battle of the eternal ages, the culmination of majestic insolence, the beginning of the sinful era, and a desperate effort of rebellious, sagacious, and powerful intellectual activities to take the reins of empire and the seat of God. It was the battle of gods in the heart of the empire, and at the seat of government. Proud Lucifer had been the tall archangel, the prime minister of the court of heaven, crowned with the belted cycles. He wore the robe of honor, the insignia of state--a thousand suns pinned together by a thousand comets, which threw back their burning tails in majestic folds and wide-spread seas of pyramidal light from pole to pole, high above his head; and expanding over all was the rainbow, radiant in the beauties of its seven colors, the God-given and sacred memento of universal and eternal peace. But the crisis is approaching. The relation between the oldest and mightiest sons of God is strained. The cables break, civic volcanoes explode, and the internecine and political convulsions unhinge the harmonies of the centuries. Fiery conclaves on steeds--ethereal currents, like flashes of lightnings-- thread and ramify the kingdoms, thrones, dominions, principalities and powers. All the heights, depths, lengths, provinces, and eternal eras, with all their multitudes, are summoned to the battle of the cycles. But proud Lucifer, the first, the greatest and the oldest of sinners, fails, as all must fail who fight against God and challenge the throne and authority of the Most High. "How art thou fallen from Heaven, O Lucifer, son of the morning." This is a great event, the beginning of sin. But Christ is born, and a greater event enters the record of the ages and the history of being. His nativity marks an era more distinguished, more interesting, and more universal than the loss of planets, or of the sinking suns and lost systems. In the starry frame of the constellated tracks of space, suns have ceased to shine, moons have waned to calcined dust, and old worlds have been honeycombed by the giant worm of decay. In the mid-ocean of the galaxies of sidereal systems, our proud earth, with her cold, chaste moon, the uncrowned pale empress of the night, is making her trip on the high seas of time. She belongs to an immediate system, and with each of her sisters is moved and warmed by the great sun; but the best message that ever fell upon her heart, in her onward flight through space, is the nativity of Christ, the Annointed of God, the Heavenly Legate, the Savior of men, and the Preserver of angels.

His name is the charm of centuries, the wand of the ages, the anthem of the nations and the inspiring melody of the spheres. God says, "I will make Thy name to be remembered in all generations, therefore shall the people praise Thee forever and ever." Quickly and strongly down through the days of the onflow of the multitudes of aspiring millions, His name, like burnt incense ascending from the golden censers of adoring seraphs, shall be the chorus of the redemption anthem, the life of every song and the sweetness of every verse.

Annalists and recording scribes may forget the name of the Cæsars, the Napoleons, and the noble founders and protectors of empires. Peoples, nations, monarchies, and republics may pass from the drama of nations. Bards, poets, and seers, and the skillful touchers of the organ keys may forget their national airs and the names of their glorified and deified heroes of a thousand battles, and their quivering strings of gold may lie silent upon their broken harps and lutes. The eternal shafts and marble piles of fretted stone and towering columns, and all the dreamers that sleep in "the rock-ribbed" and bronze-bound sarcophagi may be forgotten, and the letters of their illustrious names erased by the abrasions of centuries; yet the name of Jesus--the Christ--will never be forgotten, but will go ringing down the declivities of the world's civilizations, sweeping on in the radiant splendors of its own effulgent brightness, until every lip shall lisp His name, every tongue spread His fame, yea, until every heart is a throne, every soul a temple, and every child of man a polished gem to stud and bedeck a trophied empire, gathered and sorted out from the perverse and rebellious majesties and actualities of sin and darkness.

But the time was approaching for the great nativity. The purposes of God were ripening fast. The prophets had waited long, sung of His coming, dreamed of His triumphs, descanted in solemn lays upon their stringed instruments and played on their high-sounding cymbals the preludes to His dramatic majesty upon the public stage of nations. The magi in far distant climes of the East had calculated upon tablets of golden plate the time of His appearing. The flight of stars, the flash of comets, and the position of planets, were studied and catalogued, and the lost Pleiades, called up from the infinite plentitudes of their long disappearance, read the predictions of His coming from their fiery rings and the flitting phantasmagoria of their sheeny trails. The philosophical archives of ancient lore, and the hieroglyphics of occult syllogisms were laid open to the calm visions and the cold judgment of the deepest and the keenest occultism. The fall of meteors, the dance of the aurora borealis in awful display around the, northern hemisphere, the dull cold thud of earthquakes, the howling seas and the hum and stately tramp of receding centuries were marked, and the hands upon the dial plate of time were watched, and their epochal relations measured and weighed until the high-born beauties and majesties of the universe spoke to men in the language of the stars, and told of His coming. The last of the four great monarchies--the four great acts in the drama of human government--Rome-- was quivering upon its ancient foundations, and the kingdom of the Tiber with its hoary locks of the ages was stooping to the weight of years. "The scepter had departed from Judah," the Jewish polity was broken, and the throne of David and Solomon was a thing of the past. Up, up, the days of the centuries climb, angels watch, cherubs drop their wings, all harps are unstrung, cymbals cease to vibrate their symphonies, and the diatonic chords of the universal diapason lose their music in the sea of silence. The court of heaven is open; awful muteness that could be felt myriads of leagues from center toward circumference seals every lip and tongue, relaxes every harp sting, and the immortal celebration is hushed.

So He came, and so He was born in Bethlehem of Judea. "And the angel said unto them, 'Fear not, for behold I bring good tidings of great joy, which shall be to all people, for unto you is born this day in the City of David, a Savior, which is Christ the Lord.'" * * * "Glory to God in the highest, and on earth, peace, good will toward men." Blessed nativity! blessed birth of "the Prince of Peace!" Blessed Legate from the court of heaven!

But what of His work? He is here to stay, not in His physical manhood, but in spiritual power. He is here to deal with the nations, to elevate humanity and purify the civilizations of the world. Christmas ever calls to memory His advent, nature and work. But how sweet is the name of Christ, and of Jesus! It is associated with human happiness and human redemption. It is the light of the nations, the guiding star of the millions, and the balm for every aching heart. Some man has said in effect, that the time would come when the name of Jesus Christ would be blotted from the face of the earth. But how can it be? Who can blot it out? Who can hush the millions and erase from their "heart of hearts" the beauties of his grace, or the melody of his name? Sirs, if men should hold their peace, the very stones would cry out. Sweet carols would spring from the earth, and songs of praise from the rocks of the hills. The rivers would murmur it, the little rills would babble it, the seas with a thousand bass drum would roar it, the storms would howl it, and the winds would whistle among the glades and valleys and trees of the woods, until every leaf, bud, trunk, fruit, and flower would quiver beneath the melodies of His name and the joys of His salvation. Yea, every dead prophet, bard, seer and evangelical poet would leap from his grave, tune his golden notes afresh, call up all the choirs of the nations, and gather the broken chords of the centuries. Before His name can be blotted out every Bible must be burnt up, every church torn down, every Sunday-school annihilated, and every minister and working saint and pious heart crushed to insensibility. What will you do with David and Asaph, the sweet singers in Israel? What will you do with Milton, Watts, Toplady, Charles Wesley, and the other tens of thousands who tuned their harps on Calvary, and from its crimson summit caught the inspiration of heaven in their hearts, and poured their anthems with plastic fingers in the bosom of the rhythmic rills of heavenly lays? What will you do with the redeemed soul fresh and green in the transcendencies and beatific transitions of the new life? When rightly played man is a harp of a thousand strings, keyed, and attuned by the holy name of Jesus Christ. This harp was made after the heavenly pattern. It is the lyre of God. Its strings are of the loftiest cast and of the finest mould, whose threads never break, whose music, though old, is always new. Its songs are long, deep, melodious, sweeping down from heaven to Calvary in melting softness and dulcet strain which thunders in awful refrain in the depth of the spheres, causing to vibrate every quivering thread and living octave. Blot out the name of Jesus? It cannot be done. No! The stars would hand it down, the moon would kiss it, the sun would shine it through all the planets, and ethereal currents would waft it on wings of flame, and the lightnings of God would hurl it and burn it across the bosom of "Arcturus, Orion, Pleiades and the chambers of the South." Then let the inhabitants of the earth take up the thrilling cry and with lip and tongue, with harp and fife and drum, chant the Te Deum of the ages and the melodies of His name forever and forever.

The Unity of Force.

It is evident from the teachings of the Bible, and spiritual and physical activities, that there is but one moving, all-pervading, central, living energy. Deep down beneath and passing through and rising above all principles, things, and agencies, there is an intelligent reality, a forceful, inherent and active life. This active life is before all things, in all space, permeating every particle of universal matter and spirit, guiding, directing and controlling the countless and eternal activities. There may be rest, but not real quietism. There can be no quietism in a moving universe. Life itself is activity, and that that acts is life. Since life is activity there is nothing else to act. The life of the universe is the central or universal mentality, and is the unit of force. Force is only a part of the universal mentality, that part, or that property, or faculty, that agitates, oscillates, or stirs the elements and constituencies. Nothing can move or vibrate except as it is moved upon or vibrated by the universal mentality.

One of the most wonderful and distinguishing properties or faculties of the universal mentality is wisdom, that perfect knowledge of all the entities, results, and facts of being. State or condition has no effect upon universality. State or no state, condition or no condition, cannot destroy or annul the property of universality any more than state or condition can destroy or annihilate being. Nothing can anihilate being. It is an eternal, an indestructible, and divine entity. Being is a reality that is independent of matter, even in its highest possible mode of existence, or in its greatest volatile or ethereal vitality. There is no living factor in the universe but mind. All else is dead, mute and inert. The universe around us, above us and beneath us, acts only as it is acted upon by the spiritual, universal intelligence--the incomprehensible mentality. Matter acts, therefore, because it is acted upon by a power that is above it in degrees of those constituent properties that characterize its superiority belonging only to itself. If there were a mental force equal to another mental force, with equal intelligence, there could be no unity of force any more than there could be "the unity of nature and the reign of law." Hence all the phenomena in nature harmonize with the highest concepts of wisdom and lead us unto the temple of the enthroned and incomprehensible intelligence. There is no real inherent force, life, or action in matter, and consequently none in the universe, except this, or the universal intelligence, and all that we see or comprehend in physical nature is the product of universal mind. To comprehend the measure and the mode of the existence of mind, or even to hint at the unknowable and infinite deeps out of which it rises in resplendent unity of being and action, would eventuate in nothing, and a thousand billions of centuries would leave us as far from the solution as we are to-day. It is not a province of thought or comprehension, for in these mighty deeps and unzoned seas of mental reality, the wing of thought, or the pinions of the imagination never can rest, roll, or soar. The presentation of metaphysical syllogism teaches us that there is but one reality in the universe, and that is mind. There is no other reality in the sense that it has its own inherent and self-activities. Nothing can be a true reality but that which has self-action and unified personal proclivities and spiritual individuality.

The doctrine that teaches the unity of force does not in any sense teach the doctrine of monism, because the unit of force has intelligence that is plainly to be seen in every part of the universe. There can be no design without intelligence, or that power that designs and chooses the best and fittest means to accomplish the best and fittest ends. Wisdom is the property of mind, that mental unity of character or individualism; and since mind must act in harmony with itself, it is of necessity a unit. Monism teaches the unity of force, (but a force that is in itself blind, and has no intelligence, no personality of being or design,) and that the vast results and products of the universe arise out of the precipitant elements and the fortuitous vibrations of its parts. It denies all mental intelligence and spiritual activities, except such as arise out of the fortuitous combinations of precipitant forces and vibratory elements; it denies that there is any such thing as mind or mental character beyond that which has been produced by physical nature, and asserts that the mental faculties of man (or spirits, if there be any) are the products of mere molecular force or action with chemical combinations under happy conditions. This view leaves the universe without a designing mental individualism that we call the universal intelligence, and shuts us up to ill fatalities and capricious chance, and allows the universe, like an unguided ship upon some vast sea, to float in space without chart or compass, leaving the boundless and unnumbered worlds to ply on their own chosen orbits without let or design. Think of it. A universe running away with itself. Possibly it may come in contact or collision with another. Then what? The thought is ridiculous and also stupendous. Under it, the stoutest must quiver and the souls of towering spirits must quail as the unthinkable catastrophe photographs its shapeless image upon the undying mentalism.

So far as science is concerned, the unity of force is proved by the form or shape of all the known systems or worlds

that float in space. None of them are yet proved to be square, oblong, ovate, octangular, or rhomboidal, but all are round, or spheroidal. And so far as we know, the very molecules, or the atomic aggregations of bodies, in their most subtle particles, and in themselves, are round. One is made to correspond to all of the others in the vast machinery of the universe. It seems apparent that in no other way could perfect harmony be produced and maintained. It is believed that planets have, by some marvelous and eruptive force, been broken to pieces and forced into space, and that in process of time they have become round, because in no other way could they regain and maintain those harmonious relations and conditions that are essential to the order and happiness of the intelligent universe. If nature was the author and creator of itself, which is incapable of designs, why is it that all these worlds and systems of worlds are made round? Why is it that none of them are square, oblong, rectangular or some other shape besides the globular? Why they are formed thus, is because the universal intelligence, the infinite mentality so designed them that the beauty and harmony and glory of the universe might be a dwelling-place and a magnificent temple for "the Father of Lights" and His intelligent offsprings, the shining phalanxes and legates of His love.

The Colored Methodist Episcopal Church. (Published in The Independent, March, '91.)

This, the youngest branch of American Methodism, was organized under the auspices and authority of the Methodist Episcopal Church, South, in the city of Jackson, Tenn., December 15th and 23d, 1870. As for back as 1866, its organization was contemplated and desired by both classes of those who composed the membership of the Methodist Episcopal Church, South. In this year (1866) the General Conference of the Mother Church requested their bishops to ordain colored men to the ministry, form them into conferences, preside over and superintend the colored work in assemblies, separate and distinct from those of the whites. It was also provided "that when three or more annual conferences of colored ministers were organized and presided over by the bishops" of the Methodist Episcopal Church, South; and that also when thought befitting and agreeable to both classes of members, "a separate and independent ecclesiastical jurisdiction should be established for the colored people," with all the regularities and outfits of established Methodism.

These initiatory provisions, being agreeable to both classes of persons concerned, and being consistent with what was conceived to be the harmony and best interests of both and all, the separation was authorized--legal, formal, and productive of the best feelings and results.

It is simply justice to state that the Methodist Episcopal Church, South, at the beginning of the late war, had over two hundred thousand members of color within her pales, having churches of their own, and ministers sent to them regularly from the conferences. Often one pastor served both the white and the colored members, preaching to the whites in the forenoon and to the colored in the afternoon. Of this two hundred thousand, the great majority informally dissolved their relationship with the Methodist Episcopal Church, South, and went into other branches of Methodism, the African Methodist Episcopal Church receiving the largest share of them. However, there still remained about forty thousand who adhered to the Methodist Episcopal Church, South, and who could not be induced to disband their church relation and enter others which came upon the ground immediately after the emancipation. For some years after the war the reduced number of members of color who still remained adherents of the Methodist Episcopal Church, South, was looked after and cared for as was the case during the years of slavery. As the General Conference of the Methodist Episcopal Church, South, which met in New Orleans, May, 1866, had authorized the bishops to organize conferences of colored ministers, so, four years after, the same body held its quadrennial session in Memphis, Tenn.; and upon the petition of some of the leading colored ministers, the General Conference of the Mother Church delegated their bishops, with other distinguished ministers and laymen, to organize the colored members into a separate and distinct body, which was satisfactorily consummated in December of the same year (1810).

The organization of this branch of our common Methodism seemed necessary for several reasons.

Among them we may note the following: As a result, the war had changed the ancient relation of master and servant. The former, though divested of his slaves, yet carried with him all the notions, feelings and elements in his religious and social life that characterized his former years. On the other hand, the emancipated slave had but little in common with the former master. In fact, he had nothing but his religion, poverty and ignorance. With social elements so distinct and dissimilar, the best results of a common church relation could not be expected. Harmony, friendship and peaceful co-operation between the two peoples in the propagation of a divine and vital Christianity, were among the essential elements of a successful evangelization of the people of color. Social religious equality, as well as any other kind of social equality, was utterly impracticable and undesirable, and coveted by neither class of persons composing a churchship.

With this state of things steadily in view, we had but one horn of the dilemma left us, and that was a free, friendly and authorized separation from the mother body. Although we are become two bands, yet it is, and was understood that this does not, in any sense, release the Methodist Episcopal Church, South, from those duties and obligations that Providence seems to have imposed upon her, in aiding the American African in his Christian development.

The Colored Methodist Episcopal Church in America has had a remarkable career. As a branch or product of the Methodist Episcopal Church, South, it has been opposed by strong hands and accomplished leaders among the colored people, from its birthday to the present; though, happily for us, these oppositions are now subsiding and the young organization is taking on a firm and expanding aspect that is most interesting and extraordinary. To sustain and propagate such an institution amid so many opposing forces as those that have presented themselves for the last twenty years, seemed, at first, to be a forlorn and hopeless undertaking. Green from the fields of slavery, raw in the experiences of church tactics, in membership and ministry, without houses of worship or literature, with many of its organizing feats being performed out of doors and under trees, it overcame difficulties that make it more than a mere experiment. Being in the dews of its youth, it has not yet attained its destined dignity and power for good among the colored race. But it is advancing in every department.

Its aim is the evangelization of the colored race. First, by preaching the pure and simple gospel of Christ to the masses, in the simplest form of speech. Second, to do this in the best and most effective manner, we aim, as far as possible, to establish and maintain schools for the impartation of Christian education among our people, and especially among the ministry, and that part of the race who are expecting to be teachers. As we cannot expect to do a great deal at present, by way of educating the masses, we begin with preachers and teachers, carefully and patiently training and indoctrinating them in those great moral and religious principles that lie at the base of an elevated and sound moral manhood. It is said that man is naturally a religious being. The sense of a Supreme Power intrudes itself upon all his spiritual and moral functions, and if men in general are thus religionists, the colored man is particularly so. He seems especially susceptible of religious culture and of reaching those spiritual climaxes and benedictions that have characterized the most pious of men. While these seem apparent facts, it is also apparent that all these safeguards of the gospel, and those that have grown out of the experiences of men, should be thrown around him, lest his Christian or religious zeal should subvert, cover or hide the weightier matters of the moral law, and those principles and practices that constitute the vital flame of the reformatory moral power of Christianity. Christianity pure and simple is what he needs. As a church, we came upon the stage of being to propagate the gospel along these lines and no others. To sustain this position we have always stood aloof from politics, not as individuals, but as officials representing an organization for a certain and specific purpose.

While our ministry and members represent all political parties and creeds, yet, as ministers of the gospel, we make no stump-speeches and fight no battles of the politicians. We think it better to "let the dead bury the dead," while we follow Christ. Of course we have no control over any man's vote; whether he be minister or member, he is free to vote as he pleases. We regard Christianity not only as reformatory and redeeming, but as a moral power of civilization. At present, it must be acknowledged that Negro civilization is yet in its infancy and crude evolutions. He is now laying the foundations upon which future generations are to build those institutions that are to make him and his progeny solid Christians and valued citizens. We regard him as a part of the people, a permanent fixture in the United States of America. It is true, we hope, that many of the race will, some day, go to Africa-- their native land--but the masses will fight the battle of life here, and live and die on the American continent. We also recognize the fact that he is, and will be, singularly and collectively, a separate and distinct race from the others.

Friction in church or state cannot be productive of good to him and his children, and we think it is a legitimate part of

Christianity to ameliorate and soften those cruder conditions under which he finds himself as an element in society; hence, we seek the friendship of all, and especially and particularly the fatherly directorship of the Methodist Episcopal Church, South. Beyond and behind the immediate work of the christianization of the colored race, there lie a faith, a principle, and a practice, that seem peculiar and interesting; and as these factors have done much to unite the races in harmonious co-operation and exile any hostile feelings that may have existed in the South between the two. Their aim is to bring about peace, and perpetuate the era of mutual brotherhood and concert of action.

We claim that the spirit, nature and practice of the Colored Methodist Episcopal Church in America have done, and are doing much in this direction. Some have thought that Providence has placed it where it is for this purpose. Already it has enlisted the special attention of the Methodist Episcopal Church, South, which by legislative action has appointed a Commissioner of Education for the purpose of establishing and maintaining schools for "the education of preachers and teachers," for the Colored Methodist Episcopal Church in America. This educational interest is controlled by the two churches jointly for the benefit of the Colored Church. It is the aim of this church to prosecute the work along these lines in the fear of God and in the love of a common humanity.

The Origin and Place of Religion in Civilization.

Religion may be defined as that service, consisting in worship, adoration and sacrifice which man renders to a supreme, or some being or beings that he supposes to be superior to himself--superior to himself in wisdom, power, knowledge, and indefinite existence.

The consciousness of a supreme, enduring, and all-pervading Energy is a faculty of the human mind. It is an ineradicable and indestructible element of man's nature. It is God-given, inherent, and not acquired by practice, reason, or learning. This religious faculty in man generates those elements of moral conceptions upon which the moral government of God is founded, and is the means of communication between the finite and the Infinite, and is that ever-present and far-reaching medium by which the voice of the Creator ever rings in the hearts of the created intelligences.

That man in his native elements is a religionist, not only accords with the history of the race, but is reasonable and consonant with his nature and the highest ends of his being. It is not necessary to be sinful before being religious. Had there been no sin in the universe, or no infraction of the laws that govern it, whether these laws be physical, mental, or spiritual, the religious faculty still would be a real and constituent part of all intelligences. As man is a thinking, free moral agency, he is necessarily a part of the great whole--a part of the great intelligent system. So far as the moral nature of man is concerned, it must be like that which all other moral beings have. The different spheres in the great moral system of the universe have no tendency to change the moral constitution so as to make it different in one class of moral beings from that in another, unless there could exist two moral systems in one, which is an absurdity. As there can be but one God, there can be but one government presiding over the whole. The moral laws are, therefore, the same in principle, and have the same ends in view in every part of the intelligent creation. It is also evident that the different modes of intelligent existence have nothing to do with the inherent qualities of their moral natures. Man would be man without his body or corporeal delineations, and angels would be none the less angels if clothed in mortal parts as we have. There may be lower and higher degrees of moral capability, as there are in intelligent capacity, but the innate and controlling principles are the same. As place and mode of existence cannot change moral law and moral nature in their inherent qualities, neither can the siege of ages nor the extending cycles. In other words, conditions cannot change the moral universe so as to make it something else different from what it is. It is what it is because it is the moral system. The system cannot be changed, any more than right can be made wrong, and wrong can be made right. It may be possible to annihilate the subjects of the moral system, and any physical part that may be connected with it, but not its inherent qualities. These are what they are because they cannot cease to be, nor grow into something else. Thus the moral system must remain forever intact in all the plentitude of its primary elements. If these premises are properly taken, then the government of God is necessarily a unit. It has an eternal oneness in nature and execution in all places and times, and is unaffected by mere conditions. While the moral system itself is distinct and different from its subjects or participants, yet it presupposes their existence, while, if they do exist, they cannot evade its obligations my more than they can evade the realization of their own being. Wherever there is intelligence, there must be consciousness and moral force and sense of obligation and responsibility. These are prominent faculties of the mind, and prove the existence of it, and force the thinking creature to think of his conscious moral obligations. Here, in the virgin soil of his nature, man finds those promptings, desires and proclivities that we might well call the religious faculty--faculty of his being, or attributes of his mental constitution. It is no argument against this position that some few have been found who are destitute of moral ideas and religious proclivities, if, indeed, there ever were such beings in existence. It is not to be denied that it is possible, in some cases, to suppress to a degree that is almost latent the religious faculty, yet in such cases these are no more silent and latent than the other faculties that are as little used. In any state below and on the line of civilization the human intellect will use those faculties that are most productive of the present and greatest good, because they are factors and manufactories of his immediate wants and daily needs. Forced by hunger and thirst, and the desire for the comforts of life, man, like the birds of prey or the beasts of the field, makes every effort to supply and provide himself with the things that seem needed for his happiness and well-being. Thus all his faculties that are useful for this purpose are especially aroused, cultivated, and stimulated to high degrees. By their use they are made more prominent and distinct. So with the religious faculties. They may be active or dormant to a greater or less degree by culture or less culture. So it is with all the attributes of the human mind. The Creator gave the mind complete in all its distinct attributes or characteristics, but its progressive development is left to conditions. How far mankind is responsible for favorable or unfavorable conditions in which to culture the mind need not now be elaborated. But sufficient has been said to disprove that, because the religious faculties are not particularly active in all, they do not naturally exist in any. The fact that all the great peoples of the earth have been religious is clear evidence that man is naturally so, and it also proves that every man is religious, except where the faculties and proclivities have been overshadowed by artificial means, as in the case of the atheist.

So far as we have come, we have dwelt upon the inherent emanations of religion in its origin, and we conclude that man is naturally a religious being, that the religious faculty is organic, God-given, and is an essential element of his being, and is just as enduring and abiding as any other attribute of his nature. He is, therefore, most natural when he is religious, and most unnatural when he is not religious.

False religion, so-called, is only a part of religion corrupted by superstitions, false additions, mutilations and erroneous interpretations. From the beginning it was not so. All the different forms of religious beliefs and faiths must have had the same beginning and the same parent stem. They must be branches of the same vine, or ramifications of the same great original. All their great moral ideas that have come down to us through the ages came through different channels, but came from the same true and pure fountain whose great original is the Creator. He first gave to His human offsprings, by symbolic and oracular demonstrations, as well as by internal emanations, what He would have them do, and as the generations dispersed into different climes they carried with them the germ thoughts of religion. But being corrupted, these germ thoughts of religion did not reproduce their exact originals, and as time rolled on, the originals were more and more corrupted until complete reproduction was impossible.

Then human additions were made to take their places. Hence we have the so-called false religions. But let it be remembered, that one and all of these must have had a common origin.

The name of God, in some form, is common in all known languages, and is spelled with four letters in almost all of them, indicating the unity and oneness in the origin of religion. For instance, it is in Latin, Deus; Greek, Theos; Hebrew, Adon; Syriac, Adad; Arabian, Alla; Persian, Sjra; Tatarian, Idga; Egyptian, Aumn, or Zeut; East Indian, Esgi or Zenl; Japanese, Zain; Turkish, Addi; Scandivanian, Odin; Wallachian, Zenc; Croatian, Doga; Dalmatian, Rogt; Tyrrenian, Eher; Etruian, Chur; Margarian, Oese; Swedish, Gud; Irish, Dich; German, Gott; French, Dieu; Spanish, Dios; Peruvian, Lian; English, Deity, God.

As religion has a oneness in its origin, so the oldest form of it must have been monotheistic, and not polytheistic. And when God proclaimed himself to Israel as "one God," He merely reaffirmed the more ancient truth delivered to the first of his human offsprings. He uncovered what, in many instances, had been hidden for long ages, and the broken lines of the first principles of religion were gathered and rejoined in the brighter light of the ascending centuries. It is true that God represents himself by many names, but never as more than one Being. The Elohistic and Jehovistic views presented in Genesis present to the mind only an individual God. The first conceptions of His character and individual Being by His intelligent creatures was that of oneness. We could not suppose God to be more than one individual Being, and yet proclaiming himself to be more than one. That is, we could not suppose He would teach His natural offsprings what is not true, or false. God can only speak truth.

Again, as God is one, and religion has a oneness in origin, so its first great moral idea is one, which is the conception of Deity. The first thing in worship or adoration is the attraction of the one to be adored. And if there are, in the religions of the world, polytheistic ideas (and there are), they are subsequent additions or interpolations. But no matter what may have been the changes transpiring under varied conditions and diversified experiences of mankind, adoration has always been the central moral idea of religion. So far as we know, it is so in all religions, among all peoples and ages. And so far as this central idea goes, all religions are true when directed to the only one true God. The term, "false religions," is a misnomer, if we include the honest adoration of the heart. The object may be false, but not the adoration or the religion. It is possible for a man to be honest, even when he adores a false deity, if he knows no better way to be religious. To that extent all religions are true. The cardinal idea, then, is to worship or to adore the Supreme Being, or any being whom the worshipper supposes supreme. This is the first great moral idea in religion, whether it be the Christian or any other religion. And this great moral idea, found in all religions, and in all ages, takes us back to the oneness of origin, where God first gave His commandments to the sons of men. Religion rests, not only upon the nature of man as regards his needs, but rests equally upon philosophical bases. Of course, there is much connected with religion that is not religious, nor religion. When we go out into the kingdom and vast domain of religion, and view its subjects and the results of its long and continuous administration through the ages, we conceive that it has a powerful and indestructible grasp upon human nature. This is so, not only because religion is a fixed faculty in the nature of moral beings, but also because it rests upon philosophical bases, found in the needs of man and the government of God. If there is a supreme moral Governor of the universe, then men and angels, or all intelligences come within the limits of that supreme moral government. When, therefore, adoration is demanded by the Creator, it is the most reasonable service, and the greatest that may be rendered to the great Author of being. Man is not his own creator. He did not make himself nor institute the laws by which he came into being; he has no power to create or to spring from elements already in existence. No affinity of co-operative forces, controlling precipitant elements, could produce and round into the masterly parts displayed in the constitution of man. That which did not previously exist, could not, of itself, begin to be. If it began to be, there must have been a creative force and fiat that lay deeper and beyond. Hence, intelligent creatures are all dependent--dependent upon that creative force and fiat that gave them being. What, then, is more reasonable than the praise and the adoration which mankind is required to render to God? By this we acknowledge his supreme greatness, his authority, power, and glory. By this the moral organs and mental sensibility come in contact with the Creator, and the harmonious relations of the finite and Infinite are kept in unison throughout an indefinite line of being in the moral system. Remove religion from the intelligent sphere, and the harmonious relations between God and His intelligent creatures are broken off, and sin and rebellion are the natural results.

So far we have dwelt upon religion, pure and simple, as to the oneness of its origin, and as a faculty of the human race.

Christianity is all of religion, and more than mere religion. Religion is a part of Christianity, but not all of Christianity. Religion is the nucleus of light in the moral system. Christianity is the meridian sun of its day. One is the seed planted and germinating, the other is the ripening corn in the ear. Yet, as the seed and ear are the same, so is religion and Christianity. They are two parts of a great whole in the developing and expanding moral system. Christianity reveals God and His government, not in a contrary nature, but in the more radiant splendors of the rising day and ascending centuries. Christianity is not only the doctrines and precepts of Christ, but a farther definition and clearer interpretation of the moral faculty and adoring proclivities of intelligent agents. It calls man to the worship and service of the Supreme Creator in stronger tones and deeper accents of love. It gathers up the broken threads of the ages, and rallies the moral forces to one bright center, and by its elective affinity, gathers all the gems of truth, and wreathes them about the brow of Christ. But religion is a sleepless active force in civilization. It is not bound by continents or ages. It is more than national, and more than cosmopolitan. As it is superhuman in its origin, it is universal in its operative function. Everywhere it has left its imprint upon individual character and national life. Christianity is not an ethnic religion, but the real and absolute religion of mankind. It is the religion of the universe, because it is obedience to God, love, and righteousness. It is an unchangeable fact, and abides forever the richest inheritance of man and angels. Its career is coeval with all the intellectual offsprings of God, and cognate with their incipient conceptions of Deity. They cannot think of themselves nor contemplate the dignity and wonders of creation without contemplating the masterly Hand that gave them their being. Everywhere God impresses himself upon His works. Every spring of the intelligent mind bounds toward Him. Ethereal splendors and terrestrial wonders attract every mind and thrill every heart.

As a factor and element in human civilization, it is the strongest, and the most vivacious of all the regenerative forces among men. Step by step, it has weighed the nations in its scales, and measured the civilizations of the world. All the virtue and respect for law and order that have prevailed among the civilizations of man, have had their foundation in his religious proclivity. It awakens the most astounding inquiries respecting the greatest interests of man and God. It gives wings to the imagination, faith to the life, and light and energy to the understanding, and reveals to man that which he could not discover. It enlarges the desire, quickens the spiritual force, and expands the spiritual entities. Christianity is the only system that places man in his real and true relation to God, his Father, and man, his brother. All the great moral ideas that underlie the governments and institutions of mankind which have stood the shock of ages and the ravages of time, have lived because of those grains of religion that have more or less been prominent in their constitutional and executive fitness. The strength and durability of human governments do not lie in their mere capacity, force or power, arising from numbers, wealth and intelligence. Of course these elements are essentials of government, but not the preservatives. Back of these there must be a dominant force--a silent energy--far more reaching and widespread than mere

capacity founded upon the devices and achievements of the intellect. The cornerstone of enduring institutions must necessarily be founded upon truth and rectitude--the love of virtue and the fear of God--which are the essential parts or ideal contingencies of practical religion. To put the case in clearer light, we point with a sigh to the decay of all the great governments and empires that have acted their part in the ages and the dramas of nations. They were great, strong, rich and mighty in word and deed, but they passed away because they violated all those great principles, promptings and practices that are the only fundamental basis of enduring institutions. No law of right, whether in heaven or earth, can be violated by intelligent beings unless they suffer at some time and in some place condign punishment. Religion in civilization is, therefore, not the criterion and revealer to aspiring humanity only, but it presents the reasons
why kingdoms fail and governments perish. There is nothing in the nature and theory of human government why they should not continue indefinitely. In themselves they are neither sinful nor useless. They are the God-given instruments to promote the greatest good and the universal well-being of man. But when they defeat the ends of righteousness, only one thing can follow, and that is, "eternal sleep." Still, as from the broken trunks of fallen trees, new growths repeat the acts of sires, so new nations arise upon the stocks of their predecessors, in which is continued the civilizations of the world. Civilization is but the product, or offspring of religion. Among the earliest of religious thoughts, come those efforts and inventions that have laid the foundation for civil and social comfort, and the employment of those resources and powers of mental and physical nature by which mankind has triumphed over difficulties and made obstinate elements yield

their richest treasures to his happiness and glory. While religion is adorative in its primitive emanations, operating in the deepest centers of character, yet it begets a lively hope and struggles for the larger goal beyond, where all the elements of expanding character and mental growth seek and use the fittest means to accomplish the fittest ends. Civilization is the difference between the kingdom of Dahomey and the British Isles. In the beginning both were alike--crude, low, vulgar, and beastly--in their primitive modes. The best explanation that may be given respecting the long distance between the two is: One is Christian and the other heathen--one religious intelligently, and the other religious superstitiously. The one has great intellectual light, which is largely the force of Christianity, while the other has less light with but the alphabet of civilization. Indeed, religion and civilization are so near akin that to destroy religion or remove it entirely from the state and the thoughts of men, there would remain no more of the one than of the other. The native constitution of man with his environments forbids him to be truly civilized without religion, or the prominence of the religious faculty. The place of religion in civilization is, therefore, to force its quickening energies along its lines and serial developments, and expand its golden peripheries amid the sleepless evolution of the ages. Its office is to elevate the standard of taste, direct the moral propulsion and dignity of humanity in all its phases.

The prominent features of Christianity are its progressive and aggressive forces. It cannot absorb, but it disintegrates. It cannot change its teachings, practices, nor phases any more than it can change its origin and nature. Its momentum and agencies may be variant, but its inherent elements are changeless and eternal. There are depths and heights in the evolving problems of Christianity that can only come in the fullness of its career among the peoples of the world. Its inventory of successive manifestations constantly presents the moral and physical systems, in more exalted fitness, as the only instrumentality to bring out the highest and purest forms of social and civil life. Everywhere its theory of morals and purity of life present the highest ideal of perfection. It is the universal code without a codicil. It is so universal and minutely applicable that there is no room in the boundless sphere of being for another. No other system can take its place among intelligent beings, because it has all the place that can be occupied. It forces man to think of God, of heaven, of hell, and those solemn and substantial realities that await him in the endless future. All of its proposed measures, tenets and doctrines are directed toward the amelioration of the race of man. Man could not expect any richer inheritance from the Almighty Parent; for he had nothing better to bestow upon his offspring.

Christianity is never the foe of man, but is always the foe of his foes, and as an armed sentinel it exists to guard all the interests of the children of men, in all those great concerns and multiform relations that make up the history of being. It is not only progressive, but aggressive. It comes to assault sin and evil in all their rock-ribbed and steel-clad ramparts. It has an arm of power, backed by infinite resources, even the whole breadth, depth, and height of the changeless Absolute. Slowly but surely it is at work upon the world's civilizations, transforming society, changing sentiment and human thought, correcting judgment, enthroning reason, imparting justice and crowning wisdom with the diadem of truth. It hushes the din of battles, breaks the iron sinews of bloody strife, stops the pursuits of war, and as sweetly and softly as fall the silent rays of the setting sun, it calls the nations to the legitimate avocations of life. Christianity is here to stay as long as this terrestrial sphere is the arena of thought and action. It seeks not the favor of the rich, nor the hand of the powerful, nor does it need the doctrinal skill of the philosopher, nor the metaphysics of the metaphysician. Neither does it lean upon the arm of kings and princes, nor the subtle diplomacy of skilled statesmen. It seeks not the palaces of the great and noble lords of earth, nor the hoarded treasures of the miser. It lives with, or without the sacerdotal robe, and is often driven from the paraphernalia of priestly dignity and ecclesiastic authority. It lives through the fiercest ordeals, sparkles in the furnaces of afflictions, coming out without the smell of fire upon its garments. It lives in caves and dells, sings from the tops of mountains, shouts from the lions' den, and presides in the gorgeous palaces of kings and princes. It thrives in the midst of famine, lives in the path of blood and revolution, and shines and glows in the luster of its own diamond brightness when civil and political systems perish and dance on to annihilation. "The earth is the Lord's, and the fullness thereof."

Amalgamation or Miscegenation.

Nothing has such a tremendous and powerful influence upon racial and human destiny in their final results, as to national phases and political conditions, as the passions and unbridled lusts of men. This is especially true of that class or people that rules over another class or people. No matter how great the social chasm between the upper and the nether people dwelling together in the same country or territory, the upper will seek the lower at that point of contactability and clandestine intercourse where there is mixing, The craving, heaving and impulsive passion of men, goads them on to blacklisted indulgences that even racial prejudices, many of which are stronger than death, cannot restrain. Even when the two peoples live in separate climes, divided by wide seas, high mountains and extended plains, they will seek each other in that way so as to produce another race and a new progeny. It matters not what distinctions, racial or national, there may exist between the peoples dwelling together, those who are regarded as inferiors will be sought after and will be debased by the superior. They proceed upon the theory that those who are already debased and contaminated cannot be more debauched or lowered in the moral scale than they are, and therefore it is a matter of small import to add to the sum of villainy, vileness and crime. Not that it is a crime for the races to intermix according to the laws of the land, as it may be done in almost all the countries on the earth; but the way amalgamation has been brought about in these Southern States is enough to make the bushmen in the wild jungles blush with shame. There is nothing in amalgamation sinful or wrong, providing it is legal, or done according to the laws of the land. So far as we can see, there is nothing in the nature of the different races of mankind to prohibit legal marriages between them. There is no real fundamental or inherent constitutional differences that can be urged as an objection. It is true that many claim that some races of men are constitutionally superior to others; that the white man is naturally, inherently, superior to the African and the Negro; that Indians, Malays and Chinese are really and constitutionally the deficient races, and cannot measure or cope with the Caucassian intellectually, and are therefore inferior in their creation. If they are inferior in their creation, then they are incapable of reaching that high moral intellectual status that seems inherent in the Caucassian. But there are many things connected with this question that contradict this position: 1. It is to be acknowledged that there are degrees of differences among the races of mankind; but these differences are conditional and circumstantial rather than constitutional. No man is born higher, purer, and better than another, so far as his real nature and the faculties of his humanity are concerned. One man may be superior to another in degree of learning, refinement and intellectual acquisitions; but this is in degree and not in kinds. The difference is the same as that which is between quantity and quality in any two given substances. The difference is not in the constituent elements that make up the one or the other, but in the degrees in the best elements that have the largest and most extended part in the substance. There is a great difference between the cultivated and the uncultivated mind, and in some instances there seems to be an almost infinite difference. That is, one seems almost infinitely above the other in degrees of mind culture and mental ability; but this does not show natural or native superiority.

It only shows superior training, higher culture, and better conditions. The untrained and the uncultured have as many faculties of the mind as the refined and the intelligent. Both characters have the same mental and metaphysical constitutions. The province of knowledge is not to create, but to discover, or uncover and set in their native light the things that are already in existence. It is above the power of the human mind to create, or bring from naught to being a single atom in the universe. If new things appear to the learned and the cultured, they are not new in their elementary parts, but new only in their relations and discovery. That is, they existed and had their relations to other things before they were seen by the mind, or comprehended by the reasoning faculties. If it was possible for one mind to create--to make substance from nothing--and impossible for another mind to create, then the former would be inherently and really superior to the latter. Upon this hypothesis men would not be created free and equal, but one constitutionally superior to the other.

2. The highest culture, discovery and learning of those whose ancestry have had superior advantages for centuries (not excepting the greatest minds that have acted upon the arena of life), have never been able to make or add a single new faculty to the human mentality; but men have been found in all ages and countries and nations and conditions, to have the same kind of minds and the same number of faculties, physical and moral. Whatever, therefore, is possible for one man, is possible for the generality of men, so far as their mental qualities are concerned. All the superior intelligence and the achievements of culture that are apparent among men are not founded on a higher native ability, but on the degrees of culture and intellectual altitudes that have

been attained by education and training. They are the natural result of labor bestowed upon the mental man. Culture not only develops the mind and extends the domain of thought and widens the mental possibilities, but, as a natural consequence, the mental actions and the mental forces have much to do with the physical stature, both directly and indirectly. Directly, because the body is the outward or physical instrument of the mind. It acts as it is acted upon by the spiritual and living reality that dwells within. Ambition, desires and aspirations, like perturbation, melancholia and hypochondria, all have their mighty and changing influences upon the physical and bodily proportions. Equally is it true that joy, hope and anticipations, like angels, bring the light of heaven upon their golden wings to the despondent and unhappy, physically as well as mentally. Indirectly, men are under attending influences of which they are not always cognizant. Many things are done from the force of habit, taste and custom, when there is no real reason for it. Men are partakers of the influences that surround them in spite of any resistance which they may make. Hence, one type of social and civic life may be easily engrafted upon another, until the former loses its identity in the engulfing personnel of the latter; and what was once two distinct phases of civil life becomes one unconsciously. It is by this absorbing and assimilating process that all civilizations are to become one in fact, if not in type and phase. The aims and bottom principles of civilization are always the same, since they must act upon human nature with the same ends in view. Civic, social and religious regeneration can only reach or attain its ends by this absorbing and assimilating process, and this process is accelerated when the introduction of the better elements is made and the evils are eliminated. Hence, men yield to the conditions that surround them, and yield unconsciously.

3. If there were any real constitutional differences in the races of mankind, the process of amalgamation could not proceed at all. The great disparity between the very superior and the very inferior would prevent, on natural and philosophical principles, the possibility of a progeny. There could be no half-breeds, nor cross-bloods, nor mongrel races or peoples, but there would have been but one race; and that one race would have maintained its perfect identity and individualism through all the decades and centuries. Vile Sodomy, for which "the cities of the plains were overthrown," has never yet produced a single man or woman, nor is it a thing that is possible to be done. "The reign of law and the unity of nature" forbid the monstrosity. This goes to show, not only the superiority of man over the beasts, but it shows also the unity of the human race.

4. It is in the conception of mankind that "all men are created free and equal," because the moral requirements, at least in civilized countries, are the same for all men. The same law that presides over the intelligent, the educated and the learned, presides over the ignorant, the uneducated and the unlearned alike. Ignorance of the moral and civic features of the law makes no difference whatever on account of race, color, or condition. This is not only true as regards human laws, but the Divine government in its righteous requirements makes no difference in its application of the law on account of a man belonging to this, that or the other race. All are treated as equals before the law, in their punishments and in their rewards. From this it seems clear that if one race of

men wore innately superior to another race then more than one law would have to be established and executed for the one in distinction from the other. Or, if the same law, as now, is to be applied to all men, one race being superior to the other, then there must be degrees in the same law to be applied according to the guilt or innocence of the persons concerned. But we see the beauty of human and divine law executed alike upon all classes and races of men with the same ends in view, namely, to preserve the government of God for the happiness of the universe.

In the Southern States the colored man is treated and regarded as an inferior. The public conscience has been educated under distorted views and a vicious sentimentalism by which nearly all of his civil rights have been abridged, if not entirely destroyed; yet the shameful practice of illegal and damnable miscegenation goes on without let or hindrance. While we deplore this state of things, and while we know of no practical remedy, yet we believe that the hand of God will overrule it all in such a way as to promote the national and international harmony, peace and prosperity of universal man.

Speech Delivered Before Several Conferences of the M. E. Church, South.

Mr. President and Brethren of the Conference:

It is with great pleasure and profound respect that I appear before you on this occasion. I count it an honor as well as a pleasure to meet and to greet those lofty characters and princely heroes who bear the name and do the work of Methodist preachers. They are not only princely and heroic, but they constitute the world's greatest, and the most active moral force that comes within the limits of human agency. In their reformative movements, they are like "the living creatures" of Ezekiel's wheels who run and return at God's command, thread and ramify the zones of civil and uncivil man, filling the world with the light of God, the majesty of His love, and the splendors of His grace. It is by your grace and Christian charity that I shall attempt to speak to you upon a question of vital interest, both to your people and to mine.

In 1882, the General Conference of the M. E. Church, South, authorized the establishment and maintenance of a school for the training of preachers and teachers for "the Colored Methodist Episcopal Church in America," and accordingly in the winter of 1883 the school was organized, and the Board of Trustees gave it the name of "The Paine Institute," in honor of the then venerable Senior Bishop of the M. E. Church, South, who also, with the assistance of Bishop McTyeire organized the Colored branch of the Church, and ordained its two first Bishops. Augusta, Ga., was selected as the place of its location. For several years the school was taught in rented houses, but by the fortunate turn of events we went near the suburbs of the city and purchased the place that we now have, a beautiful site of ten acres of ground on an eminence overlooking the beautiful city of Augusta. This place was the home of a wealthy citizen, and contained his residence and outer buildings, which were his barns and stables. These were fitted up at small cost for dormitories and recitation rooms. Here the school has been taught for more than twelve years, and here it is still being taught.

Dr. Morgan Calloway, who was the Vice-President of Emory College, was its organizer and first principal, having as his assistant the Rev. George Williams Walker, of the South Carolina Conference, who has always been with the school, and is its present faithful and honored President.

The establishment and maintenance of this school is the official work of the M. E. Church, South, and the only official work which that great church is now doing for the Afro-Americans in this country. We have reached that period in its work and history where its facilities for continued service and usefulness must be enlarged or else the prosecution of its work must stop. A building is indispensable and absolutely necessary. Seeing this condition of things, the Board of Education of the M. E. Church, South, at its last session, "being fully persuaded of the imperative need of a new building at Paine Institute, Augusta, Ga., determined to undertake at once the erection of the new building," and I have been sent out by that board and the Board of Trustees to solicit your aid and co-operation, that the great work of

Christianization of the Negro race may be enlarged and continued by the Christian people of this country.

The greatest single factor in the happiness of universal humanity is ideal Christianity, and the greatest work that can be done by man is the propagation of its truths, and the practical application of its principles. You need no especial argument to prove this position to be scriptural, philosophical, and divine. Christianity is the people's religion, and comes to the great world as God's greatest gift to all the long centuries of suffering humanity. It belongs to man in the broadest sense and in its minutest and deepest application. It belongs to man in every phase of life, and in every phase and zone of his cosmopolitan character. It has like effects upon all the branches and divisions of the human race. Zones and parallels, and the character of civil, and the modes of incivil life, may change the physical aspect of man, beast, and flower, but divine Christianity knows no change, but, like the rose of eternal truth, forever buds and blooms upon its own native stock, kissing the ages of God in its own diamond brightness. Everywhere Christianity is emphatically Christianity, and everywhere it is propagated and planted in its purest forms and highest ideals, it produces itself in its native plenitude, bringing forth the cornerstone of its expanding empire, crying, "Grace, grace unto it." There is no work like that of human redemption. There is no avocation beneath the sun or amid the awful tread of the cycles that can be compared to it. Indeed, as we have said, the greatest work that man can do is that of seeking and saving the lost. Jesus Christ himself set the example when he came as the Apostle of human salvation; for, says he, "The Son of Man is come to seek and to gave that which was lost."

Whatever people, nation, or race, has Christianity in its highest ideals and purest forms, it is to that extent responsible to God and to humanity for the salvation of the world and the redemption of man. It is a joyous truth, as we as an efficient agency, to solve all great problems, to reform all civilizations, banish the errors of men, clear the moral atmosphere of the pestilential seeds of falsehood and mental debasement, and save all men from sin and that death that never dies.

On all great occasions, and in every crisis of evolving humanity, it has met the demands at the threshold of conflicting elements, adjusted the jarring forces, and filled the centers and ramified the expanding peripheries with its own greatness and ineffable fulness.

It is also a happy thought that Christianity knows no distinction of race or color or previous condition. It knows no racial lines nor national boundaries, but leaps the continents, plays on the silver-crowned waves of the seas, kisses the islands with the kisses of truth, sweeps the plains with its wing of flame, spreading its heavenly insignia over all the sorrowing sons of Adam and the weeping daughters of Eve. But as human work or labor is the greatest factor in the spread of the Gospel, and is the God-appointed method of its propagation, all Christians are called upon to contribute their quantum to the world's salvation.

Christian Europe and Christian America are at present the great receptacles of the Christian religion, the repositories of "the truth," and are the spiritual and physical dynamos that must thrill the world with its propulsions and redemptive entities and agencies. From what other point of the compass, in the moral hemisphere, shall Christianity gather its strength and radiate the circles and traverse the lines of human development?

The Negro is here and en masse he is here to stay. He is an important part of the body politic. He belongs to it as the foot or hand belongs to the human body. As such he is a factor in the growth and development of this great civilization. Providence placed him here on the American continent, and has suggested no way for his exit or elimination. Evidently he is here for a purpose. Slavery was only the occasion by which he came. It was not the end. Nay, God had greater ends in view. As there are something like two hundred and fifty millions of heathens in Africa, and as it seems evident that the educated and Christianized black man is best fitted for the preaching of the Gospel in "the Dark Continent," so Christian America, out of its eight or ten millions of Negroes, must produce that massive band of ebony-hued heroes by whom their fatherland is to be redeemed. More and more it seems apparent that American slavery was providential. It matters not how deeply hidden or intricate the threads and lines of Divine Providence may appear to be in the human concepts, one thing is clear, and that is the Negro race has lost nothing by it, but has gained a thousand pounds sterling where it lost a penny. It is true that the Master enslaved himself, and was a slave of slaves, but the asperities of the now defunct institution were struck off and wonderfully mitigated by that beautiful and lavish hand of Christian charity and evangelistic labors bestowed upon the sons and daughters of Ham by the Southern Methodist people. The Negro did not march out of slavery empty-handed, but, like Israel of old, came out with the rings and jewels of a better civilization, and with the crown of truth upon his head, and with a wreath of grace upon his brow and the golden cup of salvation in the mouth of his sack. He came out with deep touches of your Christianity and flashes of your civilization, and received an upward propulsion that he could not have obtained in his native land.

But emancipation did not abrogate moral obligation. Relations were changed, but humanity and Christianity remained intact, and the Negro is yet in the twilight dawn of a Christian civilization. He still needs help. He needs Christianity in purer phases and broader morality and higher forms in its reformative and practical ends.

We admire that noble spirit and broad Christian charity that sends your heroic and consecrated men and women flashing across the vasty deep to preach the Gospel in the regions beyond. We admire and almost adore that Christ-like devotedness shown by those who go or by those who send. It is high, holy and angelic and resplendent with the seraphic flame of love. This, it is clear, is your plainest duty, and we thank God that you are doing it. Every day you are preaching and singing to the heathens "the old, old story of Jesus and his love." You are sowing the vital seeds of the vital truth in foreign lands, and the living propagators are heralding the melodies of the redemptive scheme, and unfurling the blood-stained banner of the cross, and as the word of God cannot fail there must be fruitage in approaching days; but here at your doors, in your streets and lanes, in your great cities and rural districts, are heathens who sit "in darkness" and "in the regions and shadow of death," that need your aid, and have first claims upon your liberality and Christian charity. As their representative,

I come to rehearse and to reverberate the thrilling and all-awaking Macedonian cry.

But you know the Negro. He is no stranger to you. He has been with you all along through the diversified and changing decades of two hundred and fifty years. He is still the laborer, the mudsill of society, and the crudest part of the social fabric.

In the early decades of the American empire of sovereign and independent States, and when this now mighty empire of States was an infant of days, the Negro stood by its cradle, and helped it to break and unwind its swaddling bands of childhood, and labored to crown its youth with glory, and its manhood with a diadem of golden stars. He has been and is still a powerful factor in the development of this country, and the expansion of its civilization. His strong arm felled the forests, dried the swamps, cleared the bogs, threw the sunlight upon its shady dales, made the deserts to blush with flowers, the fields to smile with plenty, and threw up a royal highway for a triumphant civilization. He clothed your daughters with scarlet, your sisters with gowns of silk, and your queenly ladies and "high-born beauties" with jewels, and pinned the wreath of diamonds upon their brow. When the war came, and the flower of the land were slain upon its high places; when blood flowed and carnage and death swept the Southern tier of States; when your fathers, sons, and brothers were at the front upon the field of battle, the Negro stood by you. He planted the fields, sowed and reaped, and bent with devotion and silent energy over the plowshare, and made bread and clothing for the armies and the defenseless mothers, sisters, and little children at home. The black women--the sable daughters of toil and of song--nursed your children, gave them the milk of kindness from their own breasts, and with tender care, and the soft touches of love, and the dulcet strains of sweetest carols in cadence low, they sang the child angel to sweet repose. In kitchen, hall, dining room, and sick chamber, these black maidens of love and tenderness carried the sunshine of God, filled ten thousand homes with hope and comfort. Likewise "the brother in black" cared for your sick, buried your dead, wept over your slain, and with arms of iron and fingers of steel wrote angelic deeds of kindness upon the open scroll of two centuries and a half. The Negro shared in your sorrows and rejoiced in your prosperity, and in the great civil onflow of the age he is your armor-bearer. When freedom came, it came without his seeking or any effort on his part, for it was in the divine decrees that he should be free. Even then he did not forsake you nor the land of his nativity, but regathered the broken cords of an ancient civilization, and like the moving phalanx of a great army, or the steady flow of the Nile, he continued with the even tenor of his way. Nowhere has he broken friendship with you, or left the old landmarks of love and esteem. Though we are two distinct peoples, or two great bands in one great nation, there is a common interest and a common destiny. Whatever results may come from such a combination, it must take place in our common country. Whatever affects you, affects us. Whatever advances your interest, must, in a greater or less degree, advance ours. We live in the same zone, born on the same soil, breathe the same vital air, drink from the same streams, bask in the same sunshine, and in the silent cities of the dead we shall dwell together until the trump of the Archangel and the deep rolling thunders of the judgment shall summon us to stand before the Great Judge of all. We profess the same religion, read the same Bible, sing the same songs. Indeed, your religion is our religion, your church is our church, your God is our God, your Christ is our Christ, your heaven is our heaven, and your hell is our hell.

You need our brawn and muscle; we need your brain and culture. You need our sinews of brass and bones of iron. We need your steady hand to prosecute the noble ends of life, and the triumphs of a Christian civilization. You have the mental force, we have the physical power, and I come to plead for a combination of both, united in a grand national manhood, so attuned and attenuated that the national mechanism may play in harmony as the mechanism of a great steam engine. Why not?

Of course you know our church was organized by your great church, and we delight to honor our parentage and are proud of our origin. In 1870, we were "set up" as a distinct and independent branch of the great Methodist family by and under the authority of the Methodist Episcopal Church, South. I understand that we were "set up" and not "set off." In no sense does this "setting up" business destroy, neither was it intended to destroy the religious inter-racial relation that had obtained in days of old. We are the same sable sons and sable daughters whom your noble sires and princely men taught the way of life, and who the sugar zones, the rice belts and the cotton empires of the South labored to make them sons and daughters of the Lord Almighty. We are the "offspring," the legitimate ecclesiastical children of the church of which you are representatives. We have kept "the faith once delivered to the saints; and as yet" there "is no variableness nor shadow of turning." Radiating from the central sun of Wesleyan Methodism, and glowing in the heat and activity of its power, like an arrow from its bow we are striking off in straight lines of truth and love, preaching the simple Gospel of the Cross.

The new building that is now in process of erection at Paine Institute is to be called "The Haygood Memorial Hall," as a monument to that great man, who stood for so many years as a wall of brass in the defense of the Negro race in this country. In him, the Negro race had its strongest, its broadest, its truest, and its most eloquent and sincere friend. He was our Martin Luther, who with pen and voice, and with the deepest flow of soul, stood at the foot of the cross, and amid the declining decades of the dying century wrote his theses and nailed them upon the door of public opinion, and changed the tide of public sentiment in this country in behalf of the Negro race. He is not dead. He has only ascended to the city beyond the stars of God, while his thundering theses, so ably advocated, are ringing through the decades and over the surging waves of the expanding civilization, appealing to the considerate judgment, the patience and Christian charity of the Christian people of this country. Negroes should build it monument of steel to his precious memory higher than the Eifel tower, covered with gold and tipped with diamonds.

But there is a higher motive, a loftier impulse, to which we appeal. The Negro is a man, an immortal soul. Like the balance of the human race, he must be saved or lost. Christ died for him, as he died for all others. He is within the limits of the covenanted grace, a lost jewel carved out by the hand of God. He is an indestructible, self-conscious entity, "made in the image of God." Thousands, if not millions, of them were preached to and taught the way of life by the Southern Methodist preachers. They were not wise, great or rich, neither could they fathom the profundities of the intellectual deeps, or span the zones of thought, philosophy and research, but they understood the spiritual power and the essentialities of simple Christianity, and the power of saving grace. Day by day, through the long years of sweat and toil, their simple Christianity spoke to them in golden sentences, and brought to them the cheering news of God and the joys of his Christ. Tens of thousands lived in the truth of the Gospel, died in the triumphs of a living faith, and on the burning wings of the plantation melodies they swept the airy path of the ethereal seas, and fled to heaven and to God.

Religion.

Whatever may be the various phases or aspects of religion that have existed among the different branches of the human race, and which present themselves for the consideration of the thoughtful and philosophic, to be true in itself and of itself, must be of one origin and of one nature. Not only is this true, but all religion must spring from a common center, and must rest upon the basic principles, strike the same chords in human nature, and have the same ends in view, namely, to please God and to benefit and bless intelligent natures in the highest possible degree. Religion was not made for man, nor for angels; but men and angels and all the high intelligences of the intelligent systems were made for religion. Hence, there is a fitness of corresponding adaptedness of the first and second subjects. This view of the subject must be true since the ground principles of religion are increatable and exist because of the nature of God and the principles upon which His government rests. Form and symbolism in religion have no real connection with its principles and its inherent elements, Principles and natures have no forms, although they are important agencies and powerful factors in preserving, developing, and propagating original religious ideas. Every form in religion at one time, and in some state or condition, had a meaning and was a symbolic representation of an impressive idea embodied in religion, whose intent and purpose looked deeper than the mere surface. The digits are not principles themselves any more than the rainbow is peace. The former represents mathematical principles in the science of the universe, while the latter is an emblem, in its seven-fold arch, of pacification, founded upon certain natural attitudes of matter. Both are mere representatives of abstract ideas, while their material outlines are the sensitive vehicles and exterior preservatives. So the symbolisms of religion are the sensible or tangible representatives of deeper truths or basic principles that lay in the realm of the abstract. All things not only come from the center, but all things tend toward the center. All actions, elements, and forces have objects and ends to attain, although their threads of relations and infinite intricacies, with their respective bearings upon the center and the circumference are beyond the limit of human or angelic concepts. In harmonious relations and mutual conditions, they play on all the threads of infinite design to magnify their functions in those depths, expansions, and altitudes where none but the Infinite treads the golden sands or traverses the open seas of limitless spaces, forcing the entities and activities to their centers or designed ends. From this view, the principle and fundamentals of religion lay beyond their symbols and are in the central zone of the abstract. The commands of religion may not always be understood by those who are commanded to obey its precepts; neither does that class always understand the symbols or reasons why, yet they must obey, because it is possible that they have not the full capacity to understand the whole nature and design, should they be explained to them. Perhaps, also, there are things in the establishment and economies of religion that none can understand, and in the notion of the Deity and divine things, that none can comprehend; therefore, obedience upon presumptive faith is the only prerogative of intelligent activities. Accordingly religion is of faith or reliances upon those subtle substances that belong to the fundamentals in the abstract.

All ideas of God came from God, independent of the creatures who received them. Their perfect ideals and concepts are not only grounded in the dual nature of man, but they are the perfect emanations of a full and perfect God or perfect original. All the ideas of men and angels have their first perfect parts in the Deity, and as they are grasped and apprehended, they are woven into the warp and woof of creature comprehension and must be obeyed. Everywhere the threads of God and religion interramify all intelligent natures. It is God that acts upon the sphere of being and pours Himself into the activities of force and universal existence. We cannot hide from God, nor from being, nor nullify the personnel of the self-consciousness, and therefore must assume all the responsibility that belongs to intelligent personalities. To obey the precepts of religion is, therefore, to obey the law of our being and the laws that govern all being. God is more obedient to the principles of religion than men or angels. That is, the laws of righteousness that He commands us to keep are binding upon Him in the highest degree, as well as upon all the intelligent offsprings of the universal system. He does not want us to do what He does not do. He loves and obeys all righteousness. He requires us to do nothing more, and we must do nothing less. Nothing is more natural than religion, and nothing is more unnatural than irreligion. There is no such thing as supernatural religion, if we mean by that term that religion, in its nature, requirements, and principles, is contrary to or above nature. It is not even superhuman, nor superangelic except in its degrees and effects. That is, no intellect nor mental capacity, God excepted, can comprehend the depth and infinite scope of religion in those endless and countless contingencies that operate in the government of God. Religion's eternal and unending principle begins in Deity, and lingers in the endless cycles, uniting all the depths of being, intensifying their forces and activities. In essence, native reality, and requirements, religion is not only always the same, but is as universal and as extensive as the peopled empire of God. It is the law of being, the natural law of the intelligent creation, bearing upon all in a greater or less degree. There is no heaven or hell, and no punishment or rewards without it. To obey its precepts is heaven, to disobey them is hell. The mental character is so constituted in the eternity of its native elements that it carries hell and disobedience together in the same bosom, while heaven and obedience are always found in the same place. In short, the fundamentals of religion are the moral code of the universe, as well as the inherent law of being in its moral capacity, since the moral nature has much, if not everything to do with, mental purity and development. As the internal influences the exterior, giving shape and tone to life, and ameliorating the public aspect of society, so the moral force expands mentality, accelerating its momentum toward the heaven of full capacity. The moral universe is an inclined plane along whose highway countless multitudes struggle up the steep ascent of development, experiencing the wonderful transitions that lay in the road to those galaxies of mental and moral acquisitions where the eldest children of eternity are crowned and glorified in the "Father's house of many mansions." Onward the struggling multitudes and spiritual caravans of the universe move, while sinking suns and crushing systems perish, and cycles upon cycles pile, ages crumble beneath the tread of the universal armies, marching to the music of the spheres and the drum the ages. Progression, eternal progression, is the order and law of being and intelligent natures, and, consequently, perpetual evolution and struggle for personal fitness and perfection.

Southern Methodism and the Slaves.

Living in the dimness or the days of slavery, few, if any, could prognosticate the future as to the social, political or religious outcome of the system of American slavery that then prevailed in the "Union of States." However unrighteous or repugnant to a Christian civilization the institution seems to have been, and whatever changes have come over the public mind since its abolition, one thing is clear, and that is, the Negro race has lost nothing by it, but has gained a thousand pounds sterling where it has lost a penny. It was one of those mysterious acts or permissions of the Divine administrations whose complicated connections and results we could not comprehend, but one in which was displayed the wisdom, power, and goodness of Him who doeth all things well. It is a trite saying, "all is well that ends well." It is a case where it seems that disease upon the body politic was necessary to heal. Both parties--the slave and slave-holder--were at fault. For some sins unknown to us in the Hametic line, perhaps coming down through the centuries of awful sweep, culminating in national dissolution and tribal confusion, the black man of Africa, when his iniquities came to the full had to suffer; and for every transgression the God of nations demanded principal and interest. The debt had to be paid, for "the wages of sin is death." But in enslaving the Negro, the master enslaved himself, and was himself a slave of slaves. His in the final settlement--God being the arbiter--was more, perhaps, than that of the man of black skin. But the system of slavery was wonderfully mitigated, and a heavy percentage of its asperities struck off by that beautiful and lavish hand of Christian charity and evangelistic labors bestowed upon the slaves by the Southern Methodists. Everywhere the sons and daughters of Ham were preached to, looked after, and sought out by a class of Methodist preachers with a care and pure simple devotion that were angelic, heavenly, and unparalleled in the annals of Christian charity and Christ-like devotion.

In those days there were intellectual giants and blazing seraphs of oratory whose piety was deep, all-spreading and bright as the morning star. None of them were afraid or ashamed to preach the gospel to Negroes. There was nothing like the simple gospel in those days, and nothing more beautiful and consistent than those faithful and true Negro veteran Christians that were the fruit of those great and noble men's labors for the salvation and Christianization of the Negro race. When the war came the Methodist Episcopal Church, South, had more than two hundred thousand persons of color in her membership, besides there was a large number of Sunday-schools, in which the best blood, both male and female, engaged in catechising and teaching the young Negroes the simple and fundamental principles of the gospel. Thousands of churches were built especially for the colored people, and often a pastor was sent to them as to the whites. Sometimes the Negroes got the best preacher and the most talented man. No matter what Methodist Church has come into the Southern States, it has simply built on the old foundation laid by "the Methodist Episcopal Church, South." That church justly claims the ground against all comers, all invasions and invaders. It laid the foundation deep, strong, and wide, upon which all subsequent buildings have been reared as religious and intellectual institutions established for the elevation and advancement of the Negro race. Every question has two sides to it, and whatever may be said about slavery and slaveholders does not concern us at present. To recall the past with its sleepy memories of strife and bitterness, recasting its shapeless forms into post-bellum thought, and thus confusing and confounding the present, is not only unwise and suicidal, but detrimental and obstructive to the progress of the colored race in too many ways to be mentioned. The earnest, consecrated and noble Southern men who proclaimed the gospel of salvation to the aspiring sons and daughters of Ham, were doing all they could under prevailing conditions, and the established laws, customs, and institutions of the land. Neither did they whine, nor sulk in the tents of idleness, nor consult the whimsical in human nature; but they consecrated their lives, their ease, and wealth, and, as apostles of the fullest and freest salvation, went forth to the black sons of Ham and founded enduring monuments to their greatness, and built a power-house of strength whose living and propulsive energies still thread and thrill the evangelistic forces and redemptive activities of all denominations. It may be truly said that the simple Christianity impressed upon the Negro race by these men of God in ante-bellum decades was the purest, the sublimest, and the most apostolic since the days of Pentecost, vieing with that of the Waldenses, the Huguenots, and those devoted Piedmontese who dwelt in their rock-bound land of the skies. There were Christians in those days. Black men and white men, black women and white women, lived for God and heaven, and the pure and simple Christ of the New Testament was the only most exalted and consummate ideal of the Christian life, while his death of perfect resignation was the plenary gauge by which they died. While other denominations helped to some small degree in preaching the Gospel to the slaves, yet the Methodists led the way, cleared the ground, and burnt the stubble with the ardent flames of love and sacred, far-reaching devotion that was pure, splendid and heroic. By their preaching and evangelistic labors, thousands, if not millions, of Negroes lived and died in the ecstacies of a living faith, and in "the mysterious translation," that awful flight to the celestial center, they fled on the burning wing of the plantation melodies to hymn in eternal anthems that Saviour preached to them by the Southern Methodist preachers.

The Papacy.

Whatever may betide the peace, the happiness, and the development of man in the onward trend of his civilization; whatever civil forms, social aspects, or religious tendencies may claim the attention of mankind, one of the most powerful and potent agencies that is to influence the destiny of nations is that wonderful and aged organization known as the papacy or the Catholic hierarchy. While we have no hatred or malice toward any man or set of men because of their church, faith, or religious opinions, yet, because of the doctrines, claims and fearful record of the Catholic church, it presents to-day, as of old, a profound study and the deepest concern. It is not denied that there are millions of honest hearts, pure souls and good Christian people in that church. Throughout its long tramp through the ages, amid the birth and death, of years and the mutations of centuries, many of its hehoic devotees and pronounced followers have stood as monuments of honor, piety and virtue. Many of its sainted heroes and majestic apostles shine in the galaxy of blazing suns and golden stars with an enduring and unfading lustre that shall outlast the roll of years and the flight of centuries. Their ancient priests with rosary and cross have traversed sea and land, and stood among the evanescencies and reversions of states and empires, and with tenderness and love have sought to bind up the broken-hearted and dry up the tears of the widow and orphan. They have stood amid contagions, epidemics and the wide sweep of endemics and the wild play of even "the black death." In the track of blood and revolution, and the debris of broken kingdoms and shattered empires, they have remembered the sons of toll and the daughters of misery.

The papal regime has produced scholars, poets, states, men, historians, inventors, explorers, lawyers, doctors, philosophers, discoverers, painters, and sculptors. Thus far the papacy has been an aid to mankind in his betterment and the expansion of the world's civilization. But perhaps one of the most noticeable and distinguishing characteristics of the papacy's history and procedure is its skill in art and sublimity in architecture. Grandeur in style, loftiness in dignity, and immensity in height and extent, are the ponderous faculties by which the multitudes of its blind and besotted devotees are overshadowed and awed into a profound reverence that makes the physical church everything, the invisible spirit of Christianity a little thing, and the freedom of the people nothing. Mountains of superstition rise, the church is greater than Christianity, and the Roman See the only lord and potentate. If there are seven wonders of the ancient world and seven wonders of the modern, the papacy is seven times more wonderful than each, and in its stability and blind assumption stands out in greatness and singleness of a sublimity that has awed the masters of the world. The multitudes of its followers eschew reason, surrender the rights of conscience, and implicitly obey the iron mandates and cosmopolitan edicts of the Roman See. In other words, the church is everything, principles and people nothing. As an organized institution, all the rights of conscience and the rights of men and nations are held subordinate to the rule, usages, history and doctrines of the church. Throughout its wide sway and long reign it has presumed to be the only church on earth, and the Pope is the vicegerent of Christ, the master of states and empires, the ruler of kings as well as the supreme ruler and pontiff of the universal church.

Now, it is not the individual persons of the Roman Catholic church that Protestant nations fear, neither can any reasonable man who believes in religious liberty and freedom of speech and conscience object to the church nor its peculiar doctrines and forms of worship. Every man is free, and ought to be free, to select any church, believe any doctrine, or espouse any form of worship which seems right to him. But this freedom certainly gives no license to go to the extent of interfering with the rights, privileges, and freedom of others, and when the church, so-called, attempts to limit or prescribe the faith and consciences of men, it becomes non-churched, and claims more authority than Jesus Christ himself. None but God, the Master and Supreme Ruler of the universe, can dictate to the consciences of men or prescribe their religious proclivities and aspirations. Eternal conformity to established forms of religious obligations, based on the mere demands of ecclesiastical legalism, is in no sense religion nor Christianity. To bow the knee and subscribe to dogma, leaving the heart untouched and the conscience unmoved, is not only irreligious, but is also the basest form of Pharisaism, a profane prostitution of the noblest powers of manhood and the sacred functions of religion.

From whatever standpoint we view the Catholic hierarchy, it presents to the considerate mind marvels that approximate the miraculous. To the superficial view it has the appearance of a perpetual and continuous miracle. It has a wonderful amount of tact, and an extent of versatility and adaptedness of stratagem that surpass anything that has occurred in the historic transactions of men. It lives while it is dead, and is dead while it lives. The defeats, repulsions and deadly wounds which it has received from the edicts of governments and acts of reformations, have never destroyed it, nor even paralyzed its life and energies. After all its baptisms of blood and fire, it has risen from the ashes of its death, stood upon the brink of its grave and smiled in triumph in the face of its powerful foes. It yields for a time in meek submission to Protestant thrones, reserving its latent forces and energies to rekindle its fires upon the expanding arenas of advancing civilizations. It is always, rising and coming amid changeful evolutions and eventful dispensations. It is ever the same in design, but ever changeful in its methods to reach its ends. Its propoganda is unscrupulous, besotted, superstitious and full of that blind bigotry that knows nothing but to demand obedience to the papal head. Its slogan is: "The means are sanctified by the ends." It is not a question of holiness and purity of the public morals, and freedom of the conscience, but with them the only question is, the extension of the Roman See and papal authority. In its lust for power and greed for universal conquest, anything and everything is right, and nothing is worth redemption but the church and the iron rule of the supreme Roman pontiff.

Romanism is a factor in human history, government and progress. Its effects and influence upon the political status of nations and kingdoms is weighty, far-reaching, and immense in results. It is the greatest antagonist of freedom of speech, of a free press and of a free religion. It is a grand oligarchy, with immense force and push--with cunning and skilful intrigue--in whose plenipotent fingers the threads of the universal octopus centralizes its splendid capabilities in a papal head.

The Roman Catholic church is incapable of progress except so far as it is necessary to preserve the church. It antagonizes higher education for the masses, and is a deadly foe to the public school system unless the public school system is entirely and completely under the control of the priests and bishops of the Catholic regime. Ignorance and mental darkness (with them) is better than light and freedom of thought and investigation by the masses better than that education that reaches those degrees of mental endowments and capacities, where the enlightened manhood may think for itself. It is a curious fact that the so-called "Church of God" should be afraid of the light of knowledge and the keenest investigation by an intelligent citizen. If it is "the true church of God," and is the pillar and ground work of the truth, why should it fear investigation? Truth has nothing to fear, but invites the keenest investigation and the profoundest criticism. There must be something wrong in the men or those doctrines and establishments that are afraid of calm review and the crucial test of keen criticism. If it is afraid to be weighed in the judgment of men and measured by the legal tests of enlightened reason, then it must have something about it that is inconsistent with the best interests and the highest aims and aspirations of man.

But it is certain that the nations of mankind have a subtle, schemeful and powerful foe to deal with--a foe whose gigantic arm of power sweeps the seas, grasps the islands with an iron grip; and wraps the belted zones of human civilization in the meshes of its nimble fingers, and with cords of steel and bands of iron ties them on to the papal car. Papal diplomacy is the most skilled and artful, and full of that cunning and manipulation that plays on human nature and pours itself into its superstitions, thrilling its religious faculties with the grandeur, augustness and bright paraphernalia of its orders and the tinsilized symbolisms of its public worship and service. Romanism claims all the churchism and prelatical authority that is worth claiming. There is nothing true, heavenly and divine, but that that is from the Roman See, or emanates from the pope and his great conclaves. His bulls, encyclicals and edicts, as excathredra, are the essence of unerring mandates and infallibility, and "the high arcanna" of "the Most High" is profanely assumed by the Bishop of Rome.

No man of common judgment, with any degree of acquaintance with the history of the Roman church, doubts the sagacity, the wisdom, the farsightedness of its popes, premiers, statesmen, cardinals, bishops and leaders. They have astonished the world with feats of diplomacy and an eternal series of brilliant intrigues that seem at times to be almost superhuman. Its 150,000,000 of devoted followers embraces all nations, and the sun never sets upon this politico-religious empire of the Roman pontiff. He is the highest ruler and the greatest king on earth,, and the only one that wears the triple crown and dictates to the hearts and consciences of men.

But the most fearful thing connected with this gigantic power is its claims to universal power and authority, both in church and state. This is not only a spiritual, but political kingdom as well. The Pope claims all the kingdoms of the world, and looks forward to the day when he alone shall hold all crowns in his hand, and wield the golden scepter of universal sway, and dictate to all the governments of the world. The church of Rome wants nothing less than supreme political power. It will be contented with nothing short of it, and wherever and in whatever part of the habitable earth it shall gain this power, it will persecute and seek to accomplish by physical force what it cannot do by moral suasion. Where it has the control, it will not hesitate to resort to cruel tortures upon the wheel and the rack, and by fire and sword, put to death thousands and even millions who may dissent from its teachings and usages. This accords with its history and practice through its steady march of it thousand years, and there are no signs or probability of a change of doctrine, nature or practice. It is true, at present, its endeavors to put on a decent appearance and hold its political aspirations in abeyance, and politely bows to "the powers that be," but it is the same old bloody Monarch and gay beast that has scattered the bones of innocent men and women through its long reign of tyranny, persecution and death. Its "Spanish Inquisitions," its great court of death, has written its history in blood and reddened the soil with human gore. Nowhere in the annals of human history has there been presented to men, devils, or angels, greater cruelties and a more shocking, diabolical regime than those of the hellish and damnable Court of the Inquisition.

    The enormity of vileness, the plenitude of the outflow of blood and tears, the multitudes of the slain and the valleys of bleaching bones, the dark, damp pits and rock-bound dungeons, the weeping widows and sighing orphans, and the burning highway and smoking track of this so-called church of God, is enough to put a tingy blush upon the cheeks of the world's civilizations and make mankind forever hate and execrate this blood-thirsty Moloch of the centuries. All this, too, is done in the name of the religion of love, and in the name of and for that meek and lowly Son of Mary that died on the cross to save the world of sinners. If the Roman hierarchy in its history and practice during ages past is a true exponent and illustration of Christianity, then the world is infinitely better off without it, and its utter annihilation or total banishment from the abodes of men will be not only a riddance of intolerable evils in the name of God and man, but also a blessing of unmeasured depth and dimensions. Today, as of all days, she is laying plans, forging chains for the sixty millions of American freemen and American Protestantism, and doing it in a way so as to excite as little apprehension and uneasiness as possible. Quietly and silently she is stealing the hearts of men, proselyting and adding converts to her already enormous membership of nine millions of duped and devoted followers. Great schools and immense churches, nunneries and cathedrals rise in splendid trim and tower upon their mighty foundations in the heart of empire, holding the hub of American life and civilization in embrace and belting its arenas with its iron arm of power. Representatives, senators and presidents, with governors of states, mayors of great cities and councilmen, are bowing the knee, making concessions and confessions, and finally kissing the big toe of the Pope. "What fools we mortals be!"

One of these mornings the American people will awake to find themselves fettered and chained and bound hand and foot and made to do homage to the Roman See. What is the remedy? How shall the encroaching power of this mighty octopus be curtailed? Who can stand before the beast? We would reply by saying that there is no power on earth that can stop this encroachment of Rome but the civil power, and that can only be done while the mighty Roman pontiff is in the minority. In great Britain, in

Germany and the United States of America, Roman Catholicism is making rapid progress, especially in England. And, so far as we can see, she is doing much more to bring the world to herself than all of Protestantism is doing to bring the world to Christ. Everywhere she is earnestly, if not honestly, at work to conquer the world for the papal head, and to bring universal humanity under the control of the Pope. As in Britain and Germany, so in America, special efforts are being made to reach a safe majority in political influence and to control the public school system of the states and municipalities. The public press, which should be free, impartial and untrammeled as moulders of thought and public opinion, are cringing, bowing and scraping, and making concessions to a power whose aim is to make slaves of the souls and bodies of men and tread and crush the nations of man beneath the iron heel of the greatest despot that ever sat upon an earthly throne or reigned over an empire. It is truly astonishing when we see great men--senators, governors, renowned writers, Protestant ministers, political parties, and the mighty men of the nation--allowing, and even encouraging, the growth and expansion of a power that is seeking to destroy their liberty and reduce them to a foreign monstrosity nominally Christian, yet truly and intensely political.

Viewing this whole question from an impartial standpoint, we see a fearful conflict approaching--a conflict between the Catholic power and the civil power--unless there is at Work beneath the trend of events some unknown element or force that will set bounds to Popish aspirations and the subtle intrigue of the Roman See. Of course, this is a Protestant country at present, and a government of the same phase, but it may not be so very long.

Evidently two diverse elements and powers, or two antagonistic forces, are moving beneath the civil and religious surface, and there are indications of an increased ratio of procedure and concentration, or an intense aggregation of opposing elements and forces. So greatly are these forces and elements being intensified that agitation is continuous, and at the end of another decade there may be an explosion of the internal fires of the civic order. Protestants will have to fight for liberty, government and religion, and as the strife is to be internecine and intensified by the freedom of conscience on the one hand, and the blind and bigoted assumptions of the Roman pontiff on the other, the conflict will be short but fearful, bloody and dreadful beyond description, compared to which the French Revolution will be a baby. In the meantime the same sort or similar forces are at work in England and Germany, and the results, in the culmination of events, may be very much the same. At any rate, it seems clear, not only in prophetic vision, but in the quiet contemplation of the thoughtful, that something will soon have to be done to check the encroachments of the Roman church and save the people of several nations from a flow of blood unparalleled in the history of the world, and unanticipated by the wisest of mankind.

The Image of God in Man.

Whatever else may exist in the human personality, apart from its tangible attributes and component elements, it has in some way the image of the Absolute Intelligence. That intelligence is more than coextensive with matter which must within itself live above and beyond its own material creations. No matter how extensive and calculable the tangible parts of the universe may appear to human conception, there are no faculties possessed by man or any other created intelligences to measure its depths and heights and weigh its imponderable masses. Everywhere we look, conceive, or think, thought quails before the wonders, powers, forces, infinite varieties, and majesties amaze us. In this category of splendors, this endless chain of wonders, there dwells a "soulful life," a splendid and all-subduing actuality, whose potentialities are infinitely absolute. For the want of a better name, or rather the want of a capacity in man to use a better name, we call it God. In this image man is made. In Genesis it is declared that "God created man in his own image--in the image of God created he him; male and female created he them." St. Paul tells us that "he is the image and glory of God." St. Paul makes the "glory" here referred to an attribute of "the image." The glory is not the "image" of the Great Original, but is a product of that original. There is a "glory of God" and a glory in God. The former is a product "of God," the latter is an attribute, or an inherent quality, or part of his being or nature. If there is a seen and tangible universe, there must be an unseen and intangible universe, and the former must be the product of the latter. In other words, the unseen must have produced or brought into being the seen and the thinkable. Thus "In the beginning God created the heavens and the earth." The earth is a part of the scen, also the heavens that shine above us. But the Creator, or the invisible Universe, must be forever hid from man and all his intelligent associates. Now an image is the likeness of a thing either in form or substance, or in both, but not in the sense that the image is a part of or a dissepiment of the original. In that case there could be no image at all. It would simply be a part of the original, or a part of the first part, and not a product or creation of the first part. The possibility of making a perfect likeness of a thing in kind, possessing the same elements and attributes of the original, is an indispensable faculty or power that belongs to, and must inhere in the Creator alone. None but God can create, and the creative fiats and acts can only proceed from this unseen Intelligence that was always the unthinkable, the unknowable, and infinite embodiment of concepts that had no time, place, or condition from which to start into being. This is the universal Original in whose "image" man is made. To be made "in the image of God," is the only possible way that man and all intelligent creatures can be, or could have been, made or created. Angels and men, all spirits, whether they be in heaven, on earth, or in hell, or in any other part of the habitable spheres of the universe, are made "in the image of God," and therefore are like man, or man is like them. They are images of one another, just as a thousand photographs drawn from one face at one sitting are images of that face. Each one of the thousand is precisely like every other one of the nine hundred and ninety-nine. If there were but one man in the universe, and these one thousand images were the likeness of his face, and if this man should die and all his pictures be lost or burned in the flames, it would be impossible to reproduce them except from the negative, or the glass plate upon which his face was formerly photographed. This is the original from which all the thousand photographs were taken. Let us particularly note the fact, that every one of these thousand photographs was exactly alike in their fundamental outlines and constituents. In other words, every single one of them would correspond to or have those characteristics that distinguished the face from which it was taken; and every one, to all intents and purposes would be an image of that man. If any of them should become blurred or soiled, that would be a condition, and would have nothing to do with the fundamentals. It is still a photograph, although soiled and changed in the externals, and, in that sense, is bleared or dimmed, but not lost.

The mind of the universe is a mirror. It reflects and absorbs images. If an angel flies through the skies, he is mirrored in the deep track of space, and in the deeper, broader, and perfectly receptive mind of God. An angel or man may blend in the most subtle ether, or in the most attenuated elements of the nebulæ, but he is himself still, and is the same in image, and consequently retains his personal reality to that degree where he is forever himself and eternally no other self.

Every man is photographed in the absorbent universe, both in his mental and physical personal outlines. He is not only the highest (God excepted), but also a distinct rationality, equal in mental quality, if not in degree, to any other intelligence that inhabits the spheres of the universe. Everywhere man is man. Conditions dwarf his mental stature, or enlarge it, blear or clarify it, but do not, because they cannot, change his real self and vital humanity. Paradise, nor hell, nor the corrosions of centuries can have any effect upon the innate possibilities of mind, because that is the image of its Creator, and the only possible image of the Creator that can be made or can exist. God made man in His "own image," because there was in the nature of things no other way to make him. To be was to be made this way, and not to be made this way was not to be made at all. This brings us to the conclusion that man, like all other intelligent creatures, was finished in the fiat act that gave him the birth of his being. He was finished in his creation, and in those higher and deeper finalities where he became a living soul or an intelligent actuality. His nature is full-orbed in all those essentials upon which all subsequent possibilities must rest. If this is not so, then there must have, been not only one creation, as in the first fiat act of his being, but there must still be subsequent creations and consequently additions to his being, and soon the real self must become another self, and a distinctego from the original personality. This would not only destroy the nature of man, but it would unbalance the unseen universe, subvert "the unity of nature and the reign of law." Men and angels, and all the intelligences of the universe, would lose their identity of character and their moral responsibility.

Neither do actual developments nor possibilities imply a change in the fundamentals of being. These simply imply progress, those intellectual expansions where new conditions are attained. On these lines and principles there may be infinite lengths, depths and heights. There are broad areas for the mental force. They are open and clear for the eternal transitions of mind. Indeed, our mental humanity may not only have the power of perpetual development in endless space, but for all that we know there may be sleeping forces and even latent faculties that have not as yet reached those planes in evolution and those arenas in endless progression where they are needed in the mental sphere. All the powers of nature used for the improvement of mankind are not new energies or forces in themselves, but old forces and energies newly discovered, and together with new combinations and new uses they make up the discoveries of science and the inventions of civilization. Steam and electricity are as old as creation, and ether is as old as the heavens in which it floats, and all minerals were here from the foundation of the world. So nothing in creation is new in itself. If, then, man is made "in the image of God," and that image is the mental constitution, then all the intellectualities of the universe are images or photographs taken from the same negative, or, in other words, made like God. But they are made like God how? Man is not made like God in his physical properties, nor those delineations of his material embodiment that we call the body. As yet there is nothing discovered in science to prove the truth of the doctrine of anthropomophism. "God is a spirit, and they that worship him must worship him in spirit and in truth." This is not only a declaration of Holy Writ, but is a scientific certainty and an absolute necessity. God cannot be God unless he is spirit or mental individualism, including all the faculties of the universal intelligence. He can be nothing lower and nothing less than spirit or mind, and we are taught that he has neither shape nor form, nor bodily parts. That is, if he has these faculties at all, they are on a plane too high and exalted to be conceived by His intelligent offsprings. In the very nature of the metaphysical universe, we cannot see or handle spirit any more than we can see or handle thought. It exists everywhere as the all-pervading life and activity of the universe, but nowhere, so far as our knowledge goes, has it any perceptible parts or tangible properties. Rising higher and incumbent upon all space and all things therein contained, spirit is the finest, the most subtle and attenuated substance that can possibly be. While it is the highest form of existence possible, yet it exists, not only independent of all other things and beings, but because it cannot cease from existing. In other words, the universal intelligence cannot become annihilated, because it is not an entity in the sense that it ever began. It had no time, place, or conditions upon which to enter. It was here before all entities. It is the entirety of the unbeginning and universal actuality, whose qualities and altitude of faculties are too high to be reached by others.

The moral sense is only a part of the mental. If man loves, hates, obeys, or fears, it is the action of the human mentality, and not anything separate and distinct from it.

All of the mental natures of the universe are alike in the constituent elements of their being. Not only are they alike in this particular, but they are alike because they are made in the image of the Creator. This being the true metaphysical nature of beings in the sphere of life, all are related to each other, not only because they are the common inhabitants of a common universe, but especially because they are made in the same image in their mental constitution, and of the same substance. There exist between them the closest, the nearest, and highest function of affinity and kinship. Angels, devils, men, and all the intelligent inhabitants of the universe, whether they have fallen from any state of purity, or kept their state of obedience and happiness, are all our nearest and dearest brothers. All are of the same Father, possessing in common the same nature, with all that is in implied in the term. Adam was the father of his children, but not the father of their spiritual humanity. Spirit can only come from spirit. Flesh can beget flesh, but it cannot beget spirit or mental humanity. This is God's specific work, and belongs in the realm of the spiritual. The views here presented are substantiated from the facts of history, respecting man's nature in all ages, nations and conditions. In the fundamentals of human nature, Asiatics, Europeans, Africans, Americans, with all the people of Oceania, no matter how distinct in their habits and customs, present to the considerate judgment of all the same proclivities and mental aspects. The climate and the modes of life may change the color of the skin, distort the features, giving the whole physique an appearance of marked differences, but still the mental nature remains the same in all. If it can be shown that there have been several creations of man, or that the family of man had different starting points in their lower physical generation, yet this would not affect the human relation in any of its phases, nor destroy that intimate kinship that of necessity belongs to all intelligent creatures. No individual can evade or destroy the duties and relations which the constitution of his being imposes upon him, any more than he can get out of the universe. There is no way in the nature and fitness of things for any mental character to get off the spheres of being and responsibility any more than he can get out of himself or the eternal ego. As a citizen, he is one, and only one, but all of one, and can never be any less than one, or any less than the present self. The image of God cannot be lost or annihilated. The individuals themselves, whether men, angels, or devils, have no power or capacity to bring on total death to their mental being or destroy their personal identity. Mirrored in the universe, and engraved upon the potentialities of the eternal possibilities of the spiritual activities, each one of us shall ascend the scales and planes of evolution, transition and development, through long ages to come, forever retaining the image of God and the conscious self.

The Trend of Civilization.

Whatever may be the distinctions of one race from another in the qualities and inherent elements that constitute those distinctions, there is one civilization and one common destiny for all the human race. In essential qualities and characteristics, mankind is one and the same. The different phases of social, civic, and individual life that have presented themselves to the consideration of the student of history and philosophy are mere ramifications that radiate from the same centers, or parent stems. The foundation of civilization is found in the nature, conditions, necessities, and aspirations of men. Because of the desire to better his condition and to make the way of human life pleasing and joyous, he seeks to bend the powers of nature to his wants and coerces its forces and agencies along those lines and planes that will produce the greatest amount of those results by which he ascends the altitudes of civilization. The very construction of his native constituency that permeates "the human form divine" involve those agitative and sleepless precipitants that ever stir, stimulate, and woo him on to investigate, to weigh, and measure principles of the universe that draw his chariot from the individual center to the impalpable periphery. Man is nothing if not agitative and exploring. The mental attributes are the restless aggregates of divine sunbeams formed into the sphere of mind whereby man seeks those lofty climes and grasps those splendid qualities which make men become as gods, "knowing good from evil." To what extent the elements of nature and the mental and physical forces of the universe may be made to serve and develop the earthly side of humanity or to develop mankind as we see it in this state of being, can only be determined by the output of the ages and the wonders of the cycles. Like the universe around us, nowhere does man stand still. He is coming and going, living and dying, rising and falling, ascending and descending, on the ladder of evolution, dissolution and revolution. He springs forth to the depth of his own center, and from it rebounds to the utmost limits of his hemisphere, widening his own sphere of action and mental ebullitions, gaining every step he takes towards the great center of a unified and common civilization. What is wonderful to-day may be lost as insignificant to-morrow, and the raindrops of the morning may be the cloudbursts of the night. In the mental and physical immensity human expansion, in degrees of civilized life, is in its infancy. Its greatest possibility lies in the undiscovered depths of metaphysical science. There are latent forces whose vital cords are still untouched by the occultist or the metaphysician. There are gems of thought and jewels of wisdom in the bays and gulfs and deep seas of the manhood of humanity that shall be set to "the music of the spheres" and the song of the ages, in the day of their coronation amid the jubilees of an all-conquering, centralized, and unified civilization. All things move toward the center. It is the generous, free, and full combination of the elements and agencies that deify humanity and make men princes and kings, and women and little children angels.

Slowly, but surely, the oneness of civilization, like the oneness of humanity, is everywhere asserting itself and gathering its momentum until all its holding points shall center in a common unit of a civic, political, and inter-commercial metropolis, from whose brightness the earth shall be enlightened with "the fatherhood of God and the brotherhood of man."

The first great obstacle in the way of the unification of the world's civilizations is the want of the unification of the human race. As long as there are broad and deep racial distinctions, produced by the various conditions under which the different wings of the human kind have existed, there will be those racial antipathies and prejudices that have so long been the bane of society and the curse of the nations. Everywhere the blighting and withering blasts of caste and prejudice have left their deep imprint upon the social, civic, moral and political records of the peoples of the world. Race hatred is the strongest, the most enduring of all hatred. It is a despicable culmination of the hatred of all the individuals of a race or people, collected and crowded into the heart and life of many individuals of another race or people. They despise each other, not because they are the lower class of the same race, but they despise because they are of a different and distinct race. In the instincts of man, as in the instincts of the lower animals, there is, apparently at least, an inherent or natural propensity for class to seek its class. Hogs do not like the company of goats, nor horses the company of cows. The rich and the educated will not seek the association of poor and ignorant because they are of different tastes, feelings and practices in the social sphere. They live on different planes in the same country, and there is a manifest incongruity and a want of harmony in the social state that prevent that close personal contact that exists between social equals. If, then, there is such a difference among individuals of the same race, merely because of their class, then there will be a greater difference between individuals of two or more distinct races; and as long as these real and supposed differences exist between man and man, there will be a conflict of forces and interests, so directed in their exhaustive regime as to delay, if not despoil, the world of the speedy redemption from the evils that have grown up from the pestiferous soil of human prejudices. Be it understood that we do not want to make the impression that, because one man does not associate with another on account of the difference of race or class, he necessarily hates the other. This is not necessary, neither is it always the case. On the contrary, there are thousands of people in all classes and races who love all classes and races, and thousands have given their lives to ameliorate and better the condition of others. On the other hand, race hatred is perverse and criminal, and proceeds from the depraved and "downright cussedness of human nature."

Why should one man hate another because he is of a different race? Who does it, or who can it help or benefit? It makes no one better, but always makes the man who hates worse and more depraved in his nature and proclivities. Hatred contains the essential elements of murder, and the Scriptures of Holy Writ substantiate this when they declare: "He that hateth his brother is a murderer." As human nature is one and inseparable as to its real substantial qualities and tendencies, civilization is destined to become so changed and revolutionized in its works and effects that this race prejudice is to become a thing of the past; because it is in the way of those aggregated interests and intellectual propulsions that have given the world its present degree of advancement in the social state. The world moves. It dips its expanding horizon into out-lying seas and oceanic fathoms to disgorge from the deep the hidden treasures and unpolished gems that seem to sleep on the pebbly bottom. These when polished by human culture shall bedeck the crown and bestud the heavens of a triumphant and unified civilization. Nothing but physical disaster and material dissolution can absorb the force, or subtract that driving universal intellectual energy that now collects its agencies and moulds the thought, the life, and the sentiment of ages into one great intellectual, international, and inter-racial man. Then a mighty force is driving the wheels of a new civilization in a new age. Not new is it as to its ground principles and native elements, but new in the facts discovered, the truths revealed, and the exhibition of hidden life, by the touch of whose fingers the rocks are turned to silver, silver into gold, gold into diamonds, and diamonds into those lost jewels that fell from the crown of angels in the conflicting transition from the old to the new. The age itself is full of energy, drawing man upward and upward to himself--his more and perfect self. The selfhood of self is becoming more asserted. Man is rounding into that high and ethereal realization that himself is one, that he is an entity with an ineffacable identity, whose essential and divine personale shall outlast the stars, and glow in its ineffable splendors amid the ages of newer domains and brighter dispensations.

So forcible and widespread, so deep and earnest are the movements of the spiritual and intellectual energy to reach and conquer the powers of nature, in behalf of her thinking exponents, that wide seas lose their terrors, high mountains are bored through, commerce harnesses the waves, and the lightning flashes the accents of truth around the globe.

The advancements and discoveries of science have brought all nations near together, and so far as intercourse--commercial, political, and religious--is concerned, they speak to each other daily--almost face to face. The market's of London, New York,

Paris, Berlin, and Canton are so intermit, so near each other, and each so full of all the rest, that whatever affects one affects all the commercial centers of the great family of man. There are now no more strangers and foreigners, but all are of the household of the same civilization to an astonishing degree; and this tendency must increase as the interests of the world demand. Nothing will be allowed to stand in its way.

Here racial prejudice must fall and bow to the better and higher interests of man.

Nothing seems more apparent than the tendency of all the nations to become one in blood as well as in interest.

Shem, Ham, and Japhet are all nearly ill the same house and eating at the same table, saying the same prayers, singing the same songs, and worshipping the same God. These are the children of a common mother and a common sireship with a common destiny.

In the onward trend and rounding out of this great civilization, white and black, red and swarthy, with all the seven colors of the rainbow, shall be ground to dust and calcined by the stately tramp of a golden civilization, culminating in the eternal fixedness of the golden standard and crowned with the age of diamonds.

The Great Presence.

That we are in the midst of some great, all-pervading and extraordinary influence, is a most touching and signal fact. We have reached that period in the step of centuries and the cycles, and that degree of spiritual and mental development, where we seem to touch the hem of the Great Master's garment. We seem to sit at his feet, feel his throbbing heart, hear his thrilling voice, while the halo of his countenance fills the whole human hemisphere in the twilighted splendors of a majesty that comes from beyond the stars of God. The Great Galilean is visiting the islands, treading the waters and walking through the continents of human consciousness as never before in the long history of nations and ages. The very air that we breathe, and the sunbeams that gild the horizon with golden light, bear him gently, though strongly, to human consciousness, and the intelligence of universal humanity. The winds are His chariot, the clouds His throne, and the mists of the foaming deep His pavilion.

Indeed, there is a universal presence of an increasing and centralizing force that is stronger than nature, more pungent and deep-throbbing than electricity or the subtle activities of ethereal currents. Beneath the active force and energies of human progress, there is an arm of power, a thrilling somewhat that is silently at work sending its awakening influence to all parts of the mental and conscious humanity. We are in the presence of the great Christ--not the Christ of modern or ancient days, but the universal and eternal Christ of God, crowned from eternity and sceptered before the sun blazed, stars twinkled, or angels played on their harps. He is the God-sent, the divine Legate, who is to propagate and diffuse His inspiring spirituality until the august and adorable Son of Man shall stand in the presence of all men, and pour Himself into the entire drama of human life. Evidently, Christianity is crystalizing its forces, concentrating its energies, so as to give the greatest momentum to the evolutions of thought and actions. We see, as we never saw before, the moral concept and the spiritual comprehensions stricken off in clearer lines and more radiant with distinctiveness of character than in former ages. Faith is becoming more and more a tangible matter of fact, and with its spanning arches is seen to rest upon the fundamentals of the spiritual universe. Christ was a great philosopher as well as a great prophet. His teachings, along with the demonstrations of power displayed in the healing art, were based upon the laws or governing principles of nature. He took hold of nature in its deepest mental and physical phases, tied its broken cords and cables, belted their disobedient elements about His arm of power, coerced their rebellious fragments into line, commanded the molecular universe, and its activities obeyed the voice of the Son of God.

All through the long ages of human darkness He has been their rising Sun and the living Power from whose central throne the peeping and glinting rays of resplendent hope that have inspired their upliftings and aspirations have sprung. His voice is the music that wooed and thrilled the human spheres, vibrated the human mechanism and taught respondent souls the ways of divine providence, and cheered the millions with the truth of God and the realization of the eternal future. He is drawing nearer and nearer to all human hearts and human consciousness. Onwards the overshadowing presence climbs the ecliptic of the busy world, dislodging from its high places the subtle children of hell and the black squadrons. of sin and darkness. The great presence--what is it? What is that mysterious force that seems to play on the universal harp of universal humanity? What is this wondrous power, this magic wand that sweeps the zones of human devices and plays with almighty momentum on the social and civil planes of organized society? What is this that is changing the sentiment of men, expanding the mental vision and enlarging the moral periphery in the sphere of thought, philosophy and philanthropic activity? Is it mere science, progress and discovery, or the mere product of human genius? Or is the force of age upon age filing its victories upon victories, and achievements upon achievements? Nay, these are the fruits of the great presence--of the active Christ in personal transition, the living embodiment of truth and the active Jehovic Dispenser of the reforming and transforming kingdom of heaven. "The whole earth is crammed with heaven, and every common bush is afire with God," in the great personality of His Son. Mark the steps of modern civilization, read the signs of the times, and measure the strength and weigh the momentum of the trembling forces of evil. A mighty Prince with signal power and the dynamic forces of the spiritual arcana is standing at the end of the dying century, and, like the rising sun on a calm sea, the soft rays of His bright and resplendent light adumbrate His coming and depict His majestic presence. The Song of Solomon says, "The voice of my beloved! Behold he cometh, leaping upon the mountains, skipping upon the hills." Already we are immersed in the fullness of His joy and the plenitude of His presence. But as He advances upon the sphere of human thought and activity, both good and evil are intensified. The wicked grow more wicked, and the righteous more righteous.

As the conflict approaches active engagement, and as the two dissimilar powers line up in battle array, the lines of demarcation are more fully drawn. The devil will be more devilish, and the Christ more Christly. Reserved powers, latent activities, and long pent-up magazines of force will explode, and, the onslaught will be more dreadful and fearful as the Great Presence permeates the moral mass, and vibrates the centers of the human arena.

Who is it that has not felt the Great Presence? What zone or parallel is there in the habitable earth that does not feel His wondrous touch, the thrilling force of His divine magnetism and the impressiveness of His unique personality? The entire kingdom of men "is the Lord's." "His kingdom ruleth over all," and he will come "whose right it is." Say what you please and do what you please, "the kingdom is the Lord's." "It is not by might, nor by power, but by my spirit, saith the Lord." Hence, it "is not power" by which the process of redemption is carried on. Not by armies and navies or the unsheathed sword, or the skilled diplomacy and intrigue of wise statesmanship is it carried on. No flourish of trumpets, no bugle blasts, no rattling of drums, no high-sounding clarionets, no metal ring of cymbals, no chariots of iron with prancing steeds and amber wheels stained with human gore and rolling in the blood of the slain, mark His coming. Nay, verily, His coming is in silent power of the wonderful God. His steps are softer than the fragrance of the rosebud, and as gentle as the evening zephyrs laden with the music of the spheres and the breath of flowers. "The kingdom of God cometh not with observation," but like the noiseless flow of a river. He treads the veins of commerce, walks the royal highways of the world's greatness unobserved, and is found in the palaces of kings, the diamond chambers of queens, the secret precincts of premiers, and in the chair of national executives. Surely we are in the midst of a Great presence. How wonderful is this age! How forceful and resourceful is the Divine Presence! Then, children of God, look up and look around you. He is here in your midst, in the highways of your cities, plains and rural districts. He stands at your doors, turning the knob or pulling the latchstring.

> "Behold a Stranger at the door,
> He gently knocks--has knocked before!
> Has waited long--is waiting still--
> You treat no other friend so ill."

The Connection of Spirit and Body.

It is evident that there is a spirit and that there is a body. The oldest, the most real and most extensive is spirit. The difference between the two is the difference of life and death, or that that is self-active, and that that is not self-active. Spirit acts without matter or body, or acts when there is nothing to act upon, by, or through. Where there is action there must be spirit, since nothing can act without its presence, either mediately or immediately. If matter moves, takes form, or assumes condition, change, or progression, its activity is dependent upon a deeper, broader and more sensitive force, which embraces the elements or properties of a perfect entirety, or an eternal reality. As the human body is the mere instrument of the soul or spirit, so God, the Spirit of spirits, is the hidden or indwelling Life of all life, and the active forces of nature are but the instruments, as well as the manifestations, of the divine presence and power, and are the only means by which the intelligent universe can behold the power and presence of the Infinite. There are first and second causes, or rather there is a first and central cause, and all else are but second causes, results or emanations of the only cause. All second causes in the physical spheres and immensities are nothing but the moving changes or precipitations of the molecules of the whole or parts of the universal system; and as precipitant elements move as they are moved upon by the causative, they constitute molecular force. This molecular force is the tangible activities of the world and the universe which we call nature. In this sense nature, in its multiform and complex mechanism, is as much the instrument of God as the human hand or foot or tongue is the instrument of the human mind. Strictly speaking, spirit is the only perfect reality in the universe, because it is the only thing that has attributes of perception and is utterly incapable of annihilation. It is incapable of annihilation because it is not an entity in the sense of limitation. That is, it has all the faculties and properties of perfect self and perfect realization without beginning, growth or accretions of parts or combination of elements. Hence, spirit has neither body, nor parts, nor tangibility. Or, in other words, if spirit has form, or any kind of molecular constituency, its peculiar nature is so high, ethereal, and attenuated in itself, that we, in common with all intelligent creatures of the universal spheres, have no faculties by which we can comprehend its nature. This rests upon perfect and true philosophical grounds, since nothing call be greater than the greatest, and before the intelligent personalities of the universe call comprehend the Spirit of spirits, these personalities must have existed prior to, and independent of, the Eternal. The opposite conclusion is splendidly absurd and presents a solecism that distresses thought and tortures the imaginary faculties.

In their real nature there is no difference between those atoms or molecules that compose the human body and those that compose the bodies of the inferior animals, or even those that enter or compose the vegetable or mineral kingdoms, and the bodies of men are as much of earth and air as the hills, mines or other material forms and elements that compose the universe.

Hence form has nothing to do with the inherent properties of matter any more than it has to do with the nature of spirit or mental individuality. Change of state, condition or relation, cannot affect the nature, or the inherent qualities of spirit. Punishment may bring repentance and obedience to the laws of God and the requirements of righteousness in this or in some other state of conscious existence, or disobedience may bring on sin and inject the virus of wickedness into the spiritual or mental reality; but none of them can produce deterioration, or change, the real mental conscious individual. If it were otherwise, there could be no such thing as eternal or indefinite punishment. Even human laws presuppose the continuous personal conscious identity of the mental character, since men are often punished upon the supposition that they will remain the same person, or the same mental character to the end of natural life that they were when first adjudged guilty and assigned to life commitment.

There must be something in the character or nature by which every spirit or mental individual will be known of distinguished from every other such character in the universe. The very nature of government, whether it be of God or man, presupposes that every single individual is separate and distinct from every other one in the great whole, and it is a special and particular attribute of justice in the administration of government to avoid the infliction of punishment upon the innocent, and withhold rewards from the unworthy. The greatest scrutiny and care are exercised in the distribution of rewards and punishment lest the wrong person should be dealt with. In their fundamentals, there is no difference in the government of God and the government of men. Both are based upon righteousness, equity and justice. Mercy is not an attribute of government any more than it is an attribute of God. There may be a government without mercy, but there can be no government in the strict sense of the term without justice, equity and righteousness. This is government and all else is anarchy. No transgressor can claim mercy as of right or justice. It does not belong to him as a part of his inherited right, but justice belongs to him because he is a citizen of the universe and under the protection of its government and laws. Again, every intelligent being has an inherent claim on justice, because he is a conscious intelligence, and because he is in no way responsible for his being or his creation, or those eternal mental endowments or faculties of which he is possessed and which he cannot destroy or reduce to nonentity. No attribute of intelligent natures can disappear or be annihilated by any power less than itself, and therefore it is incapable of decay or inaction. Presuming that the above is predicated upon sound metaphysical reasoning, we reach the sequence that man, in common with all other intelligent existences, is an eternal conscious fixture in the universal circle of being. He is an eternal citizen with an indestructible identity, forever dwelling on a plane where annihilation can never come. This plane is in his being, or his being is in or on this plane. Here dwell in ethereal marvels and empyrean splendors all the expansive personal majesties and towering intellects in their universal home, forever aspiring in the highest, broadest and profoundest spheres of the countless and infinite activities. But as matter is incapable of punishment and rewards, and as it has no principles or faculties as a basis for responsibility, it is agreeable to truth and philosophy when we say that nothing is and nothing can be punished, or can receive rewards, but the mental or spirit man, and those capable spiritualities that belong to the intellectual sphere. Every spiritual reality must be a capacity, that is, it must have capability to that degree of volition that involves personal responsibility, and consequently this responsibility is upon the moral plane. This not only makes them subjects of rewards and punishment, but involves that high degree of individualism by which one mental character is distinguished from every other. Since this is the case, there must be some outline or characteristic inherent in all intelligent beings by, which they are to be known. It may not consist in vital or constitutional properties, but it may consist in some exterior delineations through which the piercing art of intuition may comprehend those differentia that must exist among the individuals of the populous universe. We could not perceive the identification of things or persons if every one were exactly alike; neither could we distinguish one place from another if all places were precisely alike in all that make up each of all the places. Intuition itself presupposes a differentiation among a multitude of individuals--those necessary distinguishing features by which one person may be known from every other person or mental individual. Indeed, personal identity seems to be an essential part or element of intellectual natures, as without it one person cannot be known from other conscious intellectualities. When an individual is disrobed of his earthly habiliments and wrapped in the habit of the spiritual, there can be no essential change in character because of the transition. He is still himself in all the plenitude and fundamentals of his being. He does not become an impersonal reality or a mere thing because of the change. In this world, expressions that consist in many things form those features or idiosyncracies of character and person by which one person is known from all the rest, and who knows but that spirits, men, angels and devils, and all the intellectualities of the universe, are clothed in ethereal integuments, though imperceptible to human vision and contact, yet suited to their nature, plane and occupation? Yea, "He maketh his angels winds and his ministers flames of fire." Then we reach the conclusion, upon philosophical deductions, that we carry with us into the mysterious realities beyond not only all the personal consciousness of tangible and intangible being, but we carry with us the shape, form and expressions that were given us in the creation, and which we had from the beginning of our being. The human form is divine, not in its inherent or native qualities, but in its chartered shape, expression, features and outlines. The contour of the personality is divinely appointed and stereotyped as an essential part or element of being. It cannot be thrown off, covered or disguised, and wherever the individual moves, speaks or acts in the sphere of being, he will be known as that special and specific personality. As every living actuality is a self-acting entity under law and responsibility, his history is registered in space and all the personal data are reflected and wafted in and through the radiating spheres and immensities. The acts and facts of his being cannot be obliterated, lost or forgotten, neither can they be extracted from the enfolding records of the progressive spheres. Man is a book, a history within himself. On and in the mental inlays of growth and development he engraves himself upon himself, and unconsciously he writes his own history, records his own acts and thoughts, and his life keeps its own register. As he is self-acting, he is self-registering, and the universe, with its faithful records, is a duplicating mirror in which every man and mental activity can find himself faithfully portrayed in the eternal archives of the eternal spheres.

PREPARED FOR PUBLICATION BY HISTORIC PUBLISHING

All Rights Reserved
San Antonio, Texas
©2017

Slavery Books & African American History Resources
https://slaverybooks.blogspot.com

www.ingramcontent.com/pod-product-compliance
Lightning Source LLC
Chambersburg PA
CBHW051400070526
44584CB00023B/3231